Blood on the Wave

Scottish Sea Battles

JOHN SADLER

BIRLINN

First published in 2010 by
Birlinn Limited
West Newington House
10 Newington Road
Edinburgh
EH9 1QS

www.birlinn.co.uk

ISBN: 978 1 84158 865 0 hardback
ISBN: 978 1 84341 051 5 paperback

British Library Cataloguing-in-Publication Data
A catalogue record for this book is available from the British
Library

Typeset by C. Griffiths, Cambridge
Printed and bound by MPG Books Limited, Bodmin

This one is for Doug,
for so many years of friendship

Let loose the hounds
Of war,
    The whirling swords!
Send them leaping
Afar,
Red in their thirst for war;
Odin laughs in his
Car
At the screaming of the swords!

Fiona Macleod, 'Washer of the Ford'

Contents

Preface

Cape Wrath stands at the north-westerly extremity of mainland Britain. The beacon of the lighthouse there gives note of civilisation in a barren and untamed landscape of moor and moss, rock girt coasts and sandy inlets, secret lochans and tumbled stone. Nearly forty years ago, as a boy, I travelled with my father, the pair of us bumping along the uncertain track that wound northward from the hamlet at Blairmore in a venerable Series IIA Landrover. It was a quiet and empty landscape, the mournful note of a curlew the only complement to the racket of the engine. The rutted way gritted past *Loch na Gainimh* and *Loch a'Mhuilinn* before it petered out and we ground to a halt.

Then there was only the silence. The rest of the way to the coast – a couple of miles or so – was accomplished on foot, through heather and harsh marram of the dunes, past the rectangle of Sandwood Loch and its much haunted bothy to the bay itself. This was in July, a leaden day, skies heavy and grey, fitful wind plucking at the grasses. And suddenly we were on the beach, a lordly strand of unblemished gold that stretched between distant headlands, the long finger of *Am Buachaille* pointing at the sky. A sky which, as though by mysterious alchemy, suddenly cleared to flood the blue waves in dazzling light; such was my introduction to the coasts of Alba.

This book is as much a journey as history. In 1996 my earlier work *Scottish Battles* was published. I sought to provide in that work a single-volume introduction to land based conflict in Scotland. Since then I have followed this with numerous studies of individual battles and campaigns. All of this arises from my enduring fascination with Scotland, its peoples and history. Though I may claim to be a military historian I cannot pretend to enjoy equal expertise in naval matters. This is not, therefore, a specialised naval study. It is an account intended for the general reader who, like the author, loves Scotland, history and travel in roughly equal measure.

Naval encounters in Scottish waters are perhaps less well written up than Scottish land battles, though every bit as important an element in the rich tapestry of a nation's history. The sea runs in the lifeblood of many Scots, and dramatic events on land have rarely been unaccompanied by actions at sea. The period this book seeks to cover – from the Iron Age to the Cold War – is very long and has witnessed immense changes in the technology and tactics of naval warfare. The view, therefore, which is given of each era is essentially a snapshot: an attempt, in each case, to provide a guide to the ships, men and principal actions.

Our narrative thus moves from triremes to longships, to birlinns and nyvaigs, carracks and galleons, ships of the line to ironclads, dreadnoughts and Polaris. From Romans to Scots, Norsemen, the Lords of the Isles, Andrew Wood and the Bartons, pirates, privateers and Nelson's Band of Brothers, to echoes of Jutland and the Battle of the Atlantic, the long decades of the Cold War and the continuing debate over a nuclear deterrent. It is a story of kings and kingdoms, the Wars of Independence, Jacobites and Frenchmen and the death of the German High Seas Fleet at Scapa Flow.

Thanks are due to my agent Duncan McAra; my editor at Birlinn, Hugh Andrew; Mark Lawrence of Lochaline Dive Centre; Dr Paula Martin of Morvern Maritime Centre; Sue Mowat for providing access to a valuable resource on the subject of privateering; Bob Mowat of RCAHMS; Cindy Vallar for advice on pirates, ancient and modern; Jon Addison of Scottish Maritime Museum; Martin Dean of ADUS at St Andrews University; Iain Mackenzie of the Naval Historical Branch; Susie Barrett; Tamara Templer, Lorna Stoddart and Lee Deane of National Trust for Scotland; Malcolm Poole of Mallaig Heritage Centre; Denis Rixson, author and authority on the Hebridean galley; Cron Mackay for casting light on aspects of galleys at war; Tobias Capwell of Glasgow Museums; Charlotte Chipchase of the Royal Armouries, Leeds; Helen Nicoll of the National Museum of Scotland; Ailsa Mactaggart of Historic Scotland; James Mitchell of 'The Secret Bunker'; and Sarah Beighton of the National Maritime Museum.

All errors and omissions remain, of course, the sole responsibility of the author.

Northumberland, Spring 2010

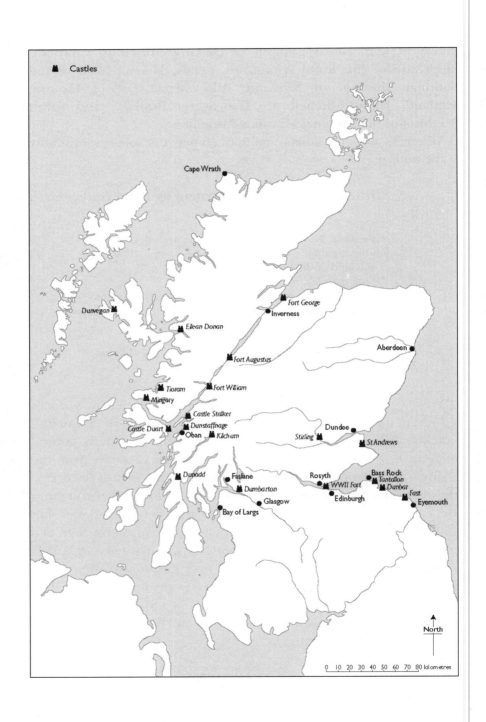

◆

ONE

Introduction: A Thundering of Waves

Caledonia! Thou land of the mountain and rock,
Of the ocean, the mist, and the wind –
Thou land of the torrent, the pine, and the oak,
Of the roebuck, the hart, and the hind;
Though bare are thy cliffs, and though barren thy glens,
Though bleak thy dun islands appear,
Yet kind are the hearts, and undaunted the clans,
That roam on these mountains so drear!

Robert Burns

SCAPA FLOW, ORKNEY IS A lagoon-like stretch of water, a mere 24km by 13km, girded by the islands of Mainland, Graemsay, Burray, South Ronaldsay and Hoy. A superb natural anchorage, it has been a haven for battle fleets, certainly from the Viking epoch. Lyness on Hoy was the HQ for the British fleets that utilised Scapa Flow during the twentieth century and throughout the course of both World Wars. Thus this desolate shelter has housed some of the mightiest assemblies of warships ever seen at a time when British naval power was both unprecedented and largely unrivalled, slab-walled hulls and the vast, gleaming ordnance of dreadnoughts riding in the swell. It was from here that the fleet ventured out to do battle with the Kaiser's navy at Jutland, and Scapa Flow remained the British navy's northern haven for the whole duration of the struggle.

BEGINNINGS
Scotland's waters are no stranger to dramatic confrontations and

encounters at sea. From Agricolan invasion to shadow play of the
Cold War, men-of-war have prowled her coasts. And it is a very long
and varied coast, one of the most challenging and dramatic in the
Western hemisphere. At 11,800km in length, it is over twice as long
as England's, longer than the coastline of the USA and accounts for
8 per cent of the entire coasts of Europe. Nobody in Scotland can be
further than 65km from the sea. The spreading expanse of the
Atlantic and the grey swell of the North Sea have provided
livelihoods for countless generations of Scots, from the time of the
earliest settlers to the harvesting of North Sea Oil.

In topographical terms, all that we see today, so seemingly ancient
it appears surely to date from the dawn of time, is quite recent.
Some 20 millennia ago, the topography was very different. This was
the time of the great ice sheet. Coastlines were some 140m lower
than at present, so that the North Sea was low-lying marshland,
which our ancestors traversed on foot. The western seaboard lay
some miles beyond the Hebrides. Scotland was shrouded in a dense
blanket of deep ice, resembling our present view of the Arctic,
entombed and sterile, pack ice forming around the coast in the
depth of long, petrified winters with icebergs cracking free of
glaciers.

When, perhaps 15,000 years ago, the ice at last began to release
its death grip, leaving a harsh, windswept upland of deep valleys and
towering peaks, sea levels began to rise, imperceptibly at first, no
more than 15mm a year, but by 8,000 BC Britain had become an
island. The rising seas flooded the lower levels leaving high ground
as a patchwork of islands, Orkney, Shetland and the Hebrides; river
estuaries swelled into the firths of Forth, Moray, Clyde and Tay. As
the glaciers retreated across the frozen ground, they scoured vast
quantities of sand and crushed rock towards the margins, and the
power of the waves then pushed thousands of tonnes back towards
the developing coastline, creating some of the country's superlative
beaches, lordly strands such as the White Sands of Morar.

Though the melting ice fuelled the inrush of the sea, the land,
released from the immense burden of weight, began to lift; the
thicker the press of the glaciers, as in the Western Highlands, the
greater the consequential uplift. Where the dead hand of the ice

sheet was thinnest, in Orkney, Shetland and the Western Isles, the land stayed calm and level. In some instances, where the earth heaved faster than the waves, the rise has left a residue of stranded ancient beaches and cliff formations. These occur particularly around Arran, Jura, Islay and the Inner Hebrides. In contrast, where the pace of change was reversed, whole areas of landscape slid beneath the encroaching waters.

We can say that by 3,000 BC the coastline was roughly that which we perceive today, but the process of change, while generally imperceptible in human terms, is nonetheless continuous. Wind and waves, the longshore drift driven by the incessant ebb and suck of the tide, all have their effect. The Northern and Western Isles continue to be affected by sea-level rise; the opposite obtains in places such as Fife, where Second World War anti-tank beach obstacles, happily never tested, are now over 100m inland! The sands shift beneath storm-lashed winds, flattening and buffeting the dunes. Shingle, those rounded pebbles ground by the ice sheet and the later actions of the waves, forms many of the beaches in the north and west, distinctive ridges or 'storm beaches' deposited by freak tides remain strewn above high-water mark

The sea was important to the early peoples of Scotland. Traces of settlement date to around 9,000 BC, showing that our ancestors followed hard upon the retreating glaciers. They were drawn by the fertile coastal plains, rich harvests to be had from the sea and the ease of communication by water; a factor that has remained constant since. Communities were small and existence precarious; they were, from necessity, in harmony with nature, the cycle of seasons and flow of the tides. In spite of the many subsequent developments, growth in population and the spread of industry and urbanisation, some 85 per cent of the Scottish coast remains essentially unaffected by the hand of man.

COAST

Coastline is unique, not only in its variety and movement but as the meeting zone between land and water, link to distant lands and continents, familiar yet ever mysterious, sparkling blue or grey, sullen, as still and subtle as a mirror, raging in white-capped fury.

Beyond the line where sea meets land, past the high-water mark, home to glasswort and sea blite, lies the fringe of dunes, salt marsh and machair. Long sandy beaches are most commonplace in Aberdeenshire, Orkney, the western coast and isles; wondrous golden expanses that seem to stretch to infinity. Dunes form around tough grasses such as the high and tussocky marram, a barrier to the scouring wind, so the dune grows like cement fill within a framework of reinforcing. In places such as Crossapol on Coll, the dunes can soar to 35m or more in height. As a boy I recall the joy of high dunes on Achnahaird Bay, north of Ullapool, when a sweep of bright sands greets the eye, an instant and arresting transition from a landscape of moorland and bog.

In the far north-west, the keen-edged blades of northerlies, driving quantities of machair sand (constituted from calcium-rich shell deposits that act as a rich fertiliser, manuring dead ground between sand and hills) create a fertile coastal strip. Rich grasslands carpeted with bright flowering in spring and early summer, dotted with saltwater lagoons, freshwater lochans and fenland. During winter months the river estuaries, mudflats and salt marsh become the habitat for thousands of waders and wildfowl, like widgeon and Brent geese. In summer the high crowding cliffs become a safe haven for guillemots, kittiwakes, fulmars, razorbills, great swarming cacophonous colonies, which cling to the near vertical rock. Manx shearwaters burrow into the steep slopes to carve out nesting platforms. Sea thrift and Scot's lovage somehow flourish even in the thin icing of salt-crusted earth that lies on ledges and in crevices. Distant St Kilda is girt with the most inaccessible of rock faces, and the inhabitants, before the evacuation, used to harvest a perilous crop of wild birds' eggs from the cliffs, lowered on ropes, swinging over the frothing Atlantic breakers below.

On a grim and darkening evening in the reign of James VI, the coastline of Ayrshire between Girvan and Ballantrae was lit by a pattern of guttering torches, flickering fitfully in the breeze, air alive with the tramping of armed men and the scouring of dogs. Several hundred of the king's subjects had embarked upon a search of the cliffs. For years, members of the local communities had been disappearing without trace. Fear and superstition stalked the steadings and townships. Now, at last, a witness had survived to give a grim account of the cause. A man and wife, riding back from the local fair, crossing the flat ground above the cliffs by Bannane Head, had been set upon by a ragged band of half-naked scavengers. Feral creatures seemed to rise from the very stones, half real, half spectral, hacking and clawing at the terrified mounts. The male, undeterred, drew his sword and laid about him manfully, beating the attackers off. His wife, heavy with child, was dragged from her horse, the carrion closed in and the screaming victim was dispatched with knives, horribly torn and dismembered, but her husband, blind with fury, fought clear.

It was he, heavy with grief and thirsting for vengeance, who had given the alarm, and the sheriff had called out the militia. The 'slewdogges' or hounds, picking up the scent of flesh, led the hunters to an unseen cave below Bennane Head, its mouth a dark gash in the rocks, sealed at high tide. Even the bravest quailed, for the sounds and odours emanating from the entrance seemed to presage the very mouth of Hell and nothing in these men's lives could have prepared them for what lay within. For this proved the lair of the cannibal Sawney Bean(e), his wife, 8 sons, 6 daughters, 18 grandsons and 14 granddaughters, mostly begotten in incest, a savage and depraved clan who lived entirely by feasting on the flesh of others.[1]

According to *The Newgate Calendar*, Alexander 'Sawney' Bean(e) was born in the mid sixteenth century, a hedge trimmer, who found the lure of honest labour unattractive. He discovered a consort as idle and vicious as he and drifted through Galloway. With the cave as a base, the Beans embarked upon their career of kidnap and murder, seizing their victims at night, dragging their prey to the lair, where the luckless victims were dismembered and consumed. The cave became a veritable shop of horrors, adorned with bones and rotting body parts. As their numbers swelled, so did their feeding patterns. Bean schooled his children in the arts of murder and cannibalistic gastronomy. By the time of their discovery, it is said they'd killed a thousand people and instigated a reign of superstitious terror, one that had led to the lynching of several supposed culprits.

Now the true perpetrators were revealed, and the full extent of this unspeakable horror became known. All were dragged in chains to Edinburgh and confined in the Tolbooth, thence, possibly to Leith where the full rigour of the law was applied (apparently without the prior accompaniment of a trial). The men were lashed to posts and had both hands and feet hacked off, the women obliged to watch their final agonies as they succumbed to exsanguination, before they too perished, at the stake.

In the south-west, the wild Galloway coast bristles with history. Looking, on its southward flank, across the Solway to England and guarded by citadels such as mighty Caerlaverock and Kirkcudbright, the rugged northern hills encircle a fertile coastal plain. Roman writers name the Celtic inhabitants as Novantae, and it was on this coast at Whithorn that St Ninian established his church in AD 397. Rerigonium, named as one of the three thrones of Britain in the post-Roman era, and likely the capital of Rheged may have been located on Loch Ryan at Dunragit (*Dun Rheged*), near Stranraer. These fierce Gallowegian warriors had a reputation for savagery. They fought for Scotland at the Battle of the Standard in 1138, where, it was said, they would carry on the fight though studded like porcupines with English arrows!

THE WEST

Northwards from Galloway, that long flank of Ayrshire coast leads to the Firth of Clyde. For generations this was home to Scotland's shipbuilding industry, though now the great days are long gone. HM Naval Base Clyde at Faslane stands some 25 miles north-west of Glasgow; home to the entirety of the UK nuclear deterrent force, four Vanguard class nuclear submarines, carrying Trident missiles. The base is now frequently beset not by warriors but the reverse, peace protesters, freshly agitated by current proposals for a new generation of Trident missiles. As an interesting postscript on the Cold War itself, the author recalls awakening at a small hotel by the shore of Loch Broom in the summer of 2000 to see a large and gleaming Russian cruise liner at anchor off Ullapool, her passengers soon flooding the shops of the delightful town; there was no sign of any hostilities, indeed there was marked cordiality all round.

Westwards, the Isle of Arran masks the long finger of Kintyre as it reaches into the cold Atlantic. Around this rugged peninsula, Jura and Islay are separated from the mainland by the Sound that leads to Argyll and the Firth of Lorne. Between Jura and Scarba whirls the Corryvrechan, a series of whirlpools, whipped into life by the gravitational pull of the moon. Loch Linnhe forms a slim fjord, guarded by the great fortresses of Dunstaffnage and Castle Stalker on the mainland and Duart on Mull. Another narrow sound divides the island from the westerly thrust of remote Ardnamurchan. Mull forms a part of that wonderfully widespread and diverse archipelago, which comprises the Inner Hebrides and includes Skye, Islay, Jura, Staffa and the Small Isles. Arran and the other islands around the Clyde Estuary do not form a part of this group. Long considered the last bastion of the Norse-Gael tongue, the Gaelic name *Innse Gall* translates as 'Isles of Foreigners': a surviving description from the Viking era.

Mesolithic settlers appear to have been the first colonists, from perhaps 8,500 BC. The magnificent stones at Callanish may have been constructed some five millennia later. In classical times, Greek chronicler Diodorus Siculus refers to the semi-mythical island of *Hyperborea*. In the twelfth century the Hebrides formed a part, perhaps even the core of the Lordship of the Isles, that long swathe of territory controlled by Somerled and, latterly his descendants, chiefs of Clan Donald. In order to try and exert some measure of sway over these fissiparous clansmen James V, in 1539, instructed navigator Alexander Lindsay to provide a *Rutter*. This comprised a series of navigational notes and aids that would facilitate the passage of crown vessels in these treacherous and, at that time, unmapped waters.

Over the often difficult waters of the Minch and the Little Minch lies a further westerly group of islands, collectively known as the Outer Hebrides. Lewis, or 'The Long Island' is by far the largest, but the archipelago also includes Harris, North Uist, Benbecula, South Uist and Barra. Compton Mackenzie's highly successful novel *Whisky Galore* was based upon real events which occurred in 1941.[2] In that darkest of years, the islanders of Eriskay received an unexpected source of liquid comfort when the SS *Politician* ran aground there. The stricken vessel contained some 24,000 cases of whisky, many of which were 'recovered' by grateful locals. The consequences of the affair were far from comic, and numbers of them were subsequently prosecuted; the legend, however, proved highly durable:

> The great ship '*Politician*'
> Her hold stacked high with grog,
> Steamed proudly past the island,
> And foundered in the fog.
>
> A case was rent asunder,
> Twelve bottles came to grief,
> When the Barra surf – like thunder –
> Came pounding on the reef.
>
> And then the scent of nectar,
> Came on the wild wind's breath.
> 'I smell it,' screamed old Hector
> 'It's whisky – sure as death'.
> Unknown, 'The SS Politician'

Westwards again, cast like pebbles in the great sweep of the Atlantic, are the Monach Islands, Flannan Isles, St Kilda and distant Rockall. The Flannan Isles are a trio of small groups possibly all that remains of a much larger land mass, encroached upon by the swelling waters after the ice retreated. The name is derived from St Flannan who may have been the seventh-century Abbot of Killaloe in County Clare. The much later lighthouse was designed by David Stevenson and built in the closing years of the nineteenth century. It became famous for the enduring mystery surrounding the disappearance of the three man crew in December 1900. The alarm was first raised on 15 December when the light was observed to be non-operational, but the relief vessel was unable to land until Boxing Day. No trace of the keepers could be found and nothing onshore could suggest what might have become of them. A search revealed that the west landing appeared to have suffered severely from storm damage. A host of rumours began to circulate concerning the men's disappearance, from straightforward accident to foul play and the actions of sea serpents. The official inquiry concluded that the keepers had been swept away by a freak wave, but an air of deep mystery has clung to the place ever since.[3]

Along its entire length, the west coast of the mainland is studded with the passages of long sea lochs, the land often bare and rugged, steep mountains rising inland. In such inhospitable terrain, with much life and industry on the islands, it is natural that the sea would offer the most attractive highway and that the waters would often be contested as Norse and Gael, as then the later clan affinities struggled to exert hegemony. In all Britain there is no other region so little changed by development. Since the dark epoch of the Clearances in the late eighteenth and nineteenth centuries, population has declined, many of the old settlements swept away; only the gaunt and abandoned walls, mute testimony to a largely vanished way of life, remain.

NORTHWARDS
To the north lie two more island archipelagos: Orkney (Orkney Islands) and Shetland. The former is some 10 miles off the coast of Caithness, comprising a grouping of over 70 islands and islets, almost a third of which are uninhabited. Mainland, some 202 square miles in area, is the largest of these. The place was inhabited long before Norse and latterly British admirals came to appreciate the advantages of Scapa Flow. First settled by Neolithic farmers, it remained, for some centuries, in the possession of the kings of Norway and was not finally annexed by the Scottish crown until 1472.

> Further than Hoy
> The mermaids whisper
> Through ivory shells
> a-babble with vowels
> George Mackay Brown, 'Further than Hoy'

Northwards again, to the furthest extremity of the British Isles, lies Shetland, washed by the Atlantic on the west and the North Sea to the east. Again, the largest island in this archipelago is named

Mainland, at 374 square miles the third largest in British waters. Of the 100 or so islands only 15 are inhabited. Colonised by early farmers and later part of the Pictish kingdoms, Shetland was conquered by Vikings by the end of the ninth century. Powerful jarls, such as Thorfinn, an ally of MacBeth, ruled independently of both Scotland and Norway. The latter remained strong in the north until the reverse at Largs in 1263. King Christian I was obliged to mortgage Orkney and Shetland to the Scottish crown when he failed to stump up the requisite cash sum needed to fund his daughter's dowry. Subsequent attempts by succeeding Scandinavian monarchs to redeem the charge were rejected.

Cape Wrath, lonely, bare, majestic – the name in Old Norse means 'turning-point' – was a handy rendezvous and re-victualling stop. Ironically the martial traditions of the Vikings are fully reflected in modern usage, for the area is home to a NATO training ground for combined arms exercises involving land, air and seaborne forces. Despite the roar of jet aircraft and rumble of guns and small arms, the *Clo Mor* cliffs, some 3 miles east of the lighthouse and the highest in Britain at over 900 feet, are home to thriving colonies of seabirds. From Cape Wrath to Duncansby Head in Caithness, the North Coast of the mainland is, in the west, punctuated by the long inlets of Loch Eriboll and the Kyle of Tongue, a pattern of points and headlands interspersed with broad, sandy beaches. The former fishing settlement of Dounreay, has, for over half a century, been taken over by what was the first of the nation's nuclear reactors. Then there is the long south-westerly sweep down to the Dornoch Firth past Wick and Helmsdale, then Cromarty and the Moray Firth and on to Inverness, the Highland capital.

EASTERLY

This long east coast is a very different fellow from the west, punctuated by deep inroads of the sea firths but devoid of sea lochs and, in the main, encroaching hills. This is the land of fishing ports and industry. Inverness was a noted centre for ship building in the medieval period. East of the city on the south bank of the Firth, at Ardersier Point, mighty Fort George guards the narrows. Built at vast expense to the public purse, following Culloden in 1746, this great artillery fort was intended to deter future rebellions. In fact, the slaughter on Drummossie Moor had already achieved that particular objective admirably.

Aberdeen, the principal settlement in the north-east, was a thriving port trading with the Continent. In the early fifteenth century, Provost Davidson augmented his living from taverns by engaging, with some success, in privateering. He was in partnership with Alexander, Earl of Mar, the illegitimate son of the notorious 'Wolf of Badenoch', Earl of Buchan. Theirs proved a fruitful partnership. From his base on the Shiprow, the provost found handy vessels, and Mar provided the necessary muscle, his 'caterans' drafted as marines. In 1410 Davidson took a hefty prize in the form of a well-laden cog out of Danzig, bound for Flanders. The French impounded the ship when the prize crew docked at Harfleur, but the Scots produced a letter of marque from the *Parlement* in Paris, which trumped the rightful owner's claims!

Now the Danzigers wanted blood. Mar's causally dismissive responses to their no doubt outraged correspondence, wherein he suggested unnamed Dutch fishermen as the true culprits, sparked a private feud between Danzig and the city of Bon Accord. And for this the Aberdonians were well and enthusiastically prepared. On 6 July 1412 a Hanseatic cog, bound for Scotland out of Rostock, loaded with flour and ale, was taken off Cape Lindesnaes. The Scottish pirates threatened to throw the luckless skipper overboard, though this was probably mere bluster, and the crew were mostly let go in the boats. Some, however, perhaps less fortunate, were transported to Aberdeen and used as forced labour on the earl's construction projects! Provost Davidson was not a party to this last venture, for he had followed Mar's standard on the fatal field of Harlaw a year earlier, when the earl led a primarily lowland force against Donald of the Isles' caterans, and there fell nobly in the fight.[4]

James VI described the ancient Kingdom of Fife as a 'beggar's mantle fringed with gold'. He was referring to the wealthy chain of coastal ports and fishing harbours, St Andrews also being justly famed as one of Europe's great universities. The ports traded with the Low Countries, exporting wool, linen, coal and salt. Southwards, across the Forth, the coastline of East Lothian is dominated by sweeping cliffs that fall, dazzlingly sheer to the sea, gaunt sentinel of the Bass Rock standing off. The bare remains of lonely Fast Castle still cling to their precarious outcrop, and Eyemouth retains traces of the defences constructed there in the 1540s by the French to counter the English strength at Berwick.[5]

DEFENDING THE COAST

In the course of the Second World War, Fife had the unexpected distinction of being the only stretch of Britain's coastline to be defended by foreign, in this case, Polish troops under General Maczek. Churchill had come to an agreement with the Polish government in exile to this effect and it was Poles, brave men who had escaped the rape of their country and vowed to fight on against the Nazi tyranny, who performed these duties. The soldiers carried out sentry duty and patrols along the beaches of Fife and the Tay estuary, as far north as Arbroath, while also keeping locals entertained with a series of parades and marches. All that now remains of this intriguing and largely forgotten aspect of the war are the lines of anti-tank obstacles that still line some beaches. It was a Polish officer, Lieutenant Josef Stanislaw Kosacki, who invented the mine detector, which would be of inestimable value to Allied troops.[6]

Coastal defence is as ancient as naval warfare. Changes in the nature of the perceived maritime threat govern the measure of response. The Dalriadic Scots built their forts, such as Dunadd, close to the water's edge. Dumbarton Rock was the chief hold of Strathclyde. Somerled, the Norse-Gael Lord of the Isles, built a chain of forts to guard and victual the galleys patrolling the sea lanes of the West, and these formed the foundation of many coastal castles, such as Dunaverty, Mingary and Tioram. Others like Tantallon, Dunbar, Berwick and Eyemouth frequently featured in the long wars with England. During the Napoleonic Wars, when the possible threat of French invasion hung in the air, a new form of coastal defence, the Martello Tower, was conceived and thrown up around the nation's coastline. These were solidly built circular brick towers, blockhouses in effect, mounting a single, traversing roof gun. One was constructed at Leith in 1809 and, six years later, a further pair was erected at Longhope in Orkney, these latter examples as a response to hostilities with America. All three were again put into repair during subsequent alarums in the 1860s.

During the twentieth century, in the course of both world wars, the need for coastal defence swelled as perceived threats developed, aggression now coming from the air as well as the seas. James IV was one of the first to construct bespoke defences covering the Firth of Forth. He was, of course, concerned about the menace from England. By 1914, road and rail communications, industry and the great naval base at Rosyth had vastly increased the attractiveness of the target area. Both shores were studded with coastal batteries and searchlights. Other positions were established on the islands, the sea approaches were sown with mines, booms and anti-submarine nets. Scapa Flow and the Cromarty Firth were likewise girded with a ring of iron. Largely decommissioned after 1918, this necklace of fortifications was almost entirely refurbished on the outbreak of fresh hostilities in 1939. Now the threat was primarily from the air and anti-aircraft ('AA') batteries became the new front line. Initially these gun emplacements were rather ad hoc, earth and sandbag redoubts with the gunners living under canvas, fat, sausage-shaped barrage balloons, billowing above. In time these primitive works were extended and dug to form concrete casemates and bunkers, linked by tunnels, canvas replaced by the ubiquitous Nissen hut.

Airfields sprouted like a rash across the land, some of these subsequently developed into civilian aerodromes and now airports. Others lie, half reclaimed by nature, only traces of the paved runways, foundations of the control tower and bases for the Nissen huts survive, hidden among weeds, spectral reminders of the desperate days of 1940. Camouflage was employed to conceal the true nature of many defensive installations, a tactic that was continued throughout the long years of the Cold War, post 1945. This coastal network was complemented by 'stop-lines' inland, secondary defensive networks, anti-tank ditches and concrete pillboxes. The long sandy beaches of the east coast were studded with tank obstacles, squared blocks of concrete, many of which remain, mute testimony to what might have been. Most of these installations were intended to endure for no longer than the period covered by the hostilities and swiftly deteriorated, others were dismantled for safety reasons, yet many survive, decaying, silent, yet still deeply resonant.

Heritage from the Sea

It is along the length of this rugged and ever-changing coastline that the history of naval actions in Scottish waters unfolds. Here ships fought in single, squadron and fleet actions; mighty navies such as Germany's in 1919 went to their watery graves; warships from birlinns to Polaris patrolled the approaches. Naval power was highly relevant in the long centuries of Anglo-Scottish conflict. Successive kings of England chose the east coast route to permit their supply ships to keep pace with the army. At the Battle of Pinkie in 1547, gunfire from an English squadron disordered one wing of the Scots' attack and had a material effect upon the outcome of the battle developing on land.

With their myriad inlets and harbours, the coasts of the Western Isles proved a haven for locals who sought to augment their meagre incomes by indulging in the more profitable game of robbery under arms. The inhabitants of Canna proved so singularly adept that the Abbot of Iona felt compelled to request a blanket excommunication for the offenders. In the sixteenth century, Pabay was a noted haunt of outlaws who earned their living by preying on ships and neighbours. Longay, off Scalpay, was another notorious haunt (in Gaelic the name means 'pirate ship'). The sea-spoilers took merchantmen and fishing vessels from Flemings, Scots and English, the lure of profit neatly transcended any nationalist sentiment. These buccaneering tendencies were by no means the sole province of disadvantaged commons; the lure was equally attractive to cash-strapped gentry or any with an eye for profit. As previously noted, the Earl of Mar, something of a rogue himself, was happy to partner Provost Davidson of Aberdeen in the fifteenth century. Later, in 1518, Calum Garbh Macleod ('Lusty Malcolm') established a base on Rona. Here was located a secret natural harbour, the *Port nan Robaireann* (literally, 'the Robbers' Port'). From his stronghold of

Brochel Castle, the MacLeod turned the various activities of individual sea-robbers into a flourishing, family-controlled enterprise.

Another sept active on the waves was MacNeil of Barra, whose bare island kingdom proved a poor space for husbandry but possessed a coastline with an abundance of sheltered coves. These formed ideal bases for swift pirate galleys, which would dart like swooping hawks upon unsuspecting merchantmen. In the reign of James VI, Ruari Og proved a most energetic predator. His penchant for attacking English vessels brought him to the attention of Queen Elizabeth who demanded action. James sent Mackenzie of Kintail to clip the pirate's wings, but MacNeil made a fool of the king's officer and pleaded his case in person. His tongue was on a par with his seamanship, for he escaped the noose.[7] In the next century, Hugh Gillespie of Caistral Huisdean, Trotternish on Skye was a noted sea-thief, captured not by the crown but by his foes from Clan Donald. He ended his life and career in the dungeons of Duntulm Castle, tormented by helpings of salt beef rations and no water.

COLD WAR

A form of conflict the piratical clansmen and later buccaneers would never have dreamt of occurs regularly around Faslane naval base and surrounding waters.[8] Here are based Vanguard Class Trident submarines: *Vanguard, Victorious, Vigilant* and *Vengeance.* On 25 October 1992, about 50 protesters from the Faslane Peace Camp and CND, loaded rather perilously into canoes and dinghies, tried, in vain, to deny a nuclear submarine access to the dock. This proved perhaps the most unequal struggle waged in Scottish waters and mercifully bloodless. The gleaming black hull of the great ship, riding the waves like an ancient leviathan, was in stark contrast to the anarchic flotilla of flimsy craft, crowded with earnest protesters, which sought to bar her passage. The weapons within her steel carapace had the capability to unleash destruction on a scale that would dwarf even a dreadnought's finest broadside, yet oddly impotent against a squadron of tiny craft, striving as the symbols of peace.

One of these minnows, complete with obligatory film crew,

rammed the bows of the submarine, a satisfyingly dramatic flourish if somewhat pointless. Swimmers, leaping from the dinghies, threw themselves in its path, to no greater effect. The protests continue today, and debate over a further generation of Trident missiles has added fresh fuel. In one sense *Vanguard* and her sister boats represent natural successors to the longships; there is an echo in their clear and uncompromising lines, combining grace with function, power and motion. Yet these nuclear submarines with their deadly armament represent the distillation of the power of the modern industrialised state, geared for war. The very terror of this fearsome arsenal could be said to have successfully acted as a deterrent to major world conflict since 1945.

The story of navies in Scottish waters is far from over.

> A shiver passed over every Viking. Strong
> Men shook as a child when lightning plays.
> Then the trembling passed. The mircath, the
> War-frenzy came on them. Loud laughter
> Went from boat to boat. Many tossed the
> Great oars, and swung them down upon the
> Sea, splashing the sub-dazzle into a yeast of foam.
> Fiona Macleod, 'Washer of the Ford'

TWO

✦

Kingdom by the Sea

A foe from abroad, or a tyrant at home,
Could never thy ardour restrain;
The marshall'd array of imperial Rome
Essay'd thy proud spirit in vain.

Robert Burns

Naval actions in Scottish waters probably occurred from an early period, but the first recorded instances of warships in northern waters arise during the time of the Roman occupation of Britain, or at least its southerly part.

THE COMING OF ROME

For warships, Rome relied upon the classical Greek trireme, though the design appears to have originated in Phoenicia. These vessels were powered by three rows of oars on each side, with one man per oar, and represented a development of the Homeric pentekonter, which had 25 oars per side. The technological advance which the trireme represented derived from its staggered seating arrangement, which facilitated three benches on each vertical. The Greek trireme most probably appeared in its developed form in the sixth century BC and went on to provide the mainstay of Greek and Mediterranean navies for centuries. A variety of offensive tactics were used. It was possible to manoeuvre around the enemy to secure an advantage, then attack from the rear, where he was more vulnerable. Less subtle, was the head-on charge, deploying a line of ships, with their fearsome rams, simply to batter a passage through an enemy formation. An obvious defence against this latter tactic was the ring or circle, the maritime equivalent of a wagon leaguer.

In earlier conflicts, before the ships became more heavily armoured around the prow and larger in size to accommodate more fighting men, or marines, favoured tactics were to ram and hole, thus sinking the enemy, or using the ram to shear his oars, rendering him immobile. In such close quarters engagements, speed and the ability to manoeuvre were paramount assets. The rowers were consummate professionals, with considerable stamina, and the captain who exercised and trained his crew most efficiently would be likely to come off best in the fight. Once a vessel was holed and sinking then prospects for those vanquished were bleak.

Driven by the need to carry more front-end armour and a greater fighting complement, larger ships were required and the trireme was, in part, supplanted by the quinquereme. The number of oars was not increased, for three banks was a practical limit, but the number of rowers grew from one man to several per oar. Fully crewed by competent oarsmen, a quinquereme could reach 10 knots in favourable conditions. Ramming was, to an extent, superseded by boarding and the use of on-board artillery to clear enemy decks. Triremes and lighter vessels were still popular, especially among smaller navies where the bigger ships required a far greater investment of resources. In battle, smaller and lighter vessels could perform scouting, skirmishing and support roles.

Rome had and continued to use a lighter form of trireme, the liburnian, developed by Liburnian seafarers and used alongside their swift galleys in pirate forays. Sea power was vital in the Mediterranean, yet Rome never valued her fleet as highly as her army. Prior to the outbreak of the first Punic war in 264 BC, she possessed no navy to speak of. The need to confront a major maritime power provided the spur. Despite an initial series of reverses, resilient Roman genius came up with the *corvus* ('raven'), a form of grappling device which lowered a wooden drawbridge affair onto an enemy deck and secured the planking with a curved attached hook, or beak, thus giving the device its name. Once the corvus was in place, Roman marines could swarm over the decks and slog it out in a miniature land battle. By this means, the navy became a vehicle simply for putting legionaries in reach of a ship-based opponent.[1]

It would be vessels of this type that Julius Agricola deployed against the native tribes of Caledonia during his attempts at conquest in the closing decades of the first century AD. During the classical period, Scotland represented the very extremity of the known world, though there is evidence of human habitation dating back to the Mesolithic period, small groups of hunter gatherers, followed by the more numerous and settled peoples of the Neolithic era, possibly as early as 3000 BC. Beaker peoples and the long centuries of the Bronze Age were followed, perhaps around 400–300 BC, by the arrival of iron. These new settlers built great strongholds and distinctive 'vitrified' forts, beginning along the eastern seaboard, while other invaders, possibly from Ireland, infiltrated the west. Latterly, perhaps two centuries before the birth of Christ, a final wave of Belgic invaders percolated from the south, proud warrior elites with their long iron swords and handy chariots.

Early seafarers made use of the hide currach (more commonly known as coracles). These were divided into river and larger seagoing craft, both constructed of hides stretched over a timber frame. This was a cheap and easy form of boat building, which persisted for centuries, though unsuitable for war. Evidence for more substantial timber-built Iron Age ships comes from Denmark: the Nydam Ships, a fascinating archaeological discovery of remains of three ships dating from, possibly, the fourth century AD. These were identified as war spoil, and a quantity of arms and war gear was found alongside. Excavation in Denmark began in the 1860s but was interrupted by war with Prussia. Further work on the site was undertaken as recently as the 1980s.

In terms of construction, the Nydam Ship (the most intact and best preserved of the three) is a clinker-built galley with a broad keel, sturdy planks and comprising five strakes. Keel and planking are finished with cleats for securing the frames. The keel is fashioned from a single oak beam some 14.4m in length, tapering to the ends. Both stem and stern posts may have been carved from a single timber and are secured to the keel by means of a short horizontal scarf, fixed with a brace of plugs. The seams are finished in a manner identical to the later Norse longships, and the overlap is luted with woollen cloth, fastened with iron rivets. She is a slender and elegant craft of probably 15 oars a side, each with a length of somewhere between 3m and 3.5m. Steering was by side rudder.[2]

It appears highly likely that Iron Age inhabitants of Scotland used such craft. Such large deposits of war gear, dating from AD 200 to 400, found with the Nydam ships gives an insight into the type of weapons Celtic marines may have carried. Spear and shield were the most common arms. Perhaps as many as a third of the warriors hefted swords: long blades, not unlike the Roman *spatha* in form, intended for both cut and thrust, and like the spear used in conjunction with the shield. Bows too were in use, finely crafted long staves in yew wood and hazel. We are forced largely into the realm of conjecture when it comes to naval tactics. Archers, as in the later Viking period, would possibly be employed either to deluge the enemy deck or pick off targets of opportunity, until the vessels closed and spears clashed.

> The third year of his campaigns opened up new tribes, our ravages on the native population being carried as far as the Taus [*this could refer either to the Tay or Solway*].
>
> Tacitus, 'The Life and death of Julius Agricola'

Having served with his mentor Suetonius Paulinus against Boudicca, Julius Agricola returned to Britain as governor in the closing months of AD 78. His attentions were initially diverted to Wales where fresh disturbances had broken out, and it was not until the following season that he could shift his gaze northwards. His objective was the subjugation of the entire island of Britain. Key to a successful outcome would be the deployment of his fleet, as his biographer and future son-in-law Tacitus confirms:

> There is however a large and irregular tract of land which juts out from its furthest shores, tapering off in a wedge like form. Round these coasts of remotest ocean the Roman fleet then for the first time sailed, ascertained that Britain is an island, and simultaneously discovered and conquered what are called the Orcades, islands hitherto unknown.

During the course of the third season in the north it appears that a number of the southern Scottish tribes, the Votadini and Selgovae submitted, and he pushed as far north as the Tay. Superior Roman technology and the system of throwing up fortified marching camps prevented any large scale attacks, though the northern climate proved as hostile as the inhabitants. At this point, as Tacitus informs, he turned his attention to Galloway and the south-west: '. . . that part of Britain which looks toward Ireland'. Agricola was contemplating an expedition against Ireland: one of the numerous sub-kings had been driven into exile and begged the governor's aid, thus opening up an opportunity. According to Tacitus, he detained the renegade 'under the semblance of friendship till he could make use of him'. The chronicler also refers to a sea-crossing: 'Agricola himself crossed in the largest ship . . .', though this may mean the Solway Firth rather than the wider expanse of the Irish Sea.

For whatever reason, his proposed Irish venture did not proceed. In AD 83 we find the governor back in the east, advancing northwards and in force from the Forth–Clyde line: 'He explored the harbours with a fleet, which, at first employed by him as an integral part of his force, continued to accompany him. The spectacle of war thus pushed on at once by sea and land was imposing . . .' This combined arms operation was the first of which we have notice to be carried on in Scotland and would subsequently be mirrored by numerous others during the long centuries of Anglo-Scottish conflicts.

Agricola's final and most dramatic campaign in Caledonia began with the dispatch of a naval squadron, whose main function seems to have been to harass the northern harbours. He then advanced his land forces, seeking solace in action from the bitter grief of losing an infant son. He brought the native hosts to battle at Mons Graupius and won a resounding tactical victory. This triumph was consolidated by a steady advance to the north, with the fleet keeping station and sweeping around through the Pentland Firth: 'Those waters, they say, are sluggish, and yield with difficulty to the oar . . .' If Julius Agricola had achieved his imperialist aims, his masters in Rome were less impressed. In balance sheet terms, the game was scarcely worth the candle. Tacitus blames the emperor's jealousy for his hero's recall, Domitian's modest triumphs in Germany being outshone by those of his subordinate in Britain. Agricola was recalled without the customary triumph, slipping back into Rome under cover of darkness and, wisely, retiring from public life. Though the Romans did return, Scotland north of the Tay remained enemy territory, wild and never subdued.[3]

DALRIADA

> O, 'tis a good song the sea makes when
> Blood is on the wave,
> And a good song the wave makes when its
> Crest of foam is red!
> For the rovers out of Lochlin the sea is a
> Good grave,
> And the bards will sing tonight to the sea-
> Moan of the dead!
> > Fiona Macleod, 'Washer of the Ford'

Should you drive southwards, along the line of the present A816, heading from Oban and passing by the southern tip of Loch Awe, through Kilmichael and Kilmartin, you will have entered an enchanted landscape where echoes of the distant past resonate as steady as beat of drum. Swelling from the plain, on the right hand, just before you pass the churchyard of Kilmachumaig, is the great hill fort of Dunadd, mighty rock-hewn fortress and capital of *Dalriada* ('*Riada*'s Portion'). For centuries it dominated the ground and withstood the assaults of hostile Pictish tribes.

A stiff scramble up the conical mound brings you to the twin plateaux that comprise the summit. On the narrow spur between the two lies the 'Inauguration Stone' – the outline of a human foot incised into the rock. Nearby, is a shallow basin, cut from the stone, with a boar in relief. It was here that the ancient kings were consecrated, each slipping his bare foot into the carving, a symbolic affirmation that the new ruler would tread the same paths as his forebears. The exact purpose of the boar's image is unclear, but the basin was used for ritual ablutions accompanying the ceremony.

With outstanding views along Kilmartin Glen and the serpentine trail of the River Add, the place vibrates with the pulse of history. The citadel echoes the cyclopean masonry of the Bronze Age settlements of Homeric Greece, great Mycenae, Tiryns and Argos.

It was in AD 258 that the Irish warlord *Cairbre Riada,* son of High King *Conar,* who already held a province named Dalriada in Ulster, landed on the coast of Argyll and established a fresh domain there. This initial phase of colonisation was little more than a beachhead, and no real expansion seems to have taken place till after AD 500, when a wave of fresh immigrants, led by Fergus mac Erc, traversed the narrow sea and established Dunadd ('The Fort of the River Add'), on the plain of *Moine Mhor,* embarking on decades of intermittent strife with their Pictish neighbours and the Strathclyde Britons. Earlier Roman writers had named these Irish Celts from Antrim as the 'Scoti' and, in the ninth century, when the Scottish chieftain Kenneth MacAlpin united the Picts and the Scots, this name was applied to the whole.[4]

Evidences for naval activity in the long, sanguinary cycle of battles between Picts and Scots, Strathclyde Britons and Northumbrian Angles is tantalisingly sparse. Picts and Scots are likely to have relied heavily upon maritime traffic for both commerce and war. Concrete references are scarce, though *The Annals of Tigernach* have an entry for 729 which asserts: 'A hundred and fifty Pictish ships were wrecked upon Ros-Cuissine [*possibly Troup Head*].' This would suggest war fleets of substantial numbers. A later entry for 733 mentions a Scottish squadron active off the Irish Coast with a battle fought in the River Bann. *Flaithbertach* is given as the commander of this expedition, and *The Annals of the Four Masters* makes reference to the same leader with his mercenaries. This suggests the Scots had been hired as free lances to intervene in an Irish dispute – such a trade in military skills has a later resonance with the Galloglas.

Ireland was regarded as militarily backward during this period, when revenge, glory seeking and spoil were prime motivators. Even the magnatial classes who led in war possessed only basic equipment, generally devoid of mail or harness. Ancient La Tene pattern swords or copies of Roman spathas, broad-headed spears, bows and axes comprised the armoury. Their descendants in Argyll, however, appear more vigorous. Dalriada was divided into three separate lordships; themselves subdivided into *davachs*, which comprised settlements of a score of households. Each of these sub-units was expected to furnish two warriors from every three households. This probably gave each of the trio of lordships a force of between 600 and 800 armed fighters able to do service on land or sea.

These immigrants imported their fine bardic lays and, sub-sequently, in the retelling, many became localised and associated with Scottish settings. Thus, the Battle of Ventry, the battle of the 'White Strand', became linked to the Big Strand in Islay. *Daire Donn*, the High King appears with his vast war fleet to assert superiority over the Hebrides. The Gaelic paladin *Finn* with his own war band the *Feine* contest the issue in a long and bloody fight, which sprawls over the white sands and the sea beyond. Much of the combat involved duels between champions, both sides paying freely with their mingled blood:

> Many a sword and shield
> Was scattered on the strand,
> The strand of Fintray of the port;
> Many dead bodies lay upon the earth,
> Many a hero with a vacant grin.
> Much was the spoil we gathered in the fight.

By comparison the Picts seem to have possessed a competent and structured military system. Warriors were grouped under war leaders (*toiseach*), and earls or *mormaers*. They were renowned for their use of war dogs. The spear was likely the dominant weapon for the foot. Warrior elites may have wielded swords not unlike those found in Ireland at the same time. The muster was based upon the manor (*petta*), and the Picts were considered hardy and competent foes, able to carry on campaigning deep into winter, hardened by their colder northern latitudes.[5]

The Annals of Ulster chronicle an earlier expedition to the Orkneys undertaken by Aedan of Dalriada in 580–581. Two contending factions from within Dalriada met to settle their differences in a sea fight in 719. Denis Rixson suggests that the Irish kings first extended and then maintained their sway into the Hebrides through naval power and that the fleets they disposed were most likely composed of skin-built currachs. *Grettir's Saga* makes mention of *Cearbhall*, King of Ossory (SE Ireland) who was exercising dominion over Barra in the late ninth century. By sea the distance is some 300 miles and argues that the Irish ruler had maritime resources at his disposal. The skin currachs of Irish warlords would be of little service against Norse longships, and the arrival of the Vikings effectively reversed the north–south axis of influence.

'A fleet [*was led*] by Muirchertach, Niall's son, and plundered and brought many spoils from the Hebrides, after obtaining victory and triumph.' This entry from *The Annals of the Four Masters* records a successful raid coming out from Ireland. As Denis Rixson observes, this would have to be accomplished using timber-hulled vessels, quite possibly Norse mercenaries. Those Scots settled in Argyll appear to have imported from their native Ireland a system of ship-service, as a form of feudal due. The *Senchus Fer n'Alban* suggests that each grouping of a score of steadings was obliged to produce so many craft of given dimensions. Thus, the prince or magnate would have the makings of his war fleet provided as a form of taxation. For a coastal, maritime people this is eminently logical. For them wealth would be counted in ships and a strong squadron the measure of a leader's potency. A similar system, known as *leiding* obtained later in the Norse lands.

For traces of Pictish ships, we are obliged to rely upon stone-carved symbols; literary allusions are extremely thin. *The Annals of Tigernach* state that 'The Orkneys were destroyed by Brude.' Clearly to transport a force to Orkney would necessitate access to a ready supply of shipping, but whether the vessels were used simply as carriers or as warships is unclear. The most celebrated carving of a ship is that found on St Orland's Stone at Cossans. On the back face near to the base is the depiction of a vessel with five or six crew. The craft itself does bear resemblance to the Nydam ship. It is without mast or sail, high at prow and stern, clinker built, steered by rudder and likely powered by oars. The image appears to be from the closing decades of the eighth century or opening years of the next.

It is generally believed to be the representation of a Pictish vessel, though there is nothing which suggests that it is necessarily a warship. It has in fact been suggested that the figures within represent Christ and the disciples on the Sea of Galilee.[6]

A further ship image was found in Jonathan's Cave, though the provenance of this depiction is not assured. It is the carving of a simple vessel, again without a mast and having a slender hull and five oars. A sixth is used as rudder or steering board. Some further, rather cruder images have been detected carved on slate at Jarlshof (Shetland). While tantalising, these few depictions scarcely amount to a significant corpus of artistic representation. Certain other images such as the 'Pictish Beast' symbol may have maritime connotations, but these are equivocal and cannot be cited to suggest that the sea and ships were more pivotal to the Picts than the very few boat carvings would indicate.

It has been suggested that a number of promontory forts may have been intended as naval bases, though this remains unsupported by any definitive evidence. Included within this tentative grouping are Burghead, Greencastle, Cullykhan, Dundarg and Dunottar. The first of these locations, Burghead, is adjacent to an excellent anchorage with extensive open sands running westwards in the curve of the bay. The fort itself was substantial, constructed in masonry with two main areas or wards, triple ramparts and ditches cutting across the spit and enclosing an area of almost 3 hectares. Greencastle was timber walled in the fourth century, but this early palisade was replaced by a more substantial affair having squared and mortised oak timbers running both vertically and horizontally. As some of the beams appear to have been recycled, it has been opined that these may originally have been former ships' timbers. While it is tempting and to a degree logical to associate these sites with Pictish fleets, there is no actual archaeology which can be adduced to support the contention. The question thus remains strictly a matter of speculation.

What also seems likely is that, during this early medieval period, the inhabitants of the Isles were already well versed in the ways of the sea-rover. Professor J.F. Watson in his *History of Celtic Place Names in Scotland* highlights the ample distribution of fortified places: 80

duns in the Hebrides, 145 on Orkney and Shetland, no fewer than 217 found around Caithness and Sutherland. He believes these indicate a Pictish hegemony throughout these areas. Gaelic legend includes fantastical tales of these sea-rovers:

> The time the Formor used to be coming to Ireland, Balor of the Strong Blows, or, as some called him, of the Evil Eye, was living on the Island of the Tower of Glass. There was danger for ships that went near that island, for the Formor would come out and take them.

One of the more enduring tales concerns St Comgall, who had his ministry on Tiree. He had quit his foundation at Bangor to pursue a vocation among the islands and continued the earlier work of St Brendan, developing a monastic settlement on Tiree. The saint, as was his custom, was labouring in the fields and, the weather being cold and damp, placed his pall over his cassock. While he was thus engaged, Pictish sea-thieves attacked in their swift galleys, taking up the village and carrying off everything of value, including slaves and livestock. When a band chanced upon the saint, seeing his pall, they were deterred, through fear, from molesting him. So enraged was Comgall, when he saw the havoc these marauders had wreaked, that he called down curses upon them and invoked God's wrath. The Almighty duly responded and stirred up a tempest, which wrecked the pirates' ships and relieved them of their spoil. Another holy man, St Donnan was less fortunate, losing his life to the sea-robbers.

Columba too, expressed saintly wrath at the depredations of the pirates, particularly King Conall of Dalriada. The saint confronted the Scot at Ardnamurchan, as the sea-reavers were loading their spoil, the third occasion they had descended on the hapless locals. Arrogantly, the king dismissed the admonitions of this holy man, laughing as Columba besought the help of God. Again the Lord took heed, raising a violent tempest that struck down the pirate ship and took the lives of all aboard. An enigmatic Irish poet, Blind Arthur MacGurkich, tells of a later, seaborne escalade mounted by the MacSeeinys (McSweens) against Castle Sween. The provenance of these verses may be suspect, but as I.F. Grant points out in that magical pre-war book *The Lordship of the Isles*, the imagery is arresting:[7]

Tall men did manage the ship,
Men, I think, to urge their way;
No hand without a champion,
A slashing, vigorous, noble hand.
With coats of black all were supplied,
In this bark, noble their race,
Bands with their broad, brown belts,
Danes and nobles were they all,
Chieftains with ivory and gold,
The crew on board this brown sailed ship,
Each with a sheaf of warrior's spears,
Shields on their hooks hung round the sides.
Widespread wings, speckled sails,
Bearing purple, all of gems;
A long handsome, gentle band,
Stood along the stout-made spars.

———◆———

THREE

Scotia: Coming of the Longships

The birlinns came on against the noon. In
The sun-dazzle they loomed black as a shoal
Of Pollack. There were fifteen in all, and
From the largest, midway among them, flew
A banner. On this banner was a disc of gold.
'It is the banner of the sunbeam!' shouted
Olaf the Red, who with Torquil the One-
Armed was hero-man to Haco. 'I know it
Well. The Gael who fight under that are warriors indeed'.
Fiona MacLeod, 'Washer of the Ford'

A FURORE NORDMANNORUM, LIBERA NOS, DOMINE –
'From the fury of the northmen O Lord, deliver us' was a litany
without need of vellum. It was graven on the hearts of men
whenever and for as long as that fury fell.
Gwyn Jones, A History of the Vikings

The *Anglo-Saxon Chronicle* records that the portents for the year AD
793 were unfavourable. If so, then for the inhabitants of
Northumbria at least, this dire forecast was to prove entirely correct.
For, in that year the community of Lindisfarne was the first to taste
the fury of the Northmen, the Vikings. They came out of a bright
clear sea, sunlight chasing movement of the oars, three long, sleek
ships of a kind not before seen in these coastal waters. They were
elegant and graceful, seeming to skim across the placid sea, but the

great square sail snarled pagan imagery, a dragon's head reared from the curved prow, and proud shields of warriors arrayed her sides.

Those men who swept ashore were tall and well proportioned, clad in gleaming ring mail, their weapons, spears, Danish axes and double-edged blades sang of death. The monks were killed or abused without pity or comment, death just a function of terror; their calling card. Anything of value was methodically looted and piled, any comely girl or youth was seized as trade. In the brief fury of the sack, laity and clergy were pillaged, settlement and monastery given to the flames, the place stripped and emptied. The Norsemen had arrived.

> Stumbling, the survivors
> Scattered from the carnage,
> Sorrowing, they fled to safety,
> Leaving their women captured.
> Maidens were dragged in shackles
> To your triumphant longships;
> Women wept as bright chains
> Cruelly bit their soft flesh.

THE NORSEMEN

Such scenes were to be enacted and re-enacted along the coasts of England, Scotland and Ireland as the sea-rovers made their presence felt. It is uncertain as to precisely which factor, or set of factors, triggered this explosive wave. Over-population of Scandinavia may have been relevant. Certainly Denmark experienced a surge in population during the course of the seventh and eighth centuries after Christ. In Western Europe the Carolingian Empire boosted trade and prosperity, commerce was fed by fat bellied merchantmen, which would attract pirates, swift as flies to a rotting carcass. Equally importantly, perhaps even paramount, the Norsemen had the means to roam the seaways at will. Developments in shipbuilding technology had resulted in firstly the longship and the less martial merchantman, the knorr. Although the former has enjoyed the more glamorous role, the latter was the tool of trade and colonisation, consolidating what the war vessels had won.

This sudden and terrible swiftness – the emerging of these pagan warriors in their rapier craft, springing from the very vastness of the oceans is a powerful image, but probably misleading. The Norse raiders were, of course, good sailors, but long voyages over open water were risky; island or coast-hopping was preferable. In all probability, Vikings had established landing places in Orkney and Shetland before they descended down the east coast, probably by the end of the third quarter of the eighth century. Unst at the north-east corner of Shetland is a bare 200 miles from Bergen. From there to the mainland is achievable by island hopping, opening up both seaboards and the approaches to Man and Ireland.

Island hopping also provided opportunities for re-victualling, at small harbours and staging posts or by raiding the *strandhogg*. Making free with handy flocks or herds of cattle could be accompanied by the lifting of local teenagers, the *materiel* of the slaving business. Where no useful harbour presented itself, the ships could be beached, ideally on a defensible island or river-loop where a defensive stockade could be thrown up. Loss of their ships was crippling to the sea-raiders, and war leaders would go to great pains to ensure secure anchorage. Two years after Lindisfarne was given to the flames, it was Iona's turn. The monastery was thoroughly pillaged then and twice again in 802 and four years after, while the precincts were still being rebuilt after the preceding devastation. Thus the *Annals of the Four Masters* records:

> I-Columcille [*Iona*] was plundered by the gaill;
> and great numbers of the laity and clergy
> were killed by them, namely sixty-eight.

Also in 795, the sea-rovers struck at Ireland taking up Innismurray and Inisbofin. By 824 even distant and desolate Skellig Michael was stripped of its meagre treasures. By 840 the Vikings were over-wintering on Lough Neagh and commenced their colonisation of Dublin in the following year. The Irish princes launched a series of concerted counter-attacks, but not until the rise of a unified Ireland under Brian Boru, in the late tenth and early eleventh centuries, did the Norsemen find themselves being put under real pressure, which climaxed with the great fight at Clontarf in 1014. When Kenneth MacAlpin united Scotia in the ninth century, the Norse inroads were again curtailed. However, this came too late for the ancient province of Dalriada, effectively under Norse control since King Eoganan fell in the course of a sea-fight in 834. Some decades later in 870, the war bands of Ivar and Olaf from Dublin captured the great rock of Dumbarton, capital of Strathclyde. Seven years later Danes, possibly from Northumberland, struck at Pictland, defeating and killing King Constantine II.

Despite the ferocity normally associated with the Vikings, their colonisation can be divided into three approximate phases. The first of these, after AD 780 till, say, 850 was a process of economic migration, a movement of settlers into Orkney and Shetland. In all probability these were entirely peaceful landings; the islands being very sparsely inhabited. After 795, however, the sea-rovers descended like wolves upon the monastic and other settlements, opportunists rather than settlers. Once Harald Fairhair had established a level of stability in Norway and appointed jarls or earls who held their grant directly from the crown, more aggressive expansion occurred. Ketil Flatnose became earl of the Hebrides and, to the south, the Norse made inroads into Galloway. Those later warriors, who claimed their mixed descent from these invaders and the native Gallowegians, became the feared Gallgaels.[1]

> In a word, although there were an hundred hard steeled
> iron heads on one neck, and an hundred sharp, ready, cool
> never-rusting, brazen tongues in each head, and an hundred
> garrulous, loud unceasing voices from each tongue,
> they could not recount, or narrate, or enumerate, or tell,
> what all the Gael suffered in common, both men and women,
> laity and clergy, old and young, noble and ignoble,
> of hardship and of injury and of oppression in every house
> from those fearless, wrathful, alien, pagan people.
> *The War of the Gaedhil with the Gaill*

THE VIKING ART OF WAR

Contrary to their wild image, these Norsemen possessed discipline to season their fire, were well-equipped and were formidable in arms. Their swift galleys, with shallow draught, enabled them to dominate coastline and estuary to deliver mailed warriors in whichever place they chose to assault, to concentrate their force for a decisive blow at any one point. An Irish chronicler of the early tenth century bore witness to these impacts:

> There were countless sea vomitings of ships and boats. Not one harbour or landing port or fortress in all of Munster was without fleets of Danes and pirates. There came the fleet of Oiberd and the fleet of Oduinn and the fleets of Griffin, Snatgar, Lagman, Erolf, Sitruic, Buidninn, Birndin, Liagrislach, Toiberdach, Eoan Barum, Milid Buu, Suimin, Suainin and lastly the fleet of the Inghen Ruaidh. All the evil Ireland had so far suffered was as nothing compared to the evil inflicted by these men. The whole of Munster was plundered. They built fortresses and landing ports all over Ireland. They made spoil land and sword land. They ravaged Ireland's churches and sanctuaries and destroyed her reliquaries and books. They killed Ireland's kings and champion warriors. They enslaved our blooming, lively women taking them over the broad green sea . . .

To Norsemen the Hebrides were known as the 'Sudreys' (the Southern Isles), in the same way as the Orkneys were named the 'Nordreys'. For a while both were under the sway of the Orkney earls, men of the calibre of Sigurd and Thorfinn. After the latter's death in 1065, authority reverted to Man, where Godfrey Crovan had established an independent minor thalassocracy. Magnus Bareleg, King of Norway, in his expedition of 1098, sought to re-establish control of the west. His methods were somewhat less than subtle, as his bard Bjorn 'Cripplehand' extolled:

> In Lewis isle with fearful blaze,
> The house-destroying fire plays,
> To hills and rocks the people fly,
> Fearing all shelter but the sky.

In Uist the king deep crimson made
The lightning of his glancing blade;
The peasant lost his land and life,
Who dared to bide the Norseman's stride.

The hungry battle-birds were filled
In Skye with blood of foemen killed,
And wolves on Tiree's lonely shore,
Dyed red their hairy jaws in gore

Having set his seal firmly and in sanguinary style upon the Isles, Magnus attempted to add Kintyre to his gains by the simple expedient of carrying or portaging his boat across the narrow neck of the isthmus, thus seeking to relegate the place to island status. The Norwegian king agreed terms with Edgar of Scotland whereby territorial limits were fixed. The Isles would be within the Norwegian sphere, but the mainland would remain Scots. Hence Magnus's attempt to define Kintyre as an island! The Norwegian next forayed against Ulster where he fell in an ambush.

Despite these exertions, the Norse grip in the west was never as certain as in the north where the Orkneys were colonised from 880. After his scattering of opponents in the great sea battle of Hafrsfjord (c.870), Harald Fairhair was opposed by émigrés based in Orkney and Shetland. These reversed the normal pattern of raids and carried out maritime forays against the Norwegian mainland. Harald responded by establishing a coastal squadron to patrol the approaches. When this expedient failed, he invaded with fire and sword; after a liberal dose of both, not only did he finish the Orkney rebels, but he extended his authority in the west as far south as Man where: 'the report of his exploits on the land had gone before him . . . and the island was left completely bare both of people and goods, so that King Harald and his men made no booty when they landed.'

Having imposed his will, the king continued by settling the subdued provinces on Earl Rognvald of Moer, who, in turn appointed his brother, the vigorous Sigurd, as jarl. He, with Thorstein the Red, carried on the Viking tradition by raiding extensively against main-land Scotland, annexing Caithness and sending a tremor through

Sutherland and Ross, establishing a base on the Moray Firth, perhaps on the present site of Inverness. Sigurd came to an unexpected and fitting end when, as the *Heimskringla* relates: 'he had killed Melbridge-tooth, a Scotch earl and hung his head to his stirrup-leather, but the calf of his leg was scratched by the teeth . . . and the wound caused inflammation in his leg, of which the earl died . . .' Poetic justice indeed.

Despite their abundant ferocity, the Norse settlers did not long remain an occupying elite; they intermarried and their descendants became Norse-Gaels. MacDonald in Norse translates as 'Summer Warriors'. Somerled and the Lords of the Isles could claim this mixed descent. It was a Norse-Gael confederacy that confronted the growing power of the English kings of Wessex in 937 on the field of Brunanburh. In this great fight the Norsemen and their confederates were decimated: 'Then the Norsemen departed in their nailed ships bloodstained survivors of spears, on Dingesmere over the deep water to seek Dublin, Ireland once more, sorry of heart.'

Brunanburh was a major upset and marked a significant power shift within the British Isles, as the kings of Wessex became rulers of Britain.[2] Power in Scotland shifted north. Sigurd the Stout of Orkney was one who fell on the field at Clontarf, but he had previously consolidated his dynasty's grip by marrying Malcolm II's daughter. Sigurd's son, Thorfinn, passed some of his youth at Malcolm's court and rose to be a great power in the north. In the 1030s he found his wings being clipped by King Olaf the Stout of Norway who insisted on partitioning the earldom, half going to his brother, or half-brother, from his father's first marriage, Brusi. After some six years this half-brother died, his estate passing to his son Rognvald. Magnus, now king in Bergen, increased his share to two-thirds, which Thorfinn accepted, at least for the moment, and entered into an uneasy alliance with his nephew. This would not last.

SHIPS AND SHIPBUILDING
For many years the two famous Viking vessels preserved near Oslo – the Osberg and Gokstad ships – were the principal source of

archaeological evidence for the methods of construction used. In 1962 a further, rich haul of five sunken boats was made off Skuldelev, in Roskilde Fjord, Zealand ('The Skuldelev Ships'). Vessels built and intended primarily for war, developed in the course of the tenth century, sometimes referred to as '*drekar*' (dragon) ships, a reference to the carved prow. The Gokstad ship is described as a '*skuta*' or '*karfi*' – a more all-purpose craft that could be employed for civil or military use. In constructional terms the man-o'-war was longer and sleeker (hence, the 'longship') than its full-bellied cousin. It possessed a shallow draft and placed greater reliance upon oars. In terms of measurement, this might be defined according to the number of oars or 'rooms' (the space between the main deck beams). The average size of Viking raiders seems to have been 16–18 'benches', making a total of 32 or 36 oars. As ships got bigger, 20–25 benches became more commonplace, though in excess of 30 was rare. The celebrated warrior-king Olaf Tryggvasson's giant warship the *Long Serpent* held 34 benches, a veritable leviathan of its day, (the late tenth century).

The Gokstad ship (850–900) is some 76 feet in length with a beam of 17- feet. Such vessels would usually have a small raised deck area at prow and stern with a lower planked deck between. The boards had to be loosely fixed to facilitate the constant baling necessary to keep the vessel from swamping. A canvas awning was rigged to shelter the crew while in harbour or riding at anchor. Many illustrations show the warriors' proud shields hung over the gunwales at sea, though most modern authorities agree this is too fanciful. The shield-array would have hampered the oars and was probably reserved for ceremony or to inspire awe. The targes were hooked in sockets cut into a continuous rail and were almost certainly displayed as a war-panoply as the ship closed to contact with the foe. Rather than fixed timber benches (no trace of which have been found), it is suggested that the seamen's chests were employed as seating for the rowers, though the Vikings might have preferred to keep their gear in hide kitbags, which could be used as mattresses. Oars were bespoke, cut to match the lines of the vessel, but averaging some 16–18 feet in length.

A lone crewman could handle a single oar but, if the ships were geared for battle, two or perhaps three rowers could be carried – this meant both more spears for the melee and greater acceleration through the water. For the decisive encounter at Svoldr (1000), the *Long Serpent* might have crammed 300 souls onto her decks, allowing for a full complement or oarsmen and additional marines. Once out of sight of land, the sail would be hoisted and this provided the means of propulsion for the bulk of the voyage, with favourable winds, perhaps going as fast as 11 knots. When contact was imminent, the sail (possibly wool or linen) was taken in and the mast lowered – typically half the length of the ship in height so it would fit snugly. Steering gear was in the form of the steerboard (starboard) oar, which was finished with a removable tiller arm. The carving of fantastical animal heads on prow and stern posts was an ancient art, pagan and deeply symbolic.

Oak, then native to Scandinavia (now, due to the requirements of the Norse shipbuilding industry almost completely denuded), was the favoured wood, though, if this was scarce it was reserved for the keel, and handy substitutes such as pine, ash, birch alder, lime or willow were pressed into service. The keel, the ship's heart, was laid first, with the prow and stern posts being fixed next. Rows of strakes were then nailed to form the hull sections, each board projecting over the one next below ('clinker-built'). Joints were caulked with tarred rope. Such was the shipwright's art that these slim-waisted vessels assumed a wondrously sleek and deadly line. Oar holes were bored in the topmost strake, sealed with small covers to resist ingress of water when she was under sail. The ribs only went in as the last structural component, bound (thus offering a measure of elasticity to the frame) rather than nailed to the strakes.[3]

SEA BATTLES

For the Norsemen, the sea was their natural element, and many battles took place upon it. In the inhospitable terrain of Scandinavia or the equally difficult ground of highlands and islands, broad water highways were the natural areas of contention. Longships were built and bred for war, yet sea fights were relatively static affairs with little scope for superior seamanship, fought in the manner of an encounter on land. The opposing fleets would form line of battle, possibly spear- or wedge-shaped formations with the heaviest forming the tip. Vessels were roped together, gunwale to gunwale, to form one large fighting platform, the prows of the longer vessels, often armoured, jutting out towards the enemy. Higher-sided merchantmen could be employed to stiffen the exposed flanks of the static squadron, their height conferring an advantage. Primitive rams or iron points – '*skeggs*' ('beards') – could be used for holing, though these seem to have been more defensive. Manoeuvring to strike was rare. The fighting platform had the advantage of providing a single space: help could be sent quickly to any area under threat; losses could be made good, dead and wounded dragged clear.[4]

For a battle to take place, both fleets would need to be in sight of each other, and the action would be confined to calm, sheltered water. Before contact, there would be the usual jostling for position. Commanders would scan the opposing vessels for size, the critical height of gunwales, the number of fighting men. Not all marines would wear mail in a sea fight: it was heavy, difficult to stow and encumbered a rower very considerably. The size of the opposing vessels was more important than overall numbers. A few big ships was preferable to a horde of smaller boats: they were higher, formed a better fighting platform and were less vulnerable to the vagaries of wind and tide. It would be the weaker side which formed the defensive raft. The attackers would close in and seek to grapple and board to their best advantage. As a 'pre-emptive strike', the weaker squadron might bunch and concentrate on targeted enemy vessels, possibly seeking to kill or capture the enemy admiral.

Shearing the enemy's oars was a popular tactic: as the masts were lowered prior to action, propulsion depended entirely on the oars. Loss of these left the foe immobilised. Grapple and board were the orders of the day. Contact was preceded by a deluge of missiles, arrows, throwing spears and axes, a rain of stones. Lighter vessels circled like hungry dogs, acting as marksmen, sniping enemy officers or pushing reinforcements into the fight. Hostilities would commence at some distance, as the ships formed up, with long-range shooting intended to pick off key figures on the enemy decks.

Once the two sides were locked together, the battle became one of attrition. Heavily armed warriors in the melee, a shield wall at sea, the decks soon crowded with dead and dying, literally awash with blood. On land either side, finding themselves hard pressed, can seek refuge in flight. Not so upon the harsh surface of the sea. There is no hiding place, no sheltering forest or moss, only small boats to gather survivors. Shield to shield, blade to point, the combatants would remain locked in a murderous embrace till one side broke or both simply fought each other to a standstill. Once either could claim the victory, the dead would be heaved overboard, enemy wounded, throats cut, sent splashing after. For the victors, captured enemy vessels were fine prizes, hopefully laden with treasure and spoil. Winning boats defined victory. Once a vessel had been cleared, the victorious attackers would likely secure their prize and investigate the spoils before, if at all, returning to the fray.

Specialised marine equipment did not really exist as such. Men wore much the same as they would on land: woollen tunics and leggings, leather or cowhide shoes or boots; fur-lined cloaks would help to keep out ice laden northern winds; striped breeches, rich woven hems were commonplace. The Viking was often something of a peacock, much concerned with his appearance;[5] hair was worn long, plaited and often dyed. Similarly, they used the same weapons they would wield on land. To arm himself, a warrior might boast a fine shirt of ring mail, the 'woven breast net' of Beowulf, a double-edged cutting sword or the shorter seax, handy for infighting when the press of the shield wall inhibited the sword swing. Long-handled Danish axes, which the Norsemen could heft with lethal ease, throwing axes, broad-bladed spears, lighter javelins, the circular shield of laminated fir planks and a round iron helmet completed his war gear. Though it relates to Olaf Tryggvasson's last stand in the Battle of Svoldr, the following extract from his saga carries the essence of a set-piece sea battle of the era:

Earl Eric was in the forehold of his ship, where a shield wall had been set up. Hewing weapons – the sword and axe – and thrusting spears alike were being used in the fighting and everything that could be used as a missile was being thrown. Some shot with bows, others hurled javelins. In fact so many weapons rained down on the 'Serpent', so thickly flew the spears and arrows, that the shields could scarcely with stand them, for the 'Serpent' was surrounded by longships on every side. At this King Olaf's men became so enraged that they ran on board the enemies' ships so as to have their attackers within reach of their swords and kill them. But many of the enemy ships had kept out of the 'Serpent's' reach so as to avoid this and most of Olaf's men therefore fell overboard and sank under the weight of their weapons.

The saga goes on to relate how an archer shoots at Earl Eric, darts thudding into the boards. The earl instructs one of his own bowmen to return the compliment, splitting the shooter's bow. Olaf's men, thinned by missiles, cling desperately to their decks, spearmen on the raised decks, fore and aft, doing the greatest execution. Amidships, where casualties are highest and the king's men are weakest, Earl Eric leads a commanded party[6] of 14 broadswords onto the blood washed deck. Fighting is savage and prolonged, but reinforcements from the foredeck drive the boarders back. As the battle rages, Earl Eric tries again, his boarding party fighting to gain a lodgement. So thinned are the defenders that portions of the deck are empty of all but the heaped corpses of the slain. Gradually, the attackers gain the upper hand, forcing Olaf and his survivors back towards the prow. Surrounded and outnumbered, the king's men sell their lives as dearly as they can. Any who try to leap overboard are killed as they jump. Olaf himself is the last to go over the side. His heavy mail drags the king under to his watery grave.

In Scottish Waters

As early as 617, a band of pirates (*Spuinneadair-mara*; sea-robbers), most likely at this early date sailing from Ireland or Man, raided the monastery of St Donan on Eigg. The pirates were gracious enough to permit the saint to conclude Mass before putting him and 50-odd monks to the sword. This was the beginning of a long tradition. Corsairs such as Sweyn Asleifsson were active off the west coast as late as the mid twelfth century. His galleys would over-winter on Gairsay then sweep down the long coastline in spring. Once he scooped a lovely prize of two fat English merchantmen laden with fabric and wine. This, the 'Cloth-Cruise', became legendary. Having consumed the alcohol, the valuable cloth was utilised to effect repairs to the ship's sail. On his final cruise, Sweyn ran out of luck. He attempted a raid upon Dublin but was outfought and killed by the inhabitants. Other Norse pirates – Thormund Thasramr, or Thormond Foals-Leg, Holmfast and his cousin Grim – infested the fine, natural harbours of the Hebrides.

We know the Norse-Gael Onund Treefoot (he'd been careless enough to lose a limb in battle against the formidable Harald Fairhair), cruising with five sail, took on a stronger squadron of eight enemy off a Hebridean island called 'Bot' (Bute). Onund cruised with his ally Thrond; the pair were opposed by two captains, Vigbiod and Vestmar. These Norwegians had chased the rival squadron and caught up with the Hebrideans off Bute. But Onund had chosen these waters with care:

> And when the Vikings saw their ships, and knew how many they were, they thought they had numbers enough, and they took their weapons and lay waiting for the ships. Then Onund bade lay his ships between two cliffs; there was a great channel there and deep, and ships could sail one way only, and not more than five at a time. Onund was a wise man; and he made the ships go forward into the strait in such a manner that they could immediately let themselves drift, with hanging oars, when they wished, because there was much sea-room behind them. There was also a certain island on one side. Under it he made one ship lie; and they carried many stones to the edge of the cliff, where they could not be seen from the ships.

Vigbiod led his ships in to the attack, deriding his foe's disability. The fight was joined in earnest and, in the narrow strait, neither could win the advantage. Onund chose his moment, allowing his flagship to drift towards the cliff as though in retreat. As the longship closed for the supposed kill, his shore party emerged at the lip of the overhanging precipice and rained down their deadly cargo of stones. Depleted and discomfited, the Norwegians sought to disengage but found the constriction of the channel and the adverse current both major impediments.

Thrond engaged Vestmar, and Onund closed with Vigbiod. Now the boaster was put to the test as the two men clashed amidships. Onund had jammed a ship's timber under his false limb to provide stability. His attacker hewed at shield and blade but his point stuck fast in the log. Onund delivered a classic killing cut to the shoulder and his assailant fell, severed arm jetting blood. Disheartened, the remaining attackers crammed into the rearward craft and made a run for it. Onund could not resist the understandable temptation to taunt his dying foe who lay rolling in the gunwales, his blood lapping the timbers, reminding him that the one-legged warrior had triumphed and come off without a scratch.[7]

Rognvald of Orkney (see p. 35) soon fell into dispute with his Uncle Thorfinn. The earl drew supporters from Orkney, Shetland and Norway while the wily and experienced Thorfinn raised forces in Caithness, the west and the Isles. Rognvald had a smaller squadron, in terms of numbers, some 30 capital ships, while his uncle amassed twice that many lesser craft. After battle was joined, however, Thorfinn received a significant and timely reinforcement of half a dozen of larger craft under Kalf Arnason. This intervention was none too soon, for Thorfinn was hard pressed:

> Each of the Earls encouraged his men as the fighting grew fierce, but soon Thorfinn began to suffer heavy losses, mostly because the ships in the two fleets differed so much in size. He himself had a big ship, well fitted out, and he used it vigorously in attack, but once his smaller ships had been put out of action, his own was flanked by the enemy and his crew placed in a dangerous situation, many of them being killed and others badly wounded.

Thorfinn was in serious difficulties. His lighter, predominantly Scottish craft were completely outclassed. The larger, more stable vessels with their critically, higher gunwales made a far better fighting platform. His vessels, mere minnows by comparison, were simply picked off (probably there was accompanying attrition through desertion). Feeling the cold breath of defeat on his neck, Thorfinn, prepared for flight, hacking through the grappling ropes and extracting his wounded. His one remaining hope was Kalf who had been a mere spectator thus far. Responding to the earl's entreaties the Norwegian brought his ships into the fray.

The effect was immediate. His larger vessels, with their markedly higher gunwales cut a swathe through Rognvald's fleet. With his victory seeming certain, it was suddenly snatched away. Part of his fleet, the Norwegian element, cut their losses and made a run for it, leaving their Orkney and Shetland allies in dire straits. Within a short time, the looming verdict was reversed. Kalf's tall-sided longships presumably struck in line and against the flanks of Rognvald's fleet. Their arrows and javelins fell into the packed ranks and did fearful execution, transfixing the earl's marines. Men so confident of victory were snatched by the arrow's song. The attackers would throw stones down onto the decks below, using the advantage of their higher gunwales to the full. The grey waters of the Pentland Firth crowded with the bobbing carcases of the dead, a mess of broken spars and cordage. It was now Rognvald's turn as his flagship came under pressure and the final victory went to Thorfinn.

Despite this triumph, Thorfinn's position was far from safe. Rognvald returned to indulge in a spot of hall-burning, a favoured Norse custom, his warriors downing ale as the flames crackled around the high posts of Thorfinn's dwelling. Any celebration would have been premature, for the quarry escaped in the smoke and presently returned the compliment, Rognvald was less fortunate. Under Thorfinn, now undisputed ruler, the power of the Orkney earls reached its apogee,[8] and the northerners retained their semi-independence from both kingdoms until 1196, when Harald Maddadsson agreed to do homage to William the Lion.

In 1136, a later Earl Rognvald was also obliged to fight for possession of Orkney. He was a client of Harald of Norway and had done the king good service in a recent civil war. The island was held, at this time, by Earl Paul, a son of that Hakon who had murdered Magnus (soon to be canonised). To stiffen the war fleet he was building, Rognvald hired the formidable Frakokk and her grandson Olvir. The cost of their hire was to be a half share in the captured province. Olvir and his active grandparent recruited men from the Scottish mainland and the Western Isles. Their squadron comprised around a dozen craft 'mostly small and poorly manned'. This unimpressive flotilla sailed at midsummer to meet with Rognvald. Aware of his enemies' intentions, Earl Paul had not been idle, amassing ships and recruiting crews.

As his fleet pulled east of Tankerness, they spied Olvir's dozen ships making straight for them, rowing eastwards from Mull Head. Paul put his vessels into a defensive array, lashing them together in the usual way. At the same moment, he received an offer of aid from Erling of Tankerness, a local landowner and his sons. The earl felt his decks were already too crowded and set these willing reinforcements to work collecting hurling stones. Olvir commanded the larger squadron, thus the total number of vessels engaged was not great. Though the majority were of the smaller type, Olvir himself skippered a large capital ship, and he steered straight for the Earl's boat.

As they engaged, Paul's ally Olaf Hrolfson, with another large ship, took on Olvir's smaller craft. Again, height proved decisive, and Olaf soon succeeded in decimating three of the crews. Undeterred, Olvir boldly pressed on, leading a boarding party aboard Earl Paul's vessel. This challenge came unstuck when Olvir was thrown overboard in the melee and, though he regained his ship, the impetus had gone from his attack. His men withdrew and presently began cutting ropes preparatory for flight. Olvir had singled out Earl Paul and brought him to the deck with a blow of his spear. The earl's life and the outcome thus hung in the balance when quick-thinking Svein Breast Rope, of the earl's affinity, intervened:

> There was a lot of shouting and just at that moment Svein Breast-Rope picked up a large piece of rock. He flung it at Olvir, hitting him such a blow on the chest that he was knocked overboard into the sea. His men managed to get hold of him but he had been knocked unconscious and nobody knew whether he was live or dead.

None of Olvir's frantic exhortations availed, and his surviving vessels scattered in flight, hotly pursued by the victorious earl. The fugitives scattered east of Mainland, beyond Ronaldsay and into the Pentland Firth. At length, the survivors made good their escape but five boats were left behind as prizes, their crews heaped lifeless on the sloshing decks. Paul had commanded a mere five ships at the outset but, these being larger, had effectively outfought more than twice their number of smaller Hebridean craft. Had Olvir avoided so reckless an attack and instead manoeuvred to join with Rognvald who had half a dozen good-sized ships of his own, the outcome could have been very different. Paul had plenty of marines, so many he could accommodate no more on deck at the outset. He was short not of men but of ships.

Denis Rixson provides an excellent unscrambling of the somewhat complex patterns of land holding in the Isles and the relationship with the ship levy. This is a form of maritime-based feudal obligation whereby the tenant must furnish the lord with vessel and crews for a specified term as a condition of tenure. The system was formalised in Norway by Hakon the Good in the tenth century, but undoubtedly dates back to a considerably earlier period. Quite simply, the king divided his realm into districts or 'shipredes', each of which owed ship-service. The tenants had to provide the vessel, its cordage, sails, oars and spars, with a competent crew, well victualled for the cruise. It is estimated that Hakon could thus muster a fleet of 300 sail. Whether this system also obtained in the Isles is unclear, but it is highly likely, as this was also a maritime society heavily influenced by and subject to Norse trends. Ships were more than just vessels; they were symbols of power, of wealth and a measure of kingship. Little wonder that magnates were reluctant to hazard their fleets in battle and why taking prizes was far more important than sinking.[9]

There is evidence that muster figures were often fixed at unreasonably high levels to keep pressure on tenants; but feudal obligation was not the only lure. Men would be drawn by affinity with their lord, by the scent of booty and an urge for adventure. It has been estimated that the full levy for Orkney amounted to some 17 vessels. In a night action off Knarston, Earl Erlend, who held half Orkney, could muster seven boats while his opponent and other co-magnate possessed eight. When Harold II of England's exiled brother, former Earl of Northumbria Tostig, sailed with Harald Hardrada towards their joint nemesis at Stamford Bridge in 1066, 17 sail from Orkney swelled the muster.

In the immediate aftermath of Tankerness, Earl Paul, still facing Rognvald, took steps to improve overall levels of turnout. He'd been obliged to face Olvir with only five capital ships in the first instance even though a further two had come up before contact:

> Then people were appointed to raise levies in different parts of Orkney. Thorstein, son of Havard Gunnason, was in charge of North Ronaldsay. His brother Magnus had Sanday, Klugi had Westray and Sigurd of Westness, Rousay. Olaf Hrolfsson went across to Duncansby in Caithness and was in charge there . . . Earl Paul presented his friends with gifts, and all of them promised him their undying friendship. He kept a large force together throughout the autumn till he heard that Rognvald and his men had cleared out of Shetland.

For Man, a further estimate suggests a dozen ships in total. When the King of Man wisely submitted in 1264, following the Norwegian king's reverse at Largs and the collapse of the Norse position, he had ten sail at his command (five carried 24 oars and the remainder half as many). Given that the Orkney earls exercised at least nominal sway over the Hebrides for the best part of a century from the 980s onwards, then ship-service was very likely the favoured form of dues. This, of itself, would not differ greatly from previous obligations to earlier magnates of Scots or Pictish provenance. The Isles and the west coast were relatively impoverished areas, where farming gave a poor yield, so the level of obligation was probably diluted.

Orkneymen were again active in the turbulent maelstrom of Norwegian politics in the late twelfth century, sailing in support of a pretender named Sigurd. These so-called 'Islanders' were opposed by the ruling claimant, King Sverre and his indigenous followers, known as 'Birchlegs'. In the spring of 1194, the king moved to deal with the opposition fleet. His initiative caught the Islanders unprepared, nine of their capital ships being dispersed, though their remaining craft still had the inestimable advantage of size. The magnate Hallkell called upon the Orkneymen to adopt a standard defensive platform, lash their ships together, prepare to use hurling stones and then arrows, as the enemy seeks to close.

King Sverre, who was attempting his manoeuvre in the half light of the spring dawn, ordered his captains to mark their craft with linen bands tied around the prows so that, in uncertain light, they might tell friend from foe. He was aware the enemy enjoyed the advantage of higher gunwales, so he urged his men to hit and run, using speed and handiness as a counter to size and weight, wearing the enemy down with missiles before closing to grapple. The odds were unfavourable. The King had a score of his small ships and, even with numbers of their muster absent, the Islanders could still count 14 sail in their line.

> In the morning, at dawn, the Islanders lay tent-less; and next they loosed their cables, and rowed out from the bay. They laid cords between their ships, both fore and aft, and rowed all in line, and intended to look for King Sverre. But because it was dark, they did not see anything before King Sverre's ships were running at them; and both sides raised the war-cry.

True to plan, the Orkneymen drew their ships together. At this point they were relying solely upon oars for propulsion, and the coming together of hulls splintered many. Presently, they were lashed into a solid fighting platform. The Birchlegs came on fast, speeding from the opaque light of dawn, their fast hulls skimming the water. A shower of missiles greeted their appearance, but the Norwegians held firm to Sverre's tactics. The sailors protected themselves with their shields, like the old Roman *testudo*, darting and lunging, showering the heavier vessels with volleys of darts and javelins. This was their type of fighting, the business second nature.

> Then they rose up under their shields and made a second affray; some threw stones, some shot and they laid their ships so close that some thrust and some hewed. The Islanders received them manfully;

47

they had now the advantage of their higher gunwales. They came with grappling hooks against the king's ship; and they slew the forecastlemen and took the standard, and cleared very nearly all the ships, to the front of the mast.

As the fight came to close quarters, the Islanders clearly established an advantage but, as they sought to board, King Sverre rallied his survivors and they met the attackers amidships with spears and sharp blades. The fight was desperate and hard fought. Men hacked and hewed. Points flickered over the shield wall, short seaxes sought out belly and groin. Men bled and died in the press, their corpses piling grotesquely on the slippery decks. Gradually the Norwegians began to press their foes back, many were driven off and obliged to scramble back to their own ships. While the Islanders took a number of the smaller ships, the larger vessels fought free, though Sverre was paying a heavy price in casualties.

Crippled by his losses Sverre was constrained to withdraw, his vessels breaking contact. Sensing victory, the Islanders cut their lines and prepared to give chase. It was now they began to miss their broken oars, with ships starting to drift on the swell and the cohesion of the platform lost. Again the Birchlegs, divining the discomfit of their enemy, returned to the attack, cutting out individual galleys and laying alongside, three or four to one. Again the outcome hung in the balance when the mainlanders received a sudden and, for them, very welcome reinforcement: a large and sturdy vessel with 100 fresh marines, all well harnessed in burnished ring mail. These laid into the scattered Islanders, wreaking havoc. The Birchlegs took one ship after another. As they cleared the decks of one enemy, they fitted spare oars and turned against the rest. The victory, and it was crushing, went to Sverre:

It is the talk of men that the battle has never been, in which men have conquered against so great gunwale-odds as there were in Floruvagar.[10]

Violence and destruction were very much elements in the Norse incursions. Before the calming effect of Christianity made itself felt, the Norsemen particularly targeted monastic settlements. These offered the richest pickings and were, besides, the major centres of influence. Terror was a tactic the Norsemen understood; striking at the established order, creating social and economic chaos, rendering the common folk more amenable to a new elite. Nonetheless, theirs was, for all the bloodletting, a noble strain, bold, adventurous, courageous and indomitable. Such men can never be enslaved.

———◆———

FOUR

Lord of the Isles: The Hebridean Galley

The reapers sing of war,
War with the shining wing;
The minstrels sing of war,
Of winged war.
                    Gododdin

Men of might in battle eager,
Boast of burning Njal's abode.
Have the princes heard how sturdy
Seahorse raiders sought revenge?
Hath not since, on foemen holding
High the shield's broad orb aloft,
All that wrong been fully wroken?
Raw flesh ravens got to tear.
                    Saga of Burnt Njal

SOMERLED MAC GILLEBRIDE, THE PROGENITOR of the
MacDonald Lords of the Isles, was of mixed Norse-Gael descent
and would claim his line stretched back to the second century AD
Irish hero, Conn of the Hundred Battles. His grandfather,
Gilladomnan, and father, Gillebride, had both married into Norse
nobility and held sway over territories in Argyll and the Isles. Their
tenure was brutally interrupted in 1098 when the rather splendid
Norwegian ruler Magnus Bareleg (so called after his fondness for
Hebridean dress) descended in force to remind his subjects where
their allegiance lay. Both Gilladomnan and his son soon found
themselves skulking in the heather, landless and pursued – a sharp
move to Ireland seemed the wisest course. Somerled, or Sumarlidi,

was thus born in exile and spent his youth in the pleasant pastures of Fermanagh and Monaghan, lands of the Macmahons and Maguires. The lad was born into the Christian faith but much of his education revolved around the discipline of arms. The Norse had won so many battles against the Gael, not because their blood ran hotter, but because they possessed discipline, stout mail and keen-edged blades:

> Not one of the champions of the Irish was able to deliver us from the tyranny of these foreign hordes. This is because of the excellence of the foreigners polished, treble plaited, heavy coats of mail, their hard, strong swords, their well-rivetted long spears, and because of the greatness of their bravery and their hunger for the pure sweet grassland of Ireland.

LORD OF THE ISLES

In 1103, Magnus Bareleg conducted one campaign too many and fell to an ambush during his final foray into Ireland. For the best part of two decades, Gillebride and his son, with their affinity, struggled to recover former holdings in Ardnamurchan and Morvern. These efforts met without success, and the young Somerled found himself again skulking around Loch Linnhe. His prowess was clearly appreciated, however, for when a chief of Clan MacInnes expired, it was to Somerled his kinsmen turned. His base in Morvern was secure and his war band swelling. Great deeds attracted keen blades, and a successful leader could quickly grow his following. Somerled made fresh war upon the Norsemen in Argyll, beating them in the field and seizing their galleys. These prizes formed the kernel of the powerful war fleet he was building. For Somerled, sea power was to be all important, and the young chieftain had come fully to appreciate that control was best exercised through fast, well-armed galleys.[1]

Ardnamurchan Peninsula, a wild, lovely and still echoingly remote landscape, still bears witness to Somerled's many triumphs: Ath Tharacaill (Atharacle), the Ford of Torquil, where more Norsemen were decimated and Glenborrowdale, where he slew Borodil, another Viking chief. Soon Somerled was master of Lorn,

Knapdale and Kintyre. By 1140 he was recognised as a powerful prince, holding sway over Lorn, Knapdale and Kintyre, and he next consolidated his position with a suitable match, marrying Ragnhild, daughter of Olaf of Man. King Olaf was a man of great estate, ruler of his own lands and secure behind the wooden walls of a powerful battle fleet.

The Isle of Man was a Norse kingdom. Olaf's grandfather had been a Viking sea-rover, Godred Crovan, whose curriculum vitae included standing in the shield wall at Stamford Bridge. By 1079 his dynasty was established on Man, which he held in an iron grip till his death in 1095. For Magnus Bareleg this was clearly a case of the overmighty subject, and taming Man had been a prime motivation behind his expedition to the west. Olaf, who succeeded his father Lagman, was described as being small in stature but exceedingly able. He was to rule for over 40 years, a very considerable achievement. Somerled may well have been married before and enjoyed the favours of a number of concubines. He'd acknowledged his son Gillecolm by one of these, and Ragnhild was to give him three more: Dougall, Ranald and Angus. Of these, the first two became progenitors of clans Dougall, Donald and Ruari. Between the date of his advantageous marriage and the death of David I of Scotland in 1153, Somerled steadily increased his power and maintained a distinct independence from the failing ebb of Norway on the one hand and the rising tide of Scotland on the other. In this, his powerful fleet was the key.

David I died in his bed; Olaf of Man was not so fortunate. His long and fruitful reign was ended by the assassin's blade, wielded by his Irish nephews. Godred Dhu ('Godred the Black'), the murdered monarch's son, stormed homeward from Ireland and harried the regicides relentlessly, gaining victory, spoil and renown. These triumphs, however, rather went to his head, and the new king of Man lacked the subtlety of touch that had kept his father on the throne for four decades. Another nephew, Torfinn Ottarson, uncowed by the beatings Godred had handed down and with his own aspirations in Dublin, courted Somerled's son Dougall. Godred, sensing his peril, reacted with customary vigour, and the rival squadrons clashed in cold waters on a winter's night at Caol Isla in the Sound of Islay. This was a land battle fought at sea; in such an engagement the defenders, after the Norse fashion, might rope their vessels together to create a wider fighting platform, those having the higher shipboards on the outside of the array. Attackers would lie alongside and attempt to board.

BATTLE IN THE SOUND

The Manxmen could muster a fine fleet, sleek birlinns and nimble nyvaigs. The former in the role of skirmishers, while the heavier vessels collided and men scrabbled and fought hand to hand:

> Let loose the hounds
> Of war,
>   The whirling
> Swords!
> Send them leaping
> afar,
> Red in their thirst for
> war;
> Odin laughs in his
> Car
>   At the screaming
> Of the swords!

Then the red mist, the blood fury, '*mircath*' would come upon the warriors, each competing for glory and renown. Subtle manoeuvre was impossible once the ships closed. The fight became a heaving, hacking frenzy of swords and long-handled Danish axes.

> Others sprang up and whirled their
> Javelins on high, catching them with bloody
> Mouths; others made sword play, and
> Stammered thick words through a surf of
> Froth upon their lips.

The cold waters of the Sound, black as ink, below a hard winter's moon. Sleek-hulled craft moving, bunched in battle formation, probably the Islesmen braced to receive the Manxmen's rush, archers shooting at the advancing decks, a volley of spears silvering the lunar light.

> The birlinns of the islanders drove swiftly
> On. They swayed out into a curve, a black
> Crescent there in the gold-sprent blue meads
> Of the sea. From the great birlinn that
> Carried the Sunbeam came a chanting voice;
>
> O, 'tis a good song the sea makes when
> Blood is on the wave,
> And a good song the wave makes when its
> Crest of foam is red!
> For the rovers out of Lochlin the sea is a
> Good grave,
> And the bards will sing tonight to the sea-
> Moan of the dead!

Contact comes as the oars cease their pull and the heavy hulls grind one against the other, spewing a torrent of mailed warriors who contest each bloodied foot of deck.

> No man knew aught of the last moments ere
> The birlinns bore down upon the Viking-
> Galleys. Crash and roar and scream, and a
> Wild surging; the slashing of swords, the
> Whistle of arrows, the fierce hiss of whirled
> Spears, the rending crash of battle-axe and
> Splintering of the javelins; wild cries, oaths,
> Screams, shouts of victors, and yells of the
> Dying . . .

Crews would form the shield wall on deck, each man's shield locked with his comrade's. Spears jabbing and thrusting, often no room for long handled weapons, better the thrust of the sword or long-bladed dagger; decks soon heaving with dead and dying. As a man goes down, he is swiftly dispatched; a wounded foe can still cause the victor's demise. The melee could last for some time, bright moon-glare reflecting from the streaming pools of spilled blood. Arrows would be shot from the decks of both the larger, capital ships, and the smaller, fleeter vessels that circled like hungry jackals. In addition to the landsman's habitual armoury, stones were still employed as secondary missiles. Primitive as this sounds, a well-aimed rock could bring down an enemy as surely as a keen-edged blade, stocks were handy and plentiful, their loss overboard inconsequential.

> Olaf the Red went into the sea, red indeed,
> For the blood streamed from head and
> Shoulders, and fell about him as a scarlet
> Robe. Torquil One-Arm fought, blind and
> Arrowspent, till a spear went through his
> Neck, and he sank among the dead. Louder
> And louder grew the fierce shouts of the
> Gael; fewer the savage screaming cries of
> The Vikings . . .

Though he had the greater press of sail, Godred could gain no advantage. Battle, like the ebb and sway of the tide, surged through the long winter's dark. Finally, both sides, battered and exhausted, shipped oars, backed off and parted, spars splintered, decks heaving with press of dead and wounded. None could claim an outright win, but it was Somerled and Dougall who gained. The Manxmen's strength had been blunted and did not recover. The *Chronicle of Man* provides a very succinct reference:

> In the year 1156 a naval battle was fought on the night of the Epiphany between Godred and Somerled and there was much slaughter on both sides . . .

To buy a truce, Godred was constrained to cede the islands south of Ardnamurchan to his rival, who two years later mustered a fleet of

50 ships and struck directly at Man. A further action was fought off Ramsey, and this time Godred was routed, fleeing back to Norway. The Manx chronicler recorded the event with customary brevity: 'In the year 1158 Somerled came to Man with fifty-three ships and joined battle with Godred and put him to flight. He ravaged the whole island and went away.'

THE WEST HIGHLAND GALLEY

The Hebridean or West Highland galley, the craft favoured by Somerled, his contemporaries and descendants for a further five centuries, was a development of the Norse longship. It was a clinker-built vessel, which could be powered by the stroke of the oars, by wind filling the single square-rigged sail or a combination of both. Prow and stern were steeply pitched but, unlike its predecessor, the Hebridean galley was steered by a stern rudder rather than a steering board. These sleek craft were fast and handy, ideally suited to the passages between mainland and islands, built for the seaborne raid or foray. They could easily be beached to unload, and their relatively small size implied they could be more easily transported or portaged over land. We understand from the sources that, during the course of Hakon of Norway's unsuccessful maritime expedition in 1263, it was the lighter galleys of his Gaelic allies which were employed in beating up the area around Loch Lomond. Vessels were portaged from the coast to the shores of the loch.

Typically, galleys were categorised by the number of oars they carried. The nimble nyvaig ('*naiblheag*', literally 'little ship') bore only eight oars. The heavier birlinn (from the Norse '*byrdingr*', a small cargo ship), with the sleek lines of the longship rather than those of the fatter bellied knorr, would have between 12 and 18 oars. Larger vessels, referred to as 'galleys' bore 18+, the biggest, as a rule, carrying 26 oars. In terms of crew size, each vessel could accommodate three rowers per oar, though the handling of reconstructions like the *Aileach* (16 oars) would suggest that the vessel cannot really carry a full complement of 48 crew. In times of war, the vessels would be crammed with fighters. Archers and spearmen would be needed aplenty in the bloody chore of sweeping enemy decks. Prize crews would be required to man captured ships.[2]

Such a great lord as Somerled could muster 80 keels for the fight against the Manx in 1156. Godred we know had more; two years later the fleet that descended on Man comprised 53 boats. For his final and fatal descent on the Clyde, Somerled mustered no fewer that 160 ships. If his host contained 4,000 or so spears, the average complement was around 25. In the thirteenth century, John of Galloway could boast 150–200 sail. John of Islay was accompanied, on the occasion of his betrothal to Margaret Stewart, by a flotilla of 60 craft. When, in 1545, Donald Dubh transported another 4,000 broadswords in a fleet of 180 galleys, the average complement thus numbered 22, a similar figure to that for Somerled's navy, nearly four centuries earlier. Individual chieftains would have one or several boats, and raiding parties could comprise anything from a mere handful to several dozen.

Large-scale naval battles were rare, even the famous fight at Bloody Bay involved fewer than a dozen ships. Most actions were focused on cutting-out raids and single-ship actions. In the dark of a northern winter, that of 1228–1229, King Reginald launched an expedition against the fleet of his brother King Olaf, cutting out the ships in the dark at St Patrick's Isle and putting all to the torch. To a sea king, this was a major disaster. His fleet represented both wealth and power, striking at the fleet inflicted both economic and military damage. Once lost, these ships would be difficult to replace and costly. Hence, in sea fights, the objective was not so much to sink the enemy as to sweep his decks and claim his vessel as prizes.

King Robert I, when assessing the feudal dues from his West Highland magnates and issuing charters, stipulated the feudatory due in terms of ship service. Each tenant in chief was to provide so many ships, with so many crewmen, for such and such a period of time. This notion of 'ship-service', as we have seen, was nothing new and dates from a much earlier period. The worth and due of the magnate was calculated in relation to the keels he could command.

Good, natural harbours were relatively scarce, so it was commonplace to beach the ships overnight. When on a hostile shore, this could prove dangerous, so the squadron might lie offshore. This could also present risks. In 1250 John of Lorn raided against Man, landing forces on St Michael's Isle. As the tide rose, some of the raiders returned to the ships while others foraged on land. The Manxmen, who had been watching the progress of their unwelcome guests with interest, waited till the swelling tide had isolated the men on board then promptly fell upon the rest, killing most.

Nimble keels, highly manoeuvrable, whose oars could lend speed and outdistance sail over short bursts were mighty handy if a warship is on your tail, or like Macneill of Barra in the rout of Bloody Bay, the enemy are three to your one and closing! That the Hebridean galley served for so long, in largely unaltered form, is a testament to its suitability. The fatal weakness was that the vessels could not mount guns. Mediterranean galleys were adapted to carry a single forward bow-chaser, but birlinns continued to rely upon archers and latterly musketeers. In the closing days, engagements such as that fought off Copeland Island in 1595 demonstrated the vulnerability of the galley when facing a man-of-war. The fall of Clan Donald, on the dissolution of the Lordship, and the gradual decline of mercenary service in Ireland also contributed to the galley's demise. The Campbells were essentially landsmen; they did not use the seas as their highway, as their predecessors had done.

THE MACSORLEYS

Somerled had reached the very zenith of his fame. The middle-aged chieftain now styled himself *Rex Insularum* ('King of the Isles'). Together with his son. He held in his palm over 25,000 square miles of territories from the west coast outwards over a necklace of some 500 islands that stretched from the Butt of Lewis to the Calf of Man. This wide sweep was united by the sea-highways of the Atlantic and the Irish Sea. Only maritime power could maintain this wave-girt domain. To sustain his galleys, as they prowled the watery marches, Somerled established a chain of supply-harbours, guarded by forts. A good example stood at Dunyvaig ('Fort of the Nyvaigs'), located on the strategically important southern tip of the Sound of Islay. It was on Islay that Somerled frequently based his rule, presiding over a council of chiefs. Their feasting and games enhanced by the telling of bards who recited great deeds of warriors and war, tracing the proud lineages of the heroes back to semi-mythical ancestors. The present stone-built keeps of Mingary, Aros, Ardtornish, Duart and Tioram were raised on the foundations of these earlier holds. Castle Sween in Knapdale and Skipness also owe their foundation to this period.

From the seas, no new threat emerged, but danger was forming on land. The Anglophile David I had begun to encourage Norman knights to follow when he, in middle age, acceded to the throne. These aggressive mail-shirted newcomers, riding their warhorses, began to filter into the lowlands. This was to be no 1066, no planned invasion, but a steady trickle of new men, skilled in war and land hungry. David, despite his sympathies for the southern kingdom, had been swift to capitalise on the anarchy of Stephen and Matilda, seeking to create a buffer zone in northern England, as far south as the Tweed. To turn this ambition into territorial reality he had demanded feudal service from the men of Lorn and the Isles, the Gallowegians had suffered particularly heavily in the reverse at Northallerton. Somerled had supported his brother-in-law Malcolm MacHeth in an abortive rising, later lending further support to Malcolm's son Donald. Both failed, and Malcolm IV made a show of entering into bonds of amity with both Somerled and Fergus of Galloway.

But a clash of cultures was brewing, Walter Fitzalan, a singularly ambitious Norman knight, raised a motte near Inchinnan, a thrust aimed at the heart of Somerled's domain. The Lord of the Isles did not immediately respond but built a formidable coalition, welding his client chiefs into a concrete alliance, perhaps 4,000 spears in all; a most formidable array against which Fitzalan could mass but a few score horse. But these were Norman knights, the heavy cavalry of their day, unimpressed by the Gael. In 1164 Somerled used his fleet to transport the host to a landfall towards Renfrew. The clash was bloody and decisive, the Gaels for all their fury could not withstand mounted knights and the Lord of the Isles perished in the fight.[3]

Somerled's death did not mark the end of the Lordship of the Isles. His successors, despite much internecine feuding, would raise the Lordship to dazzling heights but, in the aftermath of the disaster at Renfrew, his vast inheritance was divided among his legitimate sons, (Godred Dhu had darted back from exile to reassert his grip on Man). Dougall, as the firstborn, received Argyll, Mull, Coll and Tiree as his portion. Ranald took Islay, Jura and Kintyre. Angus, the junior, had to make do with areas of Ardnamurchan and Moidart with, perhaps, Rhum, Eigg and Bute (Fitzalan may already have snatched this following his victory).

It is perhaps inevitable that the sons should quarrel and seek to assert their contending claims by force of arms. Ranald, who was styling himself 'King of the Isles, Lord of Argyll and Kintyre' went to war with both his elder and younger brothers. In 1192 he was defeated by Angus but, as the feud simmered, the younger was himself, with three of his sons, cut down 18 years later. Ranald may have lived until 1221, his successors became Macdonalds and Macruaris. Dougall's descendants formed the Macdougall clan. Somerled's fractious sons, collectively known as the MacSorleys, and their equally quarrelsome offspring, enjoyed indifferent relations with the burgeoning power of the Scottish crown. In 1221, Alexander II had fitted out an expedition to tame the Islesmen and this incurred the ire of Hakon IV, whose influence had been guaranteed by an agreement dating back to 1098. By 1230 Hakon was sufficiently roused to send a squadron of his own, captained by a captain named Uspak (possibly a son of Dougall MacSorley), who may have struck at Bute where Norman influence predominated.

Alexander II offered to seek fresh terms and even buy out the Norwegian claim altogether, nominating Ewan MacDougall as his client 'King' of the Isles. Ewan held estates in Argyll, as a tenant-in-chief of the Scottish crown, and Alexander, in 1249, led an expedition calculated to remind Ewan of his true allegiance. Alexander died suddenly on Kerrera without achieving his purpose, and the matter of sovereignty in the west remained simmering while his infant successor, Alexander III, grew to manhood. One of Ranald's sons, Donald of Islay (died c.1250), was succeeded in turn by his son Angus Mor, something of a swashbuckler, whose galleys raided Ireland and stung the English settlements there. He became the first chief of Clan Donald to be honoured in verse:

Though he came round Ireland; rare is the strand whence he has not taken cattle: graceful longships are sailed by thee, thou are like an otter, O scion of Tara.

The house of Somerled, the race of Godfried, whence thou art sprung, who did not store up cattle, O fresh planted orchard, O apple branch, noble is each blood from which thou comest.

Angus may have appeared as a worthy successor to the Norse sea-rovers, but he was canny enough to detect which way the wind was blowing and named his eldest son Alexander (Alasdair). After 1260 the king, coming into his own, attempted further negotiations with Hakon but the ageing Viking proved obdurate. Alexander thus determined on a less cordial approach and began to flex his muscles. In the summer of 1263 Hakon fitted out a major expedition to enforce his right. Perhaps the memory of Magnus Bareleg's triumphant sweep of 1098 provided the necessary comfort. But matters had shifted, few among the Islesmen were prepared to respond to his call, only the Macruaries. Ewan of Argyll hastened to bend his knee to Alexander while Angus, his lands exposed to the northmen's wrath was inclined to play a waiting game, lending lukewarm support to Hakon.

THE BATTLE OF LARGS

It was late in the season when the last Norsemen sailed into the Clyde estuary. At first they were unopposed, and Angus, with Magnus of Man, enjoyed a satisfying chevauchée into Norman lands by Loch Lomond. It is said that Hakon's armada comprised some 200 keels, and the Scots could never hope to match this in a fleet engagement. Time, however, was on their side, for the Norsemen could not expect to remain in Scottish waters once the autumn gales began to howl. Some two nights after Michaelmas (1 October), as the fleet lay at anchor off the Cumbraes, 'a great storm came on, with fury, and a merchant-ship and longships were driven inshore in Scotland'. The storm drove the ships across the waters in confusion; masts and spars were lost. King Hakon's flagship drifted helplessly even with eight anchors flung against the angry waves.

Locals, with a ready eye for booty, swarmed over the beached vessels, stripping cargo and gear, but the winds had abated somewhat and Norsemen were sent ashore to drive these carrion off. Next morning the king himself landed with fresh warriors to supervise the salvage operation. Learning that Scottish forces were in the vicinity, the Norwegian king, never one to shirk a brawl, was advised to return to the ships, while a strong commanded party remained to carry out the work. Ogmund Crow-Dance was in charge of a vanguard, positioned atop a small eminence to cover the rest of the shore party. Perhaps 800–900 Vikings were ashore in total. As the Scots came up their force comprised, it is said, of 500 mounted men-at-arms and many more on foot. Faced by so many well-harnessed opponents, Ogmund, doubtless fearing he'd be cut off, began to withdraw, in good order, down towards the shore. The Scots harried them closely, deluging the northmen with rocks and missiles.

For a while the defenders' discipline held. They retreated under the cover of their shields, but, as they reached the slope leading to the shingle, the need for flight became paramount and the retreat turned swiftly into a rout. Seeing their comrades in the vanguard in disorder, the remainder of the shore party were instantly infected with panic and bolted for the boats. Many of the small craft capsized or were lost, and the stranded men formed rallying points around the bulwarks of the beached ships where they were soon joined by the wrack of Ogmund's fighters. With little alternative they hefted spears and faced front, and the Scots rushed into the attack fired by their success. It was far from one-sided, however, as the dense shingle impeded the knights' horses and many refused the hazard. Sir Piers Currie, a valiant chevalier, made a bold pass at the Norwegians, though he was cut through the thigh for his pains.

As the wind was rising again, King Hakon found he could not easily reinforce his men on the beach, though a brace of hardy captains did succeed in getting some extra men onto the shingle, and the Scots were pressed back up the slope, missiles and rocks whirling between the eddying knots of combatants. At length the invaders pushed the indigenous fighters back sufficiently to allow their survivors to disembark in relative safety. Next morning, the

Norse came again to recover their dead and fire the hulks. It was not a shattering defeat, little more than a minor tactical reverse, but Largs was enough to frustrate Hakon's efforts. As the gales increased he was obliged to withdraw the fleet. While still in Orkney that December, he died and Norse hopes expired with him.[4]

Magnus of Man and the MacSorleys were quickly brought to heel. Only Dugald Macruari remained defiant, but his stance was anachronistic and the terms of the Treaty of Perth, concluded in July 1266, confirmed Scottish sovereignty. Alexander was magnanimous in victory and sought to include the MacSorleys in the polity of Scotland. They joined with their fellow magnates in confirming the king's granddaughter, the Maid of Norway, as heir to the throne, following the untimely death of the male heir. It was another untimely and unexpected death, that of Alexander III himself, still in his prime in 1286, that plunged the nation into the abyss and began the process which was to lead to the outbreak of the Wars of Independence.

CLAN DONALD AND THE WARS OF INDEPENDENCE

As will be more fully discussed in the following chapter, sea power was to be of very great importance in determining the outcome of the long struggle for independence as three English kings fought to achieve dominance: Edward I, his son Edward II and grandson Edward III. When Alexander III was followed to the grave by his infant heiress, the succession became uncertain and it was to Edward I of England ('Longshanks') that the Scottish polity turned for arbitration. Edward was thorough and scrupulous; his decision, which fell upon John Balliol, was, in law, correct. The proviso was that the new King of Scots must do homage for his throne to the King of England, the ancient claim to overlordship.

In this submission lay the seed of strife, which blossomed in 1296, with Berwick sacked and a Scots army drubbed at Dunbar. With her king humiliated and stripped of regal status ('Toom Tabard'), her regalia pilfered and her lords cowed, the nation was reduced to a mere administrative district of a Plantagenet empire. Wallace, the following year, reignited the torch of liberty, which, though it flickered in the years to come, was never finally extinguished. In 1314, Bruce won a signal triumph at Bannockburn, though he was constrained to fight for a decade and more to come, till, dying from an unspecified illness, possibly leprosy, he concluded the terms of the Treaty of Northampton. Important as this accord was, it did not represent closure of the struggle. A new generation of the 'Disinherited' arose to renew the challenge, and the fortunes of war frequently favoured the English as the patriots grimly held on. David II, having spent his youth in secure exile, led a great raid into northern England in 1346, which ended in disaster at Neville's Cross by Durham, with the army ruined and the king made captive. Hostilities were renewed in 1369, and by now the war had taken on an international dimension, inextricably linked with English military and dynastic aspirations in France.

The MacSorleys were heavily involved, divided by personal allegiances and private feuds. Clan Dougall were related by marriage to the Comyns who supported Toom Tabard and, as such, became enemies to the Bruce faction; an acrimonious land dispute fuelled the swelling divisions between the MacSorleys. Alexander, son of Angus of Islay, gave support to Bruce at the vital time when the king's fortunes were at their lowest ebb and his military support thinned and scattered by defeats. It would be simplistic to refer to Alexander as a patriot. He was at odds with the MacDougalls, who were of the Comyn/Balliol affinity. Bruce was an ally of opportunity more than conviction. Bruce's murder of John Comyn had sparked a civil war between the factions with the Comyns remaining subservient to England. Alexander died, possibly in 1308, and may have been a casualty in the rout of the Bruce affinity at Methven. With the fugitive 'King Hobbe' skulking in the heather, he received much needed succour from Neil Campbell of Lochawe and Angus Og, who had succeeded Alexander.

> Angus of Islay then was sire
> And lord and leader of Kintyre
> The king right gladly welcomed he
> And promised him his fealty
> And offered freely out of hand

Such service as he might demand
And for a stronghold to him gave
Dunaverty, his castle safe,
To dwell therein as he might need.
Right thankfully the king agreed
And gladly took his fealty

Dunaverty in fact proved a shallow refuge, for the English took the place by storm and Bruce was again on the run. But the support of Angus of Islay kept the guttering flame of the patriot cause alive in the nadir of that grim winter. In the spring, the Bruce faction tried going over to the offensive with an amphibious descent upon Galloway. This raid misfired, and Domnal Macdougall hanged two of the king's brothers. In that year Longshanks finally died, bequeathing his war against Scotland to his less capable son. Bruce's fortunes revived, in no small measure due to the support of Angus and now Christiana Macruari, whose nimble galleys and swift footed kerns put the logistics and brawn back into the patriot cause. The 'lang swerds' of Clan Donald did good service in the fight against the Comyns and performed prodigies of valour on the crucial field of Bannockburn.[5]

All in all, Angus Og did rather well out of the war. His kerns followed Scottish spears in the harrying of northern England, Clan Donald scooped all of the old MacDougall lands in Lochaber, Ardnamurchan, Morvern and Glencoe. Edward Bruce was accompanied by Macdonalds and Macruaris on his ill-fated expedition into Ireland, and men from both septs may have fallen with him in the final debacle at Faughart. By then Angus of Islay may have already died, and his successor 'Good' John of Islay was to bring the power and prestige of Clan Donald to its very apogee. He came on to the scene at a time when the pretensions of the Disinherited threatened to undo all of Bruce's patient work of nationhood. When the patriots, defeated at Dupplin Moor in 1332 and again, massively, by the English at Halidon, a year later, found themselves under intense pressure from Edward Balliol, the more able and energetic son of Toom Tabard, it seemed as though all of Bruce's work might yet be undone.

POWER OF THE LORDSHIP

John of Islay was cannily able to play the factions off against each other to secure his own best advantage, courted by both, committed to neither. With Balliol's star in the ascendant and the pretender desperate to purchase allegiances, John submitted to Edward III at Perth in 1335. This shift brought great gains – Skye, Lewis, Kintyre and Knapdale – and as his existing holdings were confirmed by charter, John was not troubled even to lift his sword. When the patriots regained the initiative after the Battle of Culbean, he began to reconsider, offering his allegiance directly to Edward III. David II returned from exile in France in 1341, and the Bruce faction naturally regarded John of Islay with some suspicion. He was obliged to negotiate and ultimately to cede Skye but his position was otherwise inexpugnable. He was simply too powerful to alienate. By now styling himself as *Dominus Insularum*, he was at once a great feudal magnate with almost princely powers. His next coup was to wed Amy Macaruari. Her brother, childless Ranald, was lord of Knoydart, Moidart, Arisaig, Morar and held the islands of Uist, Barra, Eigg and Rhum. Early in 1346 Ranald was killed in circumstances that clearly pointed to foul play. Suspicion pointed to William, Earl of Ross, but John, by right of his wife, came into the whole of the dead man's estate.

When he died in 1387 John left his vast estate to his eldest son by Margaret Stewart, Donald of the Isles. In his lifetime John had achieved much, amassing lands and treasure with scarce any blood being shed. The culture of governance over which he presided was essentially Celtic; sea power was the main strength, now as it had been in Somerled's day. John had a number of key residences, one at Ardtornish in Morvern and another situated at the near-palatial complex of buildings constructed over two islets in Loch Finlaggan on Islay, not a fortress but a civil settlement. So great was the power of the Lordship that castle walls were not deemed necessary. That would, in later years, change altogether.

Donald became embroiled in a dispute with the avaricious Regent Albany over the vacant earldom of Ross, which he believed to be his in right of his wife. Feeling himself wronged, he resorted to arms, torching Inverness in the campaign that was to end in the blood-dimmed field of Harlaw in July 1411, when Donald's host locked with Mar's lowlanders in a fierce and bloody fight. During the minority of James II, Alexander of the Isles, as both feudal magnate and crown officer, he enjoyed considerable power. He died at his castle of Dingwall in 1449. His eldest son John assumed the mantle of the Lordship.[6]

Something of an enigma and perhaps temperamentally unsuited to the demands of the role, John became a party to the rather preposterous treaty of Westminster–Ardtornish in 1462, allying with Edward IV of England and the exiled Douglas to divide Scotland. John's leading captain was his bastard Angus Og, who proved fully adept in the arts of pillage and blackmail. The rebellion was rash and misconceived, though John suffered only modest conse-quences. However, through his inability to control his territories and a knack for failed appeasement, he alienated the redoubtable Donald Balloch and even Angus Og. In 1475 James III, now assuming his right, moved against the Lordship, stripping John of the earldom of Ross and other lands in Knapdale and Kintyre. If the Lord of the Isles was content to appear as a sheep ripe for shearing, his son was not. At some point, the growing divide between Angus and John spilled into outright confrontation, with the old man being summarily ousted, driven from his own door clad only in a nightshirt!

BLOODY BAY
This produced a clear division within the fabric of Clan Donald and its web of affinity. Some supported the fiery Angus Og; others felt obliged to stand by his father. A dispute between Maclean of Duart and the Mackenzies fuelled fissiparous flames and led to an armed confrontation at Lagabraad in Ross, where Angus duly chastised his opponents. Though he had won a victory Angus's position was by no means secure. He swiftly found himself facing a coalition of his many enemies, including by now Maclean of Duart, Macleod of Harris and Lewis together with the Macneils. The disaffected chiefs, under Maclean as admiral, brought together an impressive squadron, which took station on the Mull side of the Sound. Angus, mustering his own vessels, prepared for a confrontation at sea,

sheltering on the northern flank of the Ardnamurchan Peninsula. For five frustrating weeks contrary winds kept his boats penned, then when the weather gauge shifted Angus took his flotilla out to offer battle.

Our main account of the sea fight which ensued comes from Hugh MacDonald, historian of the clan, but he does not give us an exact date. We may, indeed we must, assume that the clash occurred sometime during the early 1480s, possibly during the summer of 1482. The fleets involved were modest. Angus Og commanded four large galleys: his own, that of Donald Gallich of Sleat, Clanranald's and his son's. Ranged against him were vessels captained by the Laird of Ardgour, Maclean of Duart, Macleod of Harris, 'the heir of Torkill of the Lewis' and MacNeill of Barra. These were the capital ships of their day. Both squadrons would have a shoal of smaller craft riding alongside, nimble and swift, ideal for scouting and the shooting of an extra handful of archers.

As Angus's squadron entered Loch Sunart they first spotted Ardgour's flag and made to attack in the mistaken assumption they were pursuing Maclean. The rest of the hostile flotilla came out in support of Ardgour. Others having set sail from Tobermory suddenly found the sanctuary of the harbour compelling and scrambled back, avoiding the fight. The battle then was fought out between four on Angus's side opposed by five under Maclean. Hugh Macdonald provides the detail:

> . . . the rest of the [Maclean] faction, seeing themselves at least in danger of losing their galleys, thought best to enter their harbour. Macdonald coming as swiftly as he could, accompanied by Donald Gallich of Sleat, Austin's son [his first cousin] and Ranald Bain, laird of Mudort's son, the last of whom grappled side to side with Macleod of Harris's galley. There was one called Edmund More O'Brian along with Ranald Bain, who thrust the blade of an oar in below the stern post of Macleod's galley, between it and the rudder, which prevented the galley from being steered.

We may presume the encounter began with the customary archery duel, arrows flicking deadly across the Sound, boats jockeying for position. The fight developed into very much a ship-to-ship encounter, contending vessels laying alongside and rival warriors coming to handstrokes as one or both sides sought to board. The tactic of immobilising the other ship by jamming the rudder was likely tried and tested, preventing the enemy from seeking to disengage and flee should the on-board melee prove disagreeable. Battle, once joined, would be fierce and bloody. Men of rank and the ships themselves had a value. It was not the objective to sink an opposing vessel but to secure the prize. As naval gunnery was in its relative infancy, no ordnance was involved. English and Continental boats were beginning to sprout gun decks, but the Hebridean galleys still relied on archers for missile troops.

On the sparkling blue waters of the Sound, summer swell running below, the galleys manoeuvred to begin the fight, rowers labouring, dancing across the white crested waves, pennants of the chiefs fluttering proud in dazzling silks from mastheads. The capital ships stalked their individual targets, battle depending on the skill and judgement of skipper and helmsman. There is little any commodore can achieve once the signal to attack is given. Oarsmen swung from line astern to line abreast, sleek vessels skimming the water like thoroughbreds, a thousand years of the shipwrights' art in their timbers and spars. Each plank now straining as archers draw, the arrow hail unleashed as men tighten straps and check their gear. Their mouths are dry, their bowels unsteady. This is the moment of dread, of constant fears before the red mist of their battle fury envelops them.

In terms of their war gear, the most reliable evidence we possess for the appearance and arming of Highland warriors in the fourteenth and fifteenth centuries is provided by images on grave-slabs. The effigy of such a fighter at Killian shows that the main body defence consisted of a padded and quilted garment, known as the aketon, which fell as far as the knees in a series of pronounced vertical pleats. The aketon was usually sewn from linen and then daubed with pitch. It was finished with full sleeves patterned in the same manner, gathered and laced at the wrist. This padding could blunt a slashing blow and deflect a thrust. That most vulnerable area around the throat was protected with an aventail or pisane, being a collar of fine ring mail. On his head, the warrior carried a conical helm or bascinet, open faced and without visor. Those of higher status also had full shirts of mail, while some effigies also show additional plate defences to the calves called greaves, which would offer protection against a cut to the hamstrings.

Most of the figures carry distinctive lobate pommelled swords. These 'longswords' were popular from 1400 onwards, elegant, tapering, double-edged blades, intended primarily for the thrust, finished either with distinctive, downswept quillons or a straight bar. Swordplay was a gentleman's birthright. The Homeric culture of Gaelic warfare naturally lauded skill at arms. Most blows would be delivered as slashing cuts, aimed at the vulnerable point in from the shoulder, where an arching blow would bite deep into tissue, nerve and bone, severing the major artery. In the Highlands small shields, little more than bucklers, were also carried. These were handy both for defensive moves, blocking and deflecting, but also striking, using the boss for punching. During the sixteenth century, the lowland author John Major gave a description of the 'wild' Highlanders of his day, their appearance is unlikely to have changed much from that of their fathers:

> From the mid leg to the foot they go uncovered, their dress is, for an overgarment, a loose plaid and a shirt saffron dyed. They are armed with a bow and arrows, a broadsword and a small halberd. They always carry in their belt a strong dagger, single edged but of the sharpest. In time of war they cover the whole body with a coat of mail, made of iron rings, and in it they fight. The common folk among the Wild Scots go out to battle with the whole body clad in a linen garment sewed together in patchwork, well daubed with wax or with pitch and with an overcoat of deerskin.

Mailed caterans would have some protection against arrows, but the more exposed rowers would not, spitting shafts transfixing men at their benches. Once the clash occurred, sword and spear would thrust and slash over the gunwales, as one side sought sufficient advantage to permit boarding. The defenders would know their very lives depended on denying the attackers space on their decks, soon slippery with gore. A sea fight is inevitably more vicious than many on land for, once engaged, once locked in this bloody embrace, the fighters have nowhere to run to, nowhere they can hide. It is a case of holding your ground or die. Kill or be killed, shuffling back amidships if the line snaps or mounting casualties leave unplugged gaps. Men falling wounded can count only upon the dagger's final, arbitrary thrust to underarm, eye socket or groin. As Macdonald relates:

> The galley of the heir of Torkill of the Lewis, with all him men was taken, and himself mortally wounded with two arrows, whereof he died soon after at Dunvegan.

This passage rather suggests that, with their skipper immobilised by wounds in the opening exchange, his crew lost heart and struck their colours, counting on the winner's clemency, which was clearly extended. Had the brawl on board begun, the losers might not have found the victors so inclined to magnanimity. Macleod's crew were less fortunate as both Angus Og and Allan of 'Mudort' (Moidart) laid alongside. Caught in the vice of enemy galleys port and starboard, Macleod's men were shot down or overpowered, a great slaughter. The laird himself, worthy of ransom, was taken. Maclean of Duart too was forced to strike, while Macneill, slippery as an eel, made a run for it and skilfully outdistanced a trio of pursuers.[7]

Angus Og had won a great and resounding victory; Bloody Bay was a considerable tactical triumph, but both his own days and those of the Lordship itself were numbered. After his assassination in 1490 and the defeat of his successor Alexander of Lochalsh by the Mackenzies in the fight at *Blar na Pairc*, the great Macdonald hegemony foundered, and James IV formally abolished the title in 1493. This did not bring order to the glens or to the sea highways of the west, quite the reverse, for into the vacuum came only anarchy and violence the *Linn nan Creach* (Age of Forays).

Well might the bard lament:

> It is no joy without Clan Donald; it is no strength to
> Be without them; the best race in the round world,

To them belongs every goodly man. . . .
For sorrow and for sadness I have forsaken wisdom and
Learning; on their account I have forsaken all things;
It is no joy without Clan Donald.

———◆———

For Freedom: Ships and the Wars of Independence

For those Scots,
I rate 'em as sots,
What a sorry shower!
Whose utter lack
In the attack
Lost 'em at Dunbar
Contemporary doggerel

WHEN, ON THE WILD AND stormy evening of 18 March 1286, Alexander III of Scotland, hurrying to do his dynastic duty by his nubile teenage bride, took a fatal tumble and was, next morning, found stiff and broken on the cold strand, few could have foreseen the full horror of what would ensue. The late king had generally enjoyed cordial relations with Edward I of England, his brother-in-law, and Longshanks had never shown any hostile intentions towards Scotland. For the northern kingdom, this sudden taking off of an otherwise vigorous monarch opened the door to potential internal dissent and anarchy.

Both of Alexander's sons had predeceased him and though the young queen, Yolande of Dreux, claimed to be with child, this proved a pious hope. Two years before his untimely end, the king had settled the succession, to which Parliament had acceded, upon his granddaughter the infant child of Eric II of Norway. As the cloud of magnatial dissent began to darken with disturbances between factions already sparking in the south-west, the interim constitutional council or 'Guardians' attempted to pick up the reins of power. It was by no means unreasonable that the Guardians should look southwards seeking a steady hand to guide the realm through such difficult times. Edward was the obvious choice, a noted lawgiver and international arbitrator of considerable standing and impeccable jurisprudence. Alarmed, after the death of the infant princess, by renewed threat of magnatial strife, the Guardians petitioned Edward to formally intervene and adjudicate on the rival claimants. Thus began the Great Cause.

THE GREAT CAUSE

From the outset, the King of England chose to regard the successful claimant as a feudal inferior, one who was bound for his throne, not just his lands in England. John Balliol, destined to be denigrated by generations of historians as 'Toom Tabard', did fealty for his throne and, had Edward exercised his right with moderation rather than arrogance, matters might have remained amicable. The increasing demands from England alienated the magnates, who forced their unwilling king's hand. This rash rebellion brought swift and bloody response. The Scots were rebels, never patriots in Edward's eye; traitors to their king's oath. Berwick was stormed and sacked, a Scottish host contemptuously dispersed at Dunbar, the kingdom reduced to a mere province, its nobility chastened and cowed.

It was thus left to William Wallace and Andrew Murray to keep the flickering patriot flame alight, and this they did, defeating the occupying power resoundingly at Stirling Bridge in 1297. Next year Longshanks came again and his tactics proved decisive; Wallace's army was cut to shreds at Falkirk. But the flame, once lit, could never be fully extinguished. Edward campaigned annually to bring the northern kingdom to heel, and for so long as he lived Scots would bear the English yoke, the magnates in seeming awe of the ageing warhorse. By 1305 and the fall of Stirling, it seemed as though all was decided and a constitutional settlement of sorts pushed through. It was far from over, for the very next year, Robert Bruce, raised his standard following the murder of John Comyn on hallowed ground in Dumfries. 'King Hobbe' enjoyed rather poor prospects, his meagre forces routed at Methven and then again, now reduced to skulking in the heather, surviving that bleak winter with the help of Clan Donald, whose naval power was to provide a boost to the recovery of the patriot cause.[1]

During the hard and savage years that followed, Bruce, with his swelling band of captains, dealt firstly with the rump of the Balliol/Comyn faction and then began the slow, patient task of attrition, clawing back territory and strongpoints from the English, slighting peles and other outposts till the impending fall of Stirling compelled Edward II to bring an army to its relief, and Bruce won a major tactical success at Bannockburn. Momentous as the victory was, this did not lead to an outbreak of peace; the war was to drag on for a full decade and a half and witness a merciless harrying of the north of England. When, after Edward's fall, terms were agreed and the terminally ill Bruce saw his great purpose come to apparent fruition, one class of interested party, those English magnates who had lands or aspirations in Scotland, found themselves excluded: the 'Disinherited'.

This bitter seed of Bruce's flawed legacy came to ripen in the minority reign of David II, when the old guard of Bruce's captains had followed their paladin to the grave. The hitherto Anglophile regent, Mar, was slain, along with a full catalogue of magnates, in the course of a disastrous clash with the Disinherited upon Dupplin Moor in 1332. Next year Berwick, so painfully recovered, was lost in the wake of a worse calamity on the slopes of another hill, Halidon. Toom Tabard's more effective son Edward Balliol enjoyed the first of several fleeting tenures, while the boy-king was removed to safety in France. Again the patriots held on by their fingertips as Edward III championed his creature Balliol.

> Blood axeth blood as guerdom dew,
> And vengeance for vengeance is a just reward
> For look what measure we to other award
> Take heed ye princes by examples past
> Blood will have blood, either first or last.
>
> *Contemporary ballad*

SEA POWER DURING THE WARS OF INDEPENDENCE
Throughout three centuries of strife between England and

Scotland, sea power was vital to both sides in the conflict. Agricola, as we recall, used his fleet both to victual his army and to act as an independent strike force. Longshanks made similar use of his navy in the campaign of 1298. Prior to its destruction in 1296, Berwick-upon-Tweed had been a vibrant sea port, and the Flemings defended their base, the Red Hall, to the last. The east coast ports naturally looked across the North Sea to the Low Countries and the rich Baltic ports. In the west, it was necessary for both sides to maintain the links to Ireland. The north-west of England and Carlisle had strong connections across the Irish Sea, as did the Norse-Gael. Man was a vital staging point in this game of naval strategy. Ships were important both for continuance of the war at sea and for commerce. For his campaign of 1300 in Galloway, Edward gathered a fleet of 30 vessels from the Cinque Ports and brought supplies across the Irish Sea to Skinburness. Despite this very considerable outlay in treasure, the campaign achieved little beyond the reduction of Caerlaverock.

Three years later, in one of his largest campaigns, the king bridged the Forth with a prefabricated structure, conveyed in sections from Lynn in a convoy of 29 craft with two warships as escort. The Red Earl of Ulster brought some 3,500 fighters out of Ireland to serve beneath the King's standard, transported in 173 ships. As a defensive mechanism, the convoy system was the obvious response to the unwelcome attentions of privateers and reflects an aspect of the form of economic warfare that was being conducted at sea. To assemble a flotilla of merchantmen was clearly a substantial logistical exercise. To commission, fit out and man ships of war entailed a further, not inconsiderable outlay. Thus the actions of privateers, even when not taking prizes, could have an effect.

After the rout at Methven, when prospects for the Bruce faction seemed very bleak indeed, it was the support of Angus of Islay that was to help keep the Patriot cause alive through the winter of 1306–1307. It would be too much to assert that any of the MacSorleys were motivated by purely nationalist sentiment; this was an infant concept, the interests of kin and affinity came first. We have surviving correspondence from 1297, a communication from, possibly, Alexander MacDonald of Islay to the court of Edward I, which details action taken against rebels, particularly the Macdougalls of Lorn and Macruaris of Garmoran. Alexander of Islay complains of the depredations of Alexander Macdougall of Argyll and of Lochlan and Roderick Macruari who had taken up Skye and Lewis, burning boats under the protection of the church – essentially a violation of sanctuary. Many of these harryings owed their origin more to private grudge than to national struggle. The destruction or, even better, cutting out of an enemy's vessels served both a tactical and economic purpose.[2]

Further correspondence from Alexander of Islay (aside from the by no means unusual reminders over unpaid expenses) details the measures taken to clip the wings of the Macruari brothers. Roderick's raiding had accounted for the lives of over a score of Alexander's men, but he was captured, while Lochlan with Alexander Macdougall of Argyll were chased beneath the walls of Inverlochy Castle,[3] his long galleys safe in the lee of the ramparts. Needless to say, the rebels were not inclined to surrender their vessels, and Alexander, regretfully, for here were two magnificent prizes, had them burnt. Macdonald of Islay had succeeded in maintaining the English position. Ships were the means of controlling territory, of transporting fighting men and of chastising your opponents. Thus depriving an enemy of his ships both diminished and emasculated him while hamstringing his war effort. Denis Rixson surmises, entirely logically, that the construction of landward forts such as Inverlochy would be accompanied by an equivalent investment in ships. The sea lanes offered the easiest route to transport, communications and supply.

In the following year, Longshanks wrote to his Irish administration giving instructions that they bring into being a squadron of four galleys. Each was to have a crew of 40, to be placed at the disposal of Hugh Bisset for such operations as he might direct against the Scots; the cost for 1298 amounted to some £160. By next season, the fiscal burden had increased as Bisset carried out raids on the islands. Ireland thus formed a handy resource for Edwardian naval operations both to launch raids and, at the same time, acting as a reminder to the king's allies, lest they be tempted to defect. It would not be entirely fanciful to surmise that a possible motivation for Edward Bruce's ill-judged intermeddling in Ireland from 1315 would be to deny the English crown maritime assistance from Irish ports. Certainly in the early period and in the wake of the Scottish collapse following Wallace's defeat at Falkirk, Alexander of Argyll appears to have been successful in curbing the excesses of Macruaris and Macdougalls who, by 6 June 1301, had swallowed their pride, accepted their losses and bent their collective knee. For the moment the west was quiescent.

Invaluable as hired men-of-war from Ireland might be, it was beyond the resources of the English crown to maintain a fleet presence off the west coast. Even had this been possible, the job of policing the network of sea lochs and islands would have been an impossible one. It was far better and more cost-effective to rely upon the loyalty of local magnates, poachers turned gamekeepers, who would employ their own fleet keels in the king's service. Naval power in the Hebrides lent itself to a form of maritime guerrilla warfare, economic rather than military. Macruaris and Macdougalls did not seek out Alexander's ships to bring on a general action; they rather attacked his tenants, harried and burnt. War galleys were a measure of power and influence, but, at this time, they were more often used as raiders than capital ships. Indeed, this form of activity was both less risky and more profitable. There was no bar to a happy contrivance of patriotic duty and garnering spoils.

Though they were brought to heel, the Macruaris were neither defeated nor cowed. In 1305 the Earl of Ross, also complaining of unpaid disbursements, was writing to Longshanks to report he'd captured (possibly) Lochlan Macruari. If so the triumph swiftly turned sour for, within a handspan of years, Ross was reporting the Macruari's impudence:

> We took the lands of the Isles from our lord the king, your father . . .
> We assigned them to Lochlan Macruari to answer to us for their
> revenues. Since he refuses, may it please you, dear lord to command
> him to answer to us as justice requires. For we have answered to your
> chamberlain for the revenues of those lands. But Lochlan is such a
> high and mighty lord, he'll not answer to anyone except under great
> force or through fear of you.

The plain fact was that independent sea power based around a handy fleet of Hebridean galleys enabled Macruari to maintain a semi-independent status, a free prince within his own island domains. Dispossessing or bringing him sharply to heel was a near impossible task for any magnate who did not count his strength in ships. Even then, Macruari and his affinity would be as nimble as fish in their own waters, slippery and elusive yet with the sharp bite of the habitual predator. When, on 10 February 1306, Robert Bruce stabbed to death John, the 'Red' Comyn,[4] or allowed his servants to complete the work he'd begun, the ripples of this sacrilegious and intemperate act spread outwards. The Macdougalls were of the Comyn/Balliol faction and thus drawn to the opposition. Enmity with the Macdougalls and Macruaris was calculated to win the friendship of the Macdonalds of Islay, a rather neat reversal of the previous skein of loyalties. Indeed it was the Macdougall, John of Argyll, who led the men of Lorn in trouncing the rump of Bruce's fleeing forces at Dalry, near Tyndrum. Islay was most likely Bruce's refuge in the closing months of 1306, a difficult year for the patriot cause by any standards, but Angus Macdonald became an ally, undoubtedly driven by the thought that 'my enemy's enemy is my friend' (Angus had apparently supplanted his brother Alexander).

An initial amphibious operation directed against Comyn lands in Galloway fared badly, defeated by Domnal Macdougall. Bruce had sent a fleet of 18 galleys, led by the Lord of Kintyre, Malcolm fitz Lengleys. Both Thomas and Alexander Bruce died traitors' deaths in consequence. Despite this dire reverse and the persistence of John of Argyll, the English position and that of the Comyn/Balliol faction was beginning to unravel. The shift that was taking place with the MacSorleys was profound; Angus of Islay was employing his considerable naval strength in the service of the patriot cause. This rendered the whole of the west coast and stretches of the Irish Sea unsafe for English merchantmen. Longshanks and his lacklustre son would find it difficult to bolster their mainland allies in Argyll and, at the same time, the shift in local power towards the Isles defined the nature of the Lordship.

By the end of January 1307, in the final year of his long reign, Longshanks wrote to the Treasurer of Ireland to advise he had commissioned Bisset to fit out a fleet for offensive operations against the Islesmen 'to repress the malice of Robert de Brus and others his accomplices, the king's rebels, who are lurking in the said islands, and to destroy the shipping of the king's said enemies'. This was intended as a cutting-out expedition; the king had correctly interpreted the menace posed by Angus Macdonald as a naval threat. At the time, Robert was able to count on a formidable array of over 30 ships, most from Angus, some undoubtedly furnished by Christina Macruari and the Campbells who'd pledged their alliance to the King of Scots. Even if the Hebridean galleys could not take on a well-armed cog, arrayed for war, merchantmen made fat prizes. The economic damage which possession of a Hebridean fleet permitted Bruce to inflict could be measured not just in terms of prizes, but in the fear and uncertainty these Islesmen spread. Merchant skippers would think twice before hazarding precious cargoes and even more precious ships.[5]

John of Argyll, ailing and now bottled up in Dunstaffnage, must have marvelled at the reverse of his fortunes; the hunter was now the hunted. Edward II, in October 1307, had appointed him as sheriff of Argyll, an empty and dangerous title if it was not to be accompanied by a supply of arms and men. In March 1308 he was glad to agree a truce and wrote to Edward II in plaintive terms:

> I was confined to my bed with illness, and have been for six months past, Bruce approached these parts by land and sea with 10,000 men they say [an improbably high figure] or 15,000. I have no more than 800 men, 500 in my own pay whom I keep continually to guard the borders of my territory. The barons of Argyll give me no aid . . . I have three castles to keep as well as a loch twenty-four miles long, on which I build and keep galleys with trusty men to each galley. I am not sure of my neighbours in any direction. As soon as you or your army come, then, if my health permits, I shall not be found wanting where lands, ships or anything else is concerned, but will come to your service.

Worse was to come. By the high summer Bruce was ready to settle his account with the Macdougalls, and the clash occurred when the latter sought to bar his advance at Pass of Brander. John of Argyll, still ailing, sought to direct the battle from the safety of his galley on Loch Awe.[6] The day went to Bruce and the patriots; by the autumn Dunstaffnage too was lost. John's father, the ageing Alexander, surrendered. John himself took refuge in flight. In the west and the Isles the patriot grip was virtually complete. Seeking refuge in Ireland, the Macdougalls received some belated subsidies from Edward II. In June 1310 both John and his father attended king and council at Westminster. Further cash grants followed, but the west coast and the Isles were lost. John would spend the remainder of his career an embittered exile, Alexander died in December 1310, and John followed a bare half-dozen years later. He did not, however, abandon the fight. In June 1311 he was appointed as commodore of a fleet being fitted out at Berwick for service in the west. The king had ordered a muster of ships at Antrim, but most of the English ports, such as New Shoreham, Barnstaple, Weymouth, Chester, Looe, Exeter, Haverford and Plymouth sent only excuses.

John did succeed in recovering Man, the only English success of 1314, when Edward's fortunes plummeted following the debacle at Bannockburn, though the island was back in Patriot hands within a couple of years. Throughout these campaigns, he was funded by the Exchequer. In 1315 he was compensated to make good his losses from the Scots and for the support of his men keeping the Isle of Man. In the final year of his life, John, indefatigable even in defeat, captured the patriot Moryauch Makenedy with a crew of nearly two dozen, who were sent from Man to Dublin, there, as John anticipated, awaiting ransom. Macdougall was clearly willing to augment his meagre stipend with kidnap and spoil.

As Denis Rixson points out, Bruce was aware of the dangers inherent in reliance upon a single magnate and his affinity. This coupled with the MacSorleys' fissiparous tendencies could imply too much power being concentrated in the hands of Angus Og, whose motives were essentially personal rather than nationalistic. The Campbells, whose overall contribution was not inconsiderable, were another important magnatial ally, useful both for their resources and as a potential counterweight to Clan Donald. At this time, the notorious enmity between the clans had not fully arisen. Barbour recounts the carefully managed spectacle of Bruce having his keel hauled over the narrow isthmus of Kintyre. This exercise indicates a careful rebuttal of the old claim put forward by Magnus Bareleg and emphasises that the western seaboard and the Isles were demonstrably a part of the Scottish polity.

Angus Og and his affinity were Scottish magnates, not free Norse-Gaels. The king carefully positioned and strengthened his outposts, never with a heavy hand but always as a reminder. Castles were, of themselves, of little value unless furnished with an attendant squadron. He himself had narrowly escaped the trap of Dunaverty Castle in the grim flight of 1306. John of Menteith had commanded a naval squadron, assisted by Irish galleys under Hugh Bisset, which mounted the successful escalade. Nobody understood the essence of controlling the west better than Bruce, whose exploitation of his ally's Hebridean galleys had transformed otherwise faltering fortunes at a pivotal moment in the war. Like Clan Donald, the Campbells reaped their reward, garnering attainted lands from the Macdougalls. Arthur Campbell received the plum captaincy of Dunstaffnage. As matters went from bad to worse in the west, traditional English maritime hegemony in the east was also under threat. In March 1315 Edward was writing to his lieutenant John de Botecourt, giving instructions for a cutting-out expedition against Scottish vessels, shipping in arms from the Low Countries:

> Order to take council forthwith with the men of Yarmouth and others whom he shall think fit, so that he may meet with sufficient power thirteen great cogs of the Scotch rebels and their adherents now in the port of Sluys in Flanders for the purpose of taking armour, victuals, and other goods thence to Scotland.

SHIPS OF WAR

Though the design of Hebridean and west coast galleys had remained largely unchanged for some time, considerable advances had been made in ship design and construction generally. In the early medieval period, most vessels engaged in naval actions were fat-bellied merchantmen simply pressed for war. Oared craft called 'balyngers' were employed against the many pirates who stalked the narrow sea lanes of the Channel. Changes in design were essentially dictated by commercial imperatives, the need to carry more and larger cargoes. In this the reliance on oars was a considerable impediment but, by the twelfth century, ships came to be powered by sail. Increasing the size and centre of gravity had a consequential effect on the beam, which had to be widened to maintain stability. Shallow draught remained a necessary requirement, and the overall length was curtailed, though vessels were still both double ended and clinker built. This type of craft, the cog, thus owed its design to the necessities of trade rather than battle at sea, but it was not long before the need to create a fighting platform spurred certain martial modifications.[7]

For military use, merchant vessels received raised timber fighting platforms both fore and aft: 'fore' and 'stern' castles. These could be manned by archers, tasked to sweep the decks of an enemy. A higher platform, secured to the mast, the 'top' castle could hold a couple of marksmen detailed to pick off targets of opportunity on the enemy deck below. As in the days of the Vikings, there was little scope for manoeuvre. Naval encounters were land battles fought at sea. Perhaps the most celebrated action of the opening decades of the fourteenth century was that fought by Edward II's successor, his son, the altogether more impressive Edward III, against a joint French, Castilian and Genoese fleet in the Bay of Sluys on 24 June 1340. This was a fleet action with perhaps 400 English sail facing rather fewer on the French side. The allies had formed their defensive array in two lines spanning the mouth of the harbour, each having the ships lashed together as a linear platform. The English came on in two lines, their cogs both bigger and bristling with longbows. Sir Thomas Morley led the van against the left of the allied line, his archers deluging the decks with a lethal hail of missiles before he closed to board. In the hacking melee, Morley's men-at-arms simply worked their way up the line, clearing ship after ship. The day went decisively to England.

Three years before the encounter at Sluys the king had commissioned John of Weasenham, master of *Grace Dieu* of Lynn to ready the vessel for an extended patrol. We know her complement was 48 seamen, 40 bowmen and 39 marines. Her mission was to seek out and intercept a squadron of Flemish craft believed to be loading materiel and war supplies for the Scots in the harbour at Sluys. Weasenham was not successful; his cruise failed to intercept the Flemings and the ancillary hunt off the east coast of Scotland, chasing phantom privateers proved equally fruitless. When, in the early fifteenth century the Welsh rebel Owen Glendower raised his standard, he appreciated how vital sea power was to the control of Wales and the Welsh coastal fortresses. The Scots, eager as ever to create a diversion, supplied ships, probably galleys, to beat the Menai Straits and support Glendower in his successful attempt on Conwy.

Shipboard artillery was provided by light versions of contemporary engines of war, the ballista, used to shoot missiles, and the stone-throwing 'Wild Ass' or onager. In an earlier sea fight in 1217 when the enterprising French admiral, Eustace the Monk, threatened the south coast of England, a home squadron used seamanship as well as force, manoeuvring so as to keep the weather gauge, gain the advantage and unleash a barrage of bagged quicklime. With their opponents floundering and blinded, the English closed to grapple and board, to decisive effect.

A further refinement in ship design was the replacement of the steering oar by rudders, which ended the double-ended appearance; ships now had a marked prow and stern. This newer steered vessel was called a nef. By the end of the fourteenth century, the temporary fighting platforms, fore and aft had become permanent features, the previously open sides fitted with planks to create enclosed deck cabins. It was vessels of this type that King Edward was alluding to in his correspondence with Botecourt. His concern was well-founded. In September 1315, a Scottish squadron, under the enterprising Thomas Dun, took up Holyhead in a well-mounted cutting-out action which relieved the king of a capital ship, *James de Karnarvon*. It was in this same year that Scottish sea power successfully conveyed Edward Bruce with 6,000 spears from Ayr to the Irish coast. The armada assembled for this invasion comprised some 300 sail, a mix of Hebridean galleys and larger cogs. The naval aspect of this ill-judged offensive has been overlooked. For the Scottish crown, still enmired in the coils of a war with England, to be able to amass such a quantity of ships and men was a very considerable feat, a mini D-Day. It speaks of a well-established maritime power, equipped not only with the swift Hebridean galleys of Angus Og and his affinity, but also with numbers of larger sailing craft – a most impressive array.

Thomas Dun, victor of Holyhead, was a constant thorn in the English king's side. On 9 May 1317, Edward issued instructions to his commodore Nicholas Dauney and a Geoffrey de Modiworthe (possibly a Macruari from Moidart) to hire a stout ship with men for crew and marines to proceed against Dun 'and others of his society, Scottish mariners, as the king understands that they sail up and down the Western seas, where they have committed divers piracies on merchants coming with their wares into the realm to trade'. The vessel was to be drawn from the south coast ports of Exeter, Tengemouth, Dartmouth, Plymouth, Looe and Fowey. The instructions mention a galley 'which the said Geoffrey built'. This may be a reference to a Hebridean craft that Geoffrey had had constructed. The expedition may not have succeeded in its purpose, for it was left to John d'Athy to bring Dun's privateering career to an end. A sea fight did take place, though details are sparse.

If there were few actual naval battles during the Wars of Independence, ships provided a number of military functions as troop transports, harrying merchantmen and undertaking cutting-out actions. As Edward Bruce's expedition began to spark a rash of local conflicts in Ireland, John of Argyll remained the English king's staunch admiral. We have records of disbursements and victuals provided for his maintenance and, in September 1315, he received the support of the powerful Cinque Ports squadron. Subsequently, he lodged a request that he might retain half a dozen of these cogs to maintain the fight over the winter months. The naval effort was continuous on both sides. So desperate was the English position a year later that Edward, John of Argyll now being dead, contracted with a Genoese captain Antoyne Pessaigne to supply a squadron of five war-galleys stuffed with 200 harnessed marines apiece, a formidable contingent.

In May 1322, when Edward was preparing to resume hostilities and ordered his Irish officers to stockpile supplies and materiel, he sent a warning that the victuals be kept safe for collection, 'as the sea between the land of Man and Ireland and Skynburnesse [*Shinburness*] is infested by the king's enemies with the intention of taking the victuals'. This is a good illustration of the worth of sea power. Depriving an enemy of his supplies frustrates his war effort as soundly as a reverse in the field and with a good deal less hazard. If the Wars of Independence do not provide any stirring accounts of fleet engagements such as Sluys, there can be no doubting that control of the seas was of vital strategic importance to both sides and that the Scots were more than able to hold their own.

War produces suffering and uncertainty, but it also operates as a spur for opportunists. Privateers, not only from Scottish ports but from France and the Low Countries, found time to combine duty with profit, preying on merchantmen. In 1316, the *St James* out of Bayonne was boarded by a mixed force of Scots and Flemings who put most of her crew to the sword. Only a last minute sighting of Botecourt's English sails saved her from final capture. Bruce, who owed his throne at least in part to west coast galleys, became an active shipbuilder, constructing cogs on the Clyde at Cardross. These were vessels which, typical of the time, could be as handily sailed for peaceful as military aims; exports of Scottish wool were once again flowing freely by the end of the hero-king's reign, some 5,000 sacks in 1327.

Bruce's death left one important aspect of the independence struggle unresolved: the position of the 'Disinherited', those magnates previously holding cross-border estates cut off from their Scottish holdings or aspirations, a problem exacerbated by the fact the king had redistributed most of the lands in question among his supporters. Edward Balliol, with Henry de Beaumont and David of Strathbogie, was not officially sponsored by the English throne for his bid in 1332, but they were conveyed from Ravenspur in an armada of English vessels, which transported them to Fife and thus facilitated their victory. In the following year, the turncoat Scottish privateer John Crabb captained a flotilla of cogs – *Gracedieu, Jonette* and *Nicholas* – which carried the artillery from York and also formed a naval blockade of Berwick.

Edward III prosecuted his war on Scotland with the aid of a powerful fleet, though, after 1335, he scaled down the naval effort, restricting activity to mercantile raiders. This was very much a two-way trade; French and Scottish privateers took several prizes off the coasts of Suffolk and the Isle of Wight. During the reigns of the first two Stewart kings, Robert I and II, sporadic naval warfare continued. When a prosperous Tayside businessman, John Mercer, was wrecked off the Northumbrian coast in 1376, his vessel and its fat cargo were lifted by the locals, the Scot being gaoled, presumably in anticipation of a ransom. Andrew Mercer, John's son, repaid the compliment by taking up Scarborough, though, two years later Andrew was himself captured by the Londoner, John Philpot. In 1406, the ageing, melancholy Robert III, whose eldest son, the rather unstable Duke of Rothesay, had died while in the custody of his uncle, Albany, took the precaution of sending his surviving boy, James (the future James I), to France. The vessel, *Maryenknyght*, with its royal cargo, was set upon by English privateers and the prince taken. Scarcely able to believe their good fortune, the pirates made haste to sell their royal captive on to Henry IV, a transaction completed in flagrant violation of the prevailing truce. This fact was delicately dealt with when the young king was finally released, ransom monies being expressed as a contribution to the cost of James's education!

During the fifteenth century, Scotland was blighted by a series of minority kingships. James I, when he finally came into his own was, like David II before him, more Anglophile than Anglophobe, having married for love a Beaufort. His son, James II, was the prey of magnatial factions and formed a particular dislike for the over-mighty Black Douglases. After the fall of Douglas and their defeat at Arkinholm in 1455, the king did campaign on the border but lost his life at the siege of Roxburgh in 1460.[8] James III, another minor, was not cast in the martial mould, an aesthete and patron of the arts with a fondness for pretty young men. His low-born courtiers were culled en masse by the Douglas of the day, Archibald 'Bell-the-Cat'[9] with the aid of rope and the handy parapet of Lauder Bridge. While this pogrom was underway, Richard of Gloucester, Shakespeare's 'Crookback Dick', had laid siege to Berwick, which he took having made use of naval power to support his campaign. The Scots retaliated, striking at English merchantmen and fishing craft in both the Channel and the Irish Sea. A sea fight occurred in 1484 in which a Scottish squadron was worsted.

ARTILLERY

Naval power, like war on land, was being affected by the growing importance of cannon. James II had a particular and fatal fascination for artillery, and a survivor from the period is the great gun 'Mons Meg', which stands in Edinburgh Castle. This monster has a barrel length of some 12 feet and could throw a shot weighing several hundred pounds a reputed distance of two miles! Ships were used initially to transport this grand ordnance. We know Edward IV of England sent his great guns 'Dijon', 'London', 'Newcastle' and 'Richard Bombartel' from the Thames to the Tyne by sea.[10] Most of these early pieces loaded at the breech, having a removable breech block, shaped not unlike a beer mug. Elevation was achieved by the insertion of wedges. Early barrels were made, hence the name, on the hoop and stave principle, though casting in brass or bronze proved more satisfactory.

As the fifteenth century progressed, handheld firearms made their appearance, though initially outmatched by the redoubtable longbow. The primitive types consisted of nothing more than a miniature gun barrel lashed to a wooden stave. This weapon was held underarm and pointed in the general direction of an enemy. Then, slow match was applied to the touch hole to ignite the wadded charge. Use of early handheld firearms demanded a certain act of faith on the part of the shooter! The advantage of guns was that their use necessitated very little training and the roar and penetrative power of shot was impressive. References to guns mounted on board ship can be traced to the early 1400s, but the art of naval gunnery only began to flower in the closing decades of the century. Initially, lighter pieces were mounted in the fore and aft castles, essentially intended as anti-personnel weapons, flensing the enemy decks with shot as with arrows. As the weight of guns and shot increased, castles needed to be constructed in a sturdier manner to bear the sharp recoil, ordnance being mounted on the internal elevations as well to clear the between decks of enemy boarders.

Cannon were to have a considerable effect upon the development of naval architecture, and the changes would effectively exclude the all-purpose merchantman/man-of-war. At the start of the fifteenth century, the cog or nef was a single-masted single-decker with only the one square sail. By the close, it had grown into a much larger vessel, possibly three-masted, with a bowsprit, five sails and double-decked. Ordnance had become both heavier, throwing a greater weight of shot, and more effective, capable of doing significant structural damage to an opposing ship. Initially, naval guns were of the cast iron, hoop and stave, breechloader variant. These were the only guns that could be easily reloaded at sea, firing as they did from a fixed wooden carriage. The sections of iron were held in place by iron rings or hoops sweated on around the external circumference. Crude carriages were finished with a heavy timber baulk at the breech, which not only held the wedge securing the removable breech, but soaked up the crashing recoil.

This primitive form was superseded late-century by an improved design, which featured a series of lengths of iron tubing, the lip being shaped like a cotton bobbin. These were secured together by a series of rings beaten around the barrel at the joints. Nonetheless, these still loaded as before, at the breech. A surviving example, salvaged from the wreck of the Tudor warship *The Mary Rose*, is of this type, and the barrel is fitted with lifting rings, probably used to lash it to the frame. As gun-casting techniques improved, a wheeled carriage was developed, which greatly facilitated loading from the muzzle. Heavier guns were placed on the main or lower deck and ships' sides were now fitted with gun ports, through which the great guns were run out to fire. These heavy deck guns might have a barrel length of 3 to 4 metres and throw a shot weighing 15 kilograms.

Powder, or 'serpentine', was milled from a mixture of sulphur, saltpetre and charcoal, being consistent neither in quality or effect. The gun barrels of the fifteenth century needed to have strength equal to 80 times the weight of the shot. As milling techniques improved this would increase to a ratio of 400 within a century. One advantage of a bronze barrel was that it would 'bulge' before bursting, a timely warning for the gunner. Iron was less accommodating, being prone to a sudden, catastrophic burst. On land this was bad, for those like James II, who had the misfortune to be in the immediate vicinity, frequently fatal. At sea it would be worse, for powder and flame added greatly to the risk of shipboard fire, a sailor's nightmare.

THE PRIVATEERS

James III of Scotland did not enjoy a popular reign. His difficulties with the magnates were not resolved after the cull on Lauder Bridge and festered till a further and final confrontation in the campaign and Battle of Sauchieburn on 11 June 1488, when the king was assassinated in murky circumstances following the rout of his forces.[11] His son's biographer, Norman Macdougall, has observed that, during James III's reign, naval hostilities continued despite any prevailing truces:

> As the Treasurer's accounts are lacking for almost all of James III's reign, these examples may not give a fair balance. What they show clearly, however, is that the principal menace to Scots shipping in the North Sea was the hostility of the English. For sea-warfare, even in time of truce, tended to form a category of its own.

The plain fact is that sea-raiding and privateering were highly profitable activities for successful captains, and the niceties of diplomacy could not be allowed to intrude upon such lucrative enterprise. At Bamburgh on the Northumbrian coast, Bishop Kennedy's fine ship *Salvator* ran aground in March 1473 and was relieved of her cargo by James Ker, despite his Teviotdale name, an Englishman. It required negotiations spanning a year and a half before James III, who may have been a stakeholder in the vessel, managed to lever any compensation. Gloucester's cog *Mayflower* had taken *Yellow Carvel*, a ship later to be associated with Andrew Wood of Largo. Sir John Colquhoun of Luss was also despoiled of shipping by Lord Grey. John Barton, brother of Andrew, had one of his vessels taken off Sluys by Portuguese pirates, who stripped the valuable merchandise and murdered a number of those on board.

In October 1474, James had succeeded in brokering a rather flimsy alliance with Edward IV, which finally broke down six years later, and the war of 1481–1482 saw a considerable amount of action at sea. In this the advantage lay heavily with the English. In 1481, Lord John Howard took his squadron into the Firth of Forth and secured a number of valuable prizes, eight Scottish vessels, taken from Leith, Kinghorn and Pittenweem. He then took up Blackness, which was thoroughly spoiled and torched, capturing another and larger vessel. This aggression did not go unopposed, for Andrew Wood led a flotilla which engaged the English, apparently gave a very good account of themselves and inflicted numerous losses. Next year, to support Gloucester's invasion, Sir Richard Radcliffe, an intimate of the duke's who was to rise in his administration, led a second expedition, probably placing his flag on the capital ship, *Grace Dieu*. He was able to occupy Leith and contributed significantly to the English victory on land and the recovery of Berwick – the final time that much beleaguered town was to change hands. Dunbar, an important bastion on the coast of Lothian, was handed over to the English in 1483 by James's traitorous sibling the Duke of Albany and remained in their possession for a couple of years. Being a coastal fortress, the English could rely on their maritime supremacy to facilitate re-supply.

Andrew Wood had been rewarded for his zeal in opposing Howard with the feu-charter of Largo, granted in 1483. The king needed Sir Andrew within his affinity in the campaign which led up to the king's defeat and subsequent death in the spring of 1488. It was Wood's ships, *Yellow Carvel* and *Flower*, which twice transported royal forces across the Firth of Forth and carried the battered survivors back. James may well have been in flight towards these ships when he was overtaken and killed. Both of Sir Andrew's ships were sizeable vessels of around 300 tons, and he was soon in action again against the English when, in 1489, his squadron took on five English raiders and captured them all in a brisk engagement off Dunbar. Wood was well rewarded for his victory, but Henry VII resented the humiliation of so sharp a reverse and commissioned Stephen Bull, an experienced mariner who commanded three competent vessels, to take up the gauntlet.

Bull took his ships into the Firth of Forth, believing, correctly, that Wood was beating back from Flanders and keeping his squadron well hidden in the lee of the Isle of May. To identify his prey, he kidnapped local fishermen who, when sails were sighted, were obliged to climb to the topmast and identify the vessels. At first, the locals temporised but, with the incentive of their release dangled, confirmed the ships were indeed *Yellow Carvel* and *Flower*. Confident of success, having numbers and weight of shot on his side, Bull broached a cask and offered his officers an additional stimulus before engaging. Undeterred by the sudden ambush, Wood cleared for action. He was surprised, outnumbered and outgunned; like his opponent he broke out the grog before the great guns thundered. With the wind steady from the south-east, the longer English guns had the advantage. Wood then beat to windward before closing the range to unleash his own broadside.

The fight which followed was both long and hard. In the constricted waters of the Firth there was little scope for extensive manoeuvring and the battle became a slogging match. Both sides sought to grapple and board, pounding each other beforehand. Amidst shrouds of foul, sulphurous smoke, seamen strove to bring the opposing vessels together, cloying air quickened by the rattle of musketry, the crash of spars and rigging as round shot tore through sails and cordage.

Battle continued all day, the combatants, like punch-drunk fighters, lurching into the open sea. Newer weapons, ordnance and handguns, were deployed alongside crossbows and broadswords. Guns added to the demonic fury of battle with their diabolical roar and the filthy, sulphurous smoke they belched out, vast clouds of the stuff, whipping and eddying in the breeze, one minute obscuring the combatants, then lifting as though with the parting of a veil. As the ships closed to grapple and board, the marines spat bolts and leaden balls from handguns Then, it was down to hand strokes. Knots of fighters boiled over gunwale and deck, screams and shouted orders bellowed in the dense-packed melee. No one had anywhere to run; axes, mallets and the lethal thrust of daggers competed in the stricken space. Darkness brought a brief lull; shattered masts and rent sails were cut free and either cobbled together or ditched overboard. Decks were littered with debris from the fight, gunwales, in several instances, awash with gore and spilt entrails. In the quiet hours, many a man slipped away and was quietly heaved towards a watery grave.

Next day, trumpets sounded and the great guns thundered again as battered vessels rejoined the fight. As Wellington would have observed, it was a very close run thing. Losses and damage were considerable on both sides, but it was Bull's Englishmen who struck their colours. A crowd of Scots had dashed along the shoreline as the battle reached the mouth of the Tay, cheering on the home side! Sir Andrew had wisely stayed to windward, herding the Englishmen towards the Fife shore. Unaware of the risk, till too late, all three of Bull's ships ran aground. The fight was over, the stranded keels boarded and towed in triumph to Dundee. James, delighted with his victory, could afford to be magnanimous, and the survivors were repatriated, but only after a spell as forced labour working on coastal defences! Wood survived into a comfortable retirement and even ordered the construction of a canal between his fine house and the parish church so that, as he journeyed to Mass he might be conveyed in his barge in a manner befitting so venerable a sea-dog.[12]

THE BARTONS

Andrew Wood, notable as his career was, never quite achieved the renown of the Bartons. John, the father, was an experienced mariner from Leith. His three sons, Robert (Hob a Barton to the English), John and, most famously, Andrew, carved a niche as the most active privateers of their day. The brothers had a singular enmity towards the Portuguese who, aside from discommoding John the younger, had plundered their father in 1476. All three sons had distinguished and energetic careers both as merchantmen and sea-thieves. The combined proceeds made each of them wealthy. Intimates and trusted servants of King James IV, numerous of their more outrageous acts were simply winked at. It has been suggested that issuing the brothers with letters of marque was a handy and cost-effective means of bestowing patronage, for the burden fell upon those despoiled in consequence. Robert was heavily involved in the king's shipbuilding programme, entrusted with the sourcing, acquisition and transport of materials. It was he who James chose to escort the Pretender Perkin Warbeck when he was conveyed from Scotland. The letters of reprisal authorising the brothers to prey on the Portuguese, while being issued, were not actually authorised and thus not effective prior to 1507. Robert promptly scooped a fat prize only to find himself under arrest in the port of Veere, his release being procured only after an energetic exercise of royal diplomacy.

Robert's career significantly outlasted that of his two siblings. Andrew died famously in battle in 1511, John, of natural courses, while serving the French two years later. Robert survived to become an important figure in Albany's regency administration and, thereafter, in the government of James V, holding the offices of treasurer, comptroller, great customar, master of the coin, master of the ordnance and conservator of the mines of Scotland. Despite his many sinecures with the combined proceeds of trade and piracy, Robert fell into serious financial difficulties and died, probably in late 1540, still beset by creditors.

Andrew was born around 1470 and did service in the business of the pretender, Perkin Warbeck. By 1505 he had risen to the command of a capital ship *Margaret*. Like his brothers, he was active in pursuing Portuguese targets after 1507, using the letter of reprisal as carte blanche to take up merchant shipping at will. Something of a swashbuckler, he was accused of plundering a Breton ship and found it expedient to cruise to Copenhagen where the King of Denmark, impressed by his fame for derring-do was anxious to procure his services. The king may have been disappointed for Andrew accepted his wages but did little in return, sailing for pickings in the Channel on board *Lion*, (probably of around 120–130 tons) and the lighter pinnace *Jennet of Purwyn*, notwithstanding that the smaller ship had been a gift from James to Hans of Denmark! By now his depredations were causing serious embarrassment in Edinburgh and, following loud protests from the Portuguese, James, suspended the letters of reprisal in the spring of 1511.

His luck finally ran out towards the end of June that year. The two Scottish vessels had been cruising in the Channel seeking prizes when the Scots encountered, off the Downs, two superior English vessels, *Barbara* and *Mary Barking*. These were commanded by Sir

Edward Howard and his younger brother Lord Thomas, sons of the Earl of Surrey. The Howards' vessels were both capital ships and the Scots were outmatched. While not detailed to hunt pirates but engaged primarily to protect merchant convoys, the English captains hoisted sail and gave chase.

Edward Hall, the English chronicler, and no ally to the Bartons, gives a rather coloured but dramatic account of the epic fight which followed. The weather was vile, high seas and wind hampering both hunters and quarry. The ships became separated with Thomas Howard taking the smaller *Jennet*, while his brother closed with the *Lion*. Broadsides thundered over the darkening waters, round shot crashing. With the waves riding so high, there was little that long-range gunnery could achieve, and the two ships closed to grapple and board. Barton directed his men with, as even the English chronicler was prepared to concede, magnificent élan. One of his singular tactics was to unleash a heavy boulder or weight from the yardarm to come crashing down onto and through an enemy deck. Howard, aware of his peril, detailed his most efficient archers to shoot any Scot seeking to clamber up and release the great weight. Two brave Scots tumbled to the bloodied decks, before Barton, who had the benefit of harness, refused to sacrifice more sailors and attempted the job himself. A first shaft glanced harmlessly from plate, and it seemed the day might yet be his, but a second well-aimed point shot under the arm, sending the pirate plummeting to the deck, mortally wounded. Facing death, his courage did not waver and, like Grenville of the *Revenge*, he continued urging his men on to continue the fight for as long as he had breath. Once their captain had expired, however, the survivors succumbed to an instant loss of zeal and hauled down their colours.[13]

James lodged a series of protests with Henry VIII, who responded with some clemency, releasing the surviving Scottish crew. The killing of Andrew Barton still seems to have rankled with James, and Thomas Howard, seeking to goad the king into fighting before Flodden, made specific, gloating reference to his part in the pirate's end. By this time the Wars of Independence were over. Through all the long decades and several centuries of bloody strife, the smaller nation had seen off the attempts of the larger to dominate. Credit for this goes to the great patriot leaders, Wallace, Bruce, Douglas, Randolph and quite rightly, but Scottish ships had, in their way, contributed as much as land forces to the eventual deliverance, and the fast, oared galleys of Angus of Islay had played a pivotal role at a time when patriot fortunes and resources were at their very lowest ebb.

———◆———

The Old Scots Navy

*I*F THE THREE PILLARS OF the medieval state comprised God, Pope and King, the Renaissance prince was a subtly different character from his forebears. Cunning and ruthlessness were expected, inspiration coming more from Machiavelli than Malory. James IV (1488–1513) was, in some ways, the mirror of the Renaissance ruler. He was cultured and learned, his interests eclectic: building and the arts, medicine and science (he was known to practise dentistry upon his courtiers). At the same time, he was romantically attached to the cult of chivalry. The founding of a Scots Royal Navy became one of his grandest passions. He was married to Henry VII of England's daughter Margaret, thus Henry VIII became his brother-in-law. Both men had a yearning to strut upon the European stage, and tension escalated in 1513 when Henry was contemplating an expedition against France in support of the Holy See and the Emperor Maximilian.

James was placed in the invidious position of having to choose an ally, to continue sitting on the fence was politically unsustainable. The King of Scots chose to support the traditional friendship with France, and a series of ultimata delivered to Henry earned nothing but derision. This created the strategic backdrop to the Scots campaign in North Northumberland, one which was succeeding admirably in its key objective of diverting English forces from the Continent, till James took the fatal decision to fight at Flodden. This battle, fought on 9 September, was an unparalleled disaster. The

Scottish army was outfought and suffered grievous loss, the cull falling heaviest on magnates and gentry. Slashed and hacked by bills, an arrow shot through his jaw, one hand virtually severed, James IV lay unnoticed among the piles of corpses.[1]

A REVOLUTION IN SHIPBUILDING

In the course of the sixteenth century, warship design and construction underwent a significant revolution. Northern round ships or carracks, with a length twice the beam, were being built up to a weight of 1,000 tons. The fact that these ships were constructed as floating gun platforms brought out the final transition from converted merchantman to purpose-built man-of-war. They were multi-masted, multi-sailed and had sufficient weight to carry soaring timber castles, bearing an increased weight of ordnance. Both James IV and Henry VIII competed in a naval arms race in the early years of the sixteenth century. The ship which was to become most closely identified with Tudor navies was the race-built galleon. Sleeker and swifter than the carrack, two or two and a half times as long as it was broad, the height of the superstructures was reduced to produce a faster and more seaworthy vessel.

A passionate debate as to the best suited of these types for naval use raged throughout most of the century. More conservative-minded captains favoured the solid bulk of the grand-carrack. In close combat these enjoyed significant advantages. The castles provided excellent and lofty gun platforms, light pivot guns, hand guns and bows could shoot directly down onto the enemy deck and shooters enjoyed good protection. Even if she were boarded, the carrack's defenders could maintain their position in the castles, making life distinctly uncomfortable for attackers. The crucial advantage enjoyed by the galleon was her superior sailing qualities. She could stand off and use her guns to batter the heavy carrack at a distance. The Spanish, whose ships were effectively floating forts, favoured the carrack, a castle on the waves.[2]

By the end of the century, *Revenge* was regarded as a fine example of the race-built galleon. Her gun deck was around 100 feet, with a total length of about 120 feet. She was 32 foot across the beam, and her main ordnance was a score of truck-mounted culverins. Fixed firing platforms had now given way to a two-wheeled timber frame carrying guns with a barrel length of some 12 feet. As yet there was still no standardisation of calibres but the gun threw an 18-pound ball. The ships were all twin-deckers, and these heavier pieces were carried on the lower level while, on the upper, was mounted a further battery of smaller guns firing 10-pound shot. Ships of this period were crammed with ordnance, and the vessel could also house a dozen or more small muzzle-loaders ('murderers') throwing a 2-pound ball, earlier breech-loaders having now been phased out.

This general lack of standardisation was the curse of naval gunnery. Several times, during intense bouts of fighting in the course of the Armada battles in 1588, the English were rendered impotent for want of shot. Bruising and effective as the galleons' fire proved against cumbersome carracks, the capital ships survived, though not without loss and considerable damage. Galleons, in order to keep the weight as low as possible, were built with the lower gun deck stepped down at rear to create a mezzanine type effect. This housed the two hindmost guns, which could be swung around as stern-chasers should circumstances dictate. Officers enjoyed elevated quarters, while the mariners were accommodated on the gun deck. Ships were also fitted with an 'orlop' deck: a further mezzanine, a couple of yards or so above the planking, which formed the quarters for the specialists on board, carpenter, surgeon and purser. In all, the vessel would require a crew of around 150, of whom 70 might be marines with 30-odd gunners.

Though Sir Richard Grenville's epic stand on the shot-torn decks of *Revenge* is not a Scottish fight, Sir Walter Raleigh, in his subsequent report, gives a vivid impression of the conditions which obtained in sea-battles of this era:

All the powder of the 'Revenge' to the last barrel was now spent, all her pikes broken, forty of her best men slain, and the most part of the rest hurt. In the beginning of the fight she had but one hundred free from sickness, and fourscore and ten sick, laid in hold upon the ballast. A small troop to man such a ship, and a weak garrison to resist so mighty an Army. By those hundred all was sustained, the volleys, boardings, and enterings of fifteen ships of war, besides those which beat her at large. On the contrary the Spanish were always supplied with soldiers brought from every squadron: all manner of arms and powder at will. To ours there remained no comfort at all, no hope, no supply either of ships, men or weapons; the masts all beaten overboard, all her tackle cut asunder, her upper work altogether razed, and in effect she was evened with the water, only the very foundation or bottom of a ship, nothing being left over head either for flight of defence.[3]

RESTLESS NATIVES

When James IV finally embarked upon the abolition of the Lordship in 1493, he doubtless contemplated the move as enabling him to cement royal power in the west. In this he was mistaken. The fall of Clan Donald ushered in an age, not of centralised authority but of murderous, internecine strife, the *Lin na Creach* ('Age of Forays').[4] In the same year he kicked away the last supports of the tottering Macdonald hegemony in the west, James's Parliament enacted that all coastal burghs should provide a well-founded vessel of not less than 20 tons with able-bodied mariners for her crew. To reinforce awareness that the ending of Clan Donald's sway was but the beginning of a new extension of the business of the state, James led a fleet to the Isles in August, accompanied by Chancellor Angus and a fine train of magnates. At Dunstaffnage, where he stayed a mere 11 days, he may have accepted the surrender of some chiefs, reaffirming their holdings by royal charter. The Macdonalds were not completely over-reached; both Alexander of Lochalsh and John of Islay received knighthoods.

In 1495, accompanied by Andrew Wood and commanding *Yellow Carvel* and *Flower*, James cruised down the Firth of Lorn, through the Sound of Mull to MacIan of Ardnamurchan's seat, Mingary Castle,[5] where a quartet of powerful magnates bent their collective knee. These included such noted seafarers and pirates as MacNeil of Barra and Maclean of Duart. While James was diverted by his flirtation with the posturing Perkin Warbeck, this policy of treating with the chiefs was undone, largely by the avarice of Argyll, who preferred force to reason. Inevitably, this merely served to alienate the Islesmen, whose galleys conferred both force and mobility. In

1496, Bute had been taken up and disorders reached a level where the king felt obliged, once again, to assert his authority by launching a naval expedition. Indeed this was the only means whereby the chiefs could effectively be brought into line. A land-based expedition would accomplish nothing; Islesmen counted wealth and power in the number of their keels.

The king's expedition of 1498 proceeded by way of Arran to his royal castles of Kilkerran, where he spent two months, and Tarbert. James, though he wished to impress his authority on the west, did not necessarily have much enthusiasm for the chore. For the royal writ to run in the west and to fill the gap in authority left by the collapse of the Lordship, power needed to be exercised by loyal and respected subordinates. Argyll had succeeded in alienating a number of the chiefs, including his own brother-in-law, Torquil MacLeod of Lewis, who was to become a fierce opponent. MacLeod had secured, by uncertain means, the keeping of the boy, Donald Dubh, would-be claimant to the defunct Lordship. Argyll was no more loved by Huntly, his successor as Lieutenant in the north-west and one who proved equally hungry for personal gain.

James was briefly diverted in 1501 by the near-fiasco of his Danish adventure and did not turn his gaze westwards again until the following year. That Torquil MacLeod should control the person of Donald Dubh was fraught with risk. MacLeod was summoned to appear, failed to do so and was outlawed as a consequence. Huntly was commissioned to take up Torquil's confiscated estates, doubtless to Argyll's fury, he being sidelined for failing to keep a grip on his own kinsman. Both Mackintosh and Mackenzie managed to escape from confinement, though the first was soon recaptured and the second killed. By 1503, disturbances had become widespread, and Huntly was engaged in wholesale dispossession of those who refused to submit. With Donald Dubh lending legitimacy to their cause (old John of the Isles died in January 1504), the rebels under Torquil struck back. Bute was again extensively despoiled.

Parliament, sitting in March 1504, commissioned Huntly to retrieve Eilean Donan and Strome castles, while a naval command, assembled under the ever vigilant eye of Sir Andrew Wood, was entrusted to Arran. The fleet was to reduce the rebels' stronghold of

Cairn na Burgh, west of Mull in the Isles of Treshnish. The capital ships, with a full complement of ordnance, soon proved their worth; naval gunnery swiftly reduced *Cairn na Burgh*. Few details of the siege have survived, but the operation would clearly have been a difficult one. The ships would come in as close as the waters permitted and deliver regular broadsides, essentially floating batteries. What weight of shot the rebels possessed is unclear; most likely it was not very great. Several rebel chiefs – Maclean of Lochbuie, MacQuarrie of Ulva and MacNeil of Barra – presently found themselves in irons. Gradually the power and authority of the crown was restored. These captured chiefs saw little prospect in continued defiance. Argyll was fully abetted by MacIan of Ardnamurchan, a ruthlessly effective pairing.[6]

Argyll, now restored to his Lieutenancy, was prepared to be more diplomatic and, from 1506, there was a return to a more conciliatory policy, rewarding those chiefs prepared to submit, even some of those who'd been implicated or involved in the recent disturbances. MacIan too did well enough, though he had few friends in the Isles and his own advancement had to be checked to avoid the greater alienation of others, especially the Macleans. Torquil Macleod kept the rebel flame firmly alight, and his example helped to inspire dissidents. The Parliament summoned for early 1506 convicted him of treason. An expedition sent against him was to be led by Huntly and involved the hire of captains such as John Smollett and William Brownhill, with ordnance supplied from the royal train. The king and his advisors had planned on a campaign of two months' duration to wrest Lewis from Macleod. In September, the king paid a sum of £30 to Thomas Hathowy as a fee for the hire of *Raven*, which had been engaged for service in the campaign. By September, it also seems likely that Huntly had succeeded in reducing Stornoway Castle and capturing Donald Dubh, though the wily MacLeod slipped the net and remained a fugitive until his death in 1511.

By now James IV was losing interest in the Isles. Control was best exercised through local magnates like Argyll, even if the Campbells, for all their avarice, were not possessed of an effective fleet of galleys. This deficiency was partly corrected by the cordial relations the earl enjoyed with the Macleans, anxious to see the ruin of Clan

Donald fully accomplished in order that they might assume the mantle of a naval power among the clans. James had by now set his heart upon, and his mind towards, the creation of a Scottish national navy. In August 1506, he'd written to the King of France intimating that this naval project was a key objective. Scotland was a small kingdom, disturbed by the fissiparous tendencies of the Islesmen and magnatial factions. It was also a poor nation, lacking the resources of England. Nonetheless, during his reign, James bought, built or acquired as prizes taken by his buccaneering captains, nearly two score of capital ships, a very considerable total for the day.

TOWARDS A SCOTTISH NAVY

This proposed Scottish Navy was not a complete innovation. The king's predecessors had been possessed of ships; as early as 1457 Bishop Kennedy of St Andrews owned the impressive *Salvator* – at 500 tons a very large vessel. Developments in naval architecture, influenced by advances in the science of gunnery, had necessitated the final differentiation between ships of war and merchantmen. The crown could no longer count upon assembling an effective fleet by hiring in merchant vessels and converting them to temporary service as men-of-war. Nations that sought to strut upon the wider stage required a navy as a tool of aggressive policy and a statement of intent. The fifteenth century had not witnessed any serious English interference before 1481–1482, and the prime consideration, in terms of sea power, was to protect Scottish ships against the unwelcome attention of privateers, for the most part English, who infested the North Sea like hungry sharks.

Richard of Gloucester's campaigns showed how exposed the Firth of Forth and indeed the whole of the east coast were to a planned attack from the sea. Here, in the east, the problem was wholly different from that of the west. No Hebridean galleys disturbed the peace, but the Forth and Edinburgh were horribly exposed to English hostility. While Henry VII proved less inclined to attack Scotland than his despised predecessor and actually ran down the navy he'd acquired, the Perkin Warbeck crisis of 1497 highlighted the continuing exposure. Even when a more cordial atmosphere prevailed, the activities of privateers continued regardless; Andrew Wood and the Bartons persisted in their piratical activities as did their English opposites.

In 1491, the Scots Parliament empowered John Dundas to erect a fort on the strategically sited rock of Inchgarvie. Wood had already thrown up a defensive work at Largo. Conversely, the legislature had previously ordered the slighting of Dunbar Castle, the English occupation being the requisite spur (later, after 1497, the ubiquitous Wood was to oversee its rebuilding). Such defensive measures and the encouragement of privateers like Sir Andrew and the Bartons were entirely sound but, of themselves, insufficient to undertake coastal defence and the wider protection of the sea lanes. For this greater task, only a fleet would suffice. With James the creation of a navy rapidly rose to become a near-obsession; policy was overlaid with prestige. For the first ten years of his quarter-century reign, James spent under £1,500 Scots in total on his ships, a very modest outlay. This climbed to something in the order of £5,000 per annum after 1505, and by the end of the reign he was spending over £8,000 per annum on his new navy. To give a comparison, during the years he was on the throne, the king's income roughly trebled but his expenditure on the navy increased sixty fold!

A switch of emphasis from west to east characterised James's policy towards ships and shipbuilding. Dumbarton remained both as a base and a shipyard, but he considerably improved the facilities of Leith's existing dockyards, constructed a new yard at the New Haven (Newhaven) and, latterly, another at the Pool of Airth. Not only did Scotland lack adequate facilities for the construction of larger men-o'-war, but she lacked the requisite craftsmen and these had to be imported, primarily from France. In November 1502, the Treasurer's accounts reveal the hire of a French shipwright, John Lorans, working at Leith under the direction of Robert Barton. This first importation was soon complemented by others. Jennen Diew and then Jacques Terrell were engaged and, due to a shortage of hardwood, obliged to source timber for their new keels abroad. In June 1506, the great ship *Margaret* (named after the king's Tudor consort) slid into the placid waters of the Forth. This vessel was a source of great pride to the king – as indeed she might be, the cost of her construction had gobbled up a quarter of a whole year's royal revenue. She was four-masted, weighed some 600 or 700 tons and bristled with ordnance. James's chivalric obsession with the panoply of war found a natural outlet in the building of his great ships. He appointed himself Grand Admiral of the Fleet and dined aboard the *Margaret*, wearing the gold chain and whistle of his new office.[7]

The fiasco of the Danish expedition in 1502 acted as a further spur towards creating a purpose-built navy. This botched inter-meddling represented an attempt by James, at least in part, to establish himself and his realm as a player on the wider European stage. The result was scarcely encouraging and, despite the 'spin' placed upon the outcome, the affair proved something of a debacle. In 1501–1502, King Hans of Denmark found he was confronted by rebellious subjects in his client territories of Norway and Sweden and had lost control of a swathe of key bastions, including the strategically significant hold of Askerhus near Oslo. James was bound to the Danes by earlier treaty, and the situation raised possibilities for a decisive intervention by the Scots. The king hurried to make preparations for an expedition: *Eagle* and *Towaich* were made ready, together with *Douglas* and *Christopher*. The total cost of the fleet and accompanying troops was a whopping £12,000, and the burden fell on the Scottish taxpayers. From the start there were difficulties. Lord George Seton had been paid to make ready his vessel *Eagle*, but his part ended in acrimonious litigation and impounding of the ship, which does not ever appear to have weighed anchor. Raising the requisite number of infantry, ready to serve in the proposed campaign, proved arduous; far from the number of 10,000 postulated, it seems unlikely that the force amounted to more than a fifth of that total.

When the truncated fleet finally sailed towards the latter part of May, 1502 it comprised *Douglas, Towaich, Christopher*, together (possibly) with *Jacat* and *Trinity*, under the flag of Alexander, Lord Hume, wily borderer and chamberlain. In the two months of campaigning, little was in reality, achieved. The Scots likely suffered loss in an abortive escalade of Askerhus. Others sat down before Bahus and Elvsborg. A significant number simply deserted. For James, who'd had equal difficulties in securing payment of the taxes due to fund the business, there was nothing but frustration, tinged with humiliation. This was not at all what he'd envisaged.

Construction of *Margaret* was followed by the commissioning of *Treasurer*, built by Martin le Nault of Le Conquet at a further cost of £1,085 Scots. More vessels were purchased including Robert Barton's *Colomb*, which was quickly engaged in the west, cruising from Dumbarton under the capable John Merchamestone to recover Brodick Castle, seat of the Earl of Arran, seized by Walter Stewart. When King James wrote to Hans of Denmark in August 1505, he had to concede that he had no capital ships available, such were the demands of home service, making good storm damage, wear and tear, with other vessels detached on convoy duty. In part, this deficiency could and had to be made up by hire or joint venture agreements with merchants/privateers such as the Bartons, but it was clear more capital ships were needed. By 1507, work on the construction of the New Haven was already far advanced and the king was considering the possibilities of Pool of Airth, well to the west of the fort at Invergarvie and thus far more sheltered from attack. By the autumn of 1511, three new docks had been built under the direction of Robert Callendar, Constable of Stirling Castle, who had received £240 Scots to meet the costs involved.

Impressive as the construction of the great ship *Margaret* had been and as much as she represented the best in contemporary warship design, she was insufficient to satisfy James's obsession with capital ships. As early as 1506, the king had engaged James Wilson of Dieppe, a Scottish shipwright working in France, to begin sourcing suitable timbers for a yet larger project. This new vessel, *Michael*, was to define the Scots Navy of James IV. A later chronicler estimates its cost as not less than £30,000 Scots, a truly vast outlay. Finding adequate supplies of timber to build her hull and furnish the planking gobbled up much of Scotland's natural resource with much else imported besides. She would have weighed at least 1,000 tons with a length of 150–180 feet. Her main armament probably totalled 27 great guns with a host of smaller pieces, swivels and handguns. Henry VIII, not to be outdone in what was developing into a naval arms race, commissioned *Great Harry*, which went into the water a year later. For James this was imitation as flattery; the fact that *Michael* was afloat, moved Scotland into the first rank of maritime powers. A Scots Navy had now fully 'arrived'. The new ship took to the water for the first time on 12 October 1511. She had been nearly five years in the making and carried a full complement of around 300 of whom 120 were required to serve the great guns.

James took an enormous pride in his flagship. At that moment, she was likely the most powerful and advanced warship that had ever sailed. Her very existence heralded Scotland as a European power. His nascent navy now comprised in addition to *Michael* and *Margaret*, the capital ships *Treasurer* and *James* with smaller but still potent men-of-war in *Christopher* and *Colomb*, plus a couple of substantial row-barges and lesser craft. This royal squadron could be further up-gunned by the private vessels of the Bartons and seafarers such as Brownhill, Chalmers, Falconer and, of course, Sir Andrew Wood. Not only had the king created a navy, but the sea was his passion to a far greater extent than appears to have been the case with any of his forebears. It was thus the crowning irony of his reign that this fine instrument of war was never really tested in battle. For James, the great trial came on land, in the rain, at the end of a wet summer in September 1513, not on some great field of European destiny but the habitual graveyard of North Northumberland. The catastrophe of Flodden cast a perpetual dark shadow over the king's memory, his creation of a Scottish navy a mere footnote by comparison. In the final, dolorous act, the regency council sold *Michael* to their French allies for something less than half of what she'd cost to construct. It was an ignominious and inglorious ending to so great an enterprise.

What then did James achieve, if anything? For a brief and untried moment he projected the image of Scotland as a power of the first rank, or very close, a status she had not enjoyed before and would not resume. The cost in treasure to the nation had been very considerable, though the yards provided much employment and created a more sophisticated shipbuilding industry. It is true that, during his reign, no successful attacks were launched against the Forth. Lack of a naval presence would bear bitter fruit during the harrying of the Rough Wooing in the 1540s. To that extent, James's policy of aggressive defence was a success, and his victories over the dissident clans and Islesmen in the west should not be overlooked.

In spite of these very real achievements, it is impossible to escape the fact that this fledgling navy did not survive his violent death. The construction of the fleet had been due in no small part to the French alliance and the king's ability to source skilled men and sound materials from French ports and forests. Had the disaster at Flodden not occurred, the naval history of Scotland might have followed a different course. In those few hours of frenzied, doomed carnage James and his realm lost all he had created.

THE ENTERPRISE OF ENGLAND

> And it is no marvel that the Spaniard should seek by false and slanderous pamphlets, advisos and letters to cover their own loss, and to derogate from others their due honours . . . seeing they were not ashamed in the year 1588, when their purpose was the invasion of this land, to publish in sundry languages in print, great victories in words, which they pleaded to have obtained against this Realm and spread the same in a most false sort over all parts of France, Italy and elsewhere. When shortly after it was happily manifested in very deed to all nations how their Navy which they termed invincible, consisting of 240 sail of ships, not only of their own kingdom, but strengthened with the greatest Argosies, Portugal carracks, Florentines and huge Hulks of other countries; were by thirty of her Majesty's own ships of war, and a few of our own Merchants, by the wise, valiant and most advantageous conduction of the Lord Charles Howard, High Admiral of England, beaten . . .
>
> *Sir Walter Raleigh*

In the late summer of 1588, survivors of Philip II's great Armada, which was to have encompassed the destruction of heretic England, were beating northwards into the cold and unforgiving waters of the North Sea. Great carracks and galleasses wallowed in harsh seas, intense cold and pervading bleakness further lowering the morale of crews disheartened by defeat. The Duke of Medina Sidonia, Grand Admiral of the Fleet, hoped to lead his battered squadrons around the north of Scotland and then down the west coast of Ireland. Here a number of the ships foundered, driven onto rocky promontories. Scotland, under James VI was, in theory at least neutral, the situation obfuscated by the fact Mary had, under the terms of her will of 1577, bequeathed her claim to the throne of England, not to her Protestant son but to Philip II of Spain. James, however, was putative heir to Elizabeth and had a particular and vested interest in ensuring this 'Enterprise of England' should fail.

And it did indeed fail. Those wrecked on the barren shores of Ireland could hope for little mercy from the locals even if they were co-religionists: 'It is the custom of these savages [the Irish] to live like wild beasts in the mountains . . . their great desire is to be thieves and plunder one another' as one Spanish survivor recalled. Despite the nature of their reception, the idea of large numbers of Spanish soldiers, well-armed and led, being deposited in Ireland filled the administration with deep consternation. The available defenders were no more than 2,000 at best, ill-armed and worse trained, whose function was to control near a million Catholic Irish. At least one capital ship *San Juan de Sicilia* reached Tobermory where it was subsequently destroyed by explosion; an act of sabotage generally credited to the Anglophile Sir Lachlan Mor Maclean, and intended to rob Clan Donald of any advantage. Maclean may have been precipitate as the legend persists the doomed vessel carried a fortune in gold, a tale that has drawn treasure hunters ever since.

Alonso de Leyva managed to keep his large ship's company together when the great *Santa Ana* was grounded on the rocks of Loughros More Bay. His command comprised some 700 souls, well-armed and with a leavening from the very cream of Spanish magnatial families. His men managed to join with the crew of the damaged galleass *Gerona* and, under his direction, repair the stricken vessel and make for the relative safety of Scotland. The clumsy ship, unsuited to northern tidal waters and northern tempests made heavy weather of the difficult passage. A bare 40 sea miles from Scotland, their luck ran out as her rudder broke and the ungainly craft, loaded with some 1100–1200 men, drifted helplessly on to rocks beneath the ramparts of Dunluce Castle. The garrison was not much troubled, however, for only a mere handful escaped the wreck.

A more fortunate, if sorely tried, survivor was the spirited

Francisco de Cuellar. He had been stripped of his command for disobedience and was in disgrace, a prisoner aboard *La Lavia* when she was driven inshore by strong winds off Streetdagh Strand. Those who struggled ashore were manhandled and mistreated by the rapacious locals bent purely on spoil; any English officers, fearing an insurrection, would have been heartened. Despite his injuries and being a non-swimmer de Cuellar made it to the sands and survived the attentions of the indigenous predators. After many adventures, hampered by his wounds, the gallant Spaniard wandered the wastes of Ireland, sometimes befriended, often robbed and abused. With a handful of companions he stoutly defended a M'Glannagh pele against the English before making good his escape.

THE ULSTER PATROL

For several centuries, though most evidence arises during the later period, Hebrideans had been exporting military manpower to Ireland where the fighting skills of the '*Gall-Gaidhil*' ('Foreign' Gaels) were continuously in demand. Principal reasons for this continual migration were essentially economic. The Hebrides are poor and, in large part barren, thus a young man with a strong arm and fire in his belly might find ready employment with the Irish chiefs frequently at odds with the English, each other or both. These warriors evolved into an elite caste, the *Gallolaigh* or, in its anglicized form, galloglass. A significant contribution to the supposed superiority of the Islesmen was their naval capacity. Clinker-built galleys would always be superior to the currachs of the Irish lords. In his excellent and definitive study of the Hebridean galley, Denis Rixson points out that this was a clear paradox; a region that was economically backward and relatively sparsely populated could prey at will on a larger, more populous and wealthier neighbour by dint of a clear technological advantage.

The new age of internecine bloodletting after 1493 proved a further spur to military/economic migration to Ireland. Ties of blood and marriage also played their part. Bruce had married the Red Earl of Ulster's daughter and a whole web of allegiances had subsequently bound the MacSorleys and other chiefs since. In 1595, one correspondent wrote that a recently arrived company of Scots had been offered local wives, each a spouse appropriate to his degree. The letter concludes with an observation that the Scots had, on receipt of the offer, immediately departed whence they'd come! In financial terms, the more unsettled affairs in Ireland stood, the stronger the Hebrideans' bargaining position. In 1594, O' Donnell was offering high wages – double the norm – to tempt extra recruits. One year later, Macleod of Harris received an advance of £500, a very sizeable sum, from the O'Neill Earl of Tyrone and was able to raise a brigade of Islesmen 2,500 strong. Further cash bonuses accrued with the promise of harness and mounts. To poor men from the impoverished Hebrides, this was largesse indeed. Equally, other Islesmen, motivated by dislike of their neighbours, might sign on with the English. The 1590s would be bumper years for galloglasses. The native earls of Ulster were fighting a sustained and, for a long time, very successful guerrilla campaign against the encroaching English. Their final defeat at the battle of Kinsale would clearly have a proportionately adverse effect on the market.

To promote and facilitate this commerce in armed men, Hebridean galleys remained the perfect maritime vehicle. In design largely unchanged from previous centuries, the galley persisted through the sixteenth century. In terms of developments in naval and artillery technologies, galleys were redundant as warships in any action with an Elizabethan man-of-war, though her oars and handiness could still give her the edge in inland and island waters. English commander George Thornton, with decades of service in Irish and Scottish waters, clearly appreciated the usefulness of the galley's oars, that they could outstrip pursuit even by a fast pinnace, unless the wind was sufficient to close the gap. The galley could be beached and was thus not dependent upon a sound anchorage. Its use in war was not restricted to ferrying troops. It could be used to victual the armies, to transport lifted livestock or harvest local fish stocks. Numerous accounts from the late sixteenth century record Scottish sea-rovers relieving Irish owners of their beasts.[8]

In 1589, a raid of industrial proportions descended on Mayo, perpetrated by those experienced pirates, the MacNeills of Barra. Some 400 raiders slaughtered 600 head and stole near as many.

These were in due course also killed, converting the haul into hides and tallow. This was pure brigandage, reminiscent of the Norse practice of 'strand-hogg'. MacNeill was not a numerous or powerful name like Clan Donald but the remoteness of their island fastness and their skill as seafarers provided ample compensation.

From time to time the English would snap at the involvement of the clans in Irish affairs. Thomas Radcliffe, third Earl of Sussex, campaigned vigorously in Ireland during the reign of Mary Tudor. In 1557 he fought, with no small success, against Donough O'Connor and the murderously formidable Shane O'Neill. He subsequently intervened in a dispute between factions of the O'Briens, restoring the ousted Earl of Thomund. Exasperated by the continual presence of Scottish spears in the glens of Antrim, he resolved to discourage their industry and, by way of warning, took up Kintyre and several of the more southerly isles. In naval terms he was unopposed, though the lesson was largely wasted. Throughout the sixteenth century, the Irish administration was more concerned with securing the exclusion of the Scots than exerting any particular influence over them. In 1540, James V undertook his cruise through the western seaboard and the Isles with a powerful squadron of a dozen well-found vessels, bristling with ordnance. By this time there was no question that a fleet of galleys, however swift and numerous, could take on capital ships in an open engagement. Equally, for the crown, the cost of mounting such a show of force, however impressive, was very considerable, to the extent the game was scarcely worth the candle.

Though the Scots might possess the technological advantage over their Irish cousins, at least two native Irish clans – the O'Malleys and the O'Flahertys – were possessed of effective galley squadrons. To counter these, the Anglo-Irish deployed both conventional warships and galleys of their own. In June 1602, Sir Oliver Lambert petitioned the Lord-Deputy to authorise the acquisition by purchase of an English crewed galley to take on these two clans who were clearly active in raiding and piracy, taking many prizes. Sir Oliver had in mind a vessel of 15 oars a side and carrying a complement of 50 marines. Clearly, he tended to the view that it was necessary to set a thief to catch a thief in terms of the most suitable craft for the work.

Like Scotland, the west coast of Ireland was a confusion of narrow inlets and tiny natural harbours, inaccessible to a galleon. Both the O'Malleys and the O'Flahertys had a similar opportunist approach to the MacNeills and appear to have operated in similar freebooting style. The formidable Grany (Grace) O'Malley (*Grainne Ni Mhaille*), a lady of conspicuous skill as a pirate,[9] had, through a judicious choice of consort, united the two clans into a single thriving consortium. More than happy to contract to the English if the terms were attractive, she could bring a score of galleys and 200 broadswords. In 1598, her son Donald was bargaining for a commission to deny Scottish galleys any approach to Ulster:

> He will take upon him to keep from the north both the Highland and Lowland succour of Scotland, if Her majesty will build him two galleys in Wexford or Carrickfergus, the one of twenty-four oars, and the other of thirty.

These were indeed substantial vessels, and both Wexford and Carrickfergus were possessed of established yards and the size of O'Malley's proposed flagship, presumably the larger of the two, invites comparison with the nearest Hebridean equivalent, the 'Rodel' galley. This is shown, carved on one of the panels of the tomb of Alexander Macleod (d.1528), interred in St Clement's church, Rodel on Harris. It has 17 oars a side, a total of 34, and thus a likely crew of more than 100. Competent as the O'Malleys undoubtedly were, there is no record of any sea fight between their galleys and those of the Scots. As previously noted, the main English intention was to stop up the sea passage and deny the Irish their hired help, to control access via the North Channel.

With Elizabeth's naval resources concentrated against the very real threat from Spain, her officers could not afford a significant deployment off Ireland. However, for the best part of half a century, a small squadron, which became known as the Ulster Patrol, remained active. Details of a number of the vessels, which from time to time performed this thankless and inglorious chore, have been preserved, and it is immediately clear that there was a wide disparity in the type of craft employed, ranging from diminutive vessels such as the *Spy* of 50 tons, a crew two score strong and mounting only nine guns, up to the altogether more potent *Swiftsure* – 40 guns and more and with a couple of hundred mariners and marines on board. The disparity should be considered in the light of observations that the English would require a ship of no more than 30 tons to take on the O'Malleys. This implies that boats such as *Spy*, *Moon* (60 tons, 9 guns) and *Charles* (70 tons, 16 guns) were sufficient in terms of weight of shot, but the bigger ships *Swiftsure* and *Foresight* were there to provide 'shock and awe'.

The task facing English skippers, doughty George Thornton and others, such as captains Rigges and Moyle, was an unenviable one. Climate and coastline were hostile, the enemy numerous, well-prepared and with a deep local knowledge; their galleys were no match in a fight but damnably elusive otherwise. Ships were precious, representing a very considerable outlay in men and treasure. Storm damage was frequent and costly; pay and supply were frequently scarce or non-existent. Corruption and a whole raft of inefficiencies combined to render the task yet more difficult. Yet there were some successes. A report from 1584 records the destruction of six Scottish galleys taken or drowned – the latter perhaps as a consequence of ramming rather than gunfire.

In the summer of 1595 a large fleet of Hebridean craft at least 100 strong – larger galleys, birlinns and nyvaigs – was known to be sea bound, probably, from Arran for Ulster. On board, in addition to supplies, were perhaps as many as 3,000 mercenaries, raised for service by Donald Gorn Macdonald of Sleat, MacLeods of Lewis and Harris. They probably sailed on or about 22 July. George Thornton, at this point, had *Poppinjay*, while Gregory Rigges was master of *Charles*. It was not the entire Hebridean fleet which encountered the Ulster Patrol off Copeland Island, but a substantial contingent nevertheless. Accounts differ as to the exact details of the fight, but there is a consensus that the Hebrideans were badly mauled in the first clash, perhaps up to three being sunk, two more captured and others run ashore. A standoff then ensued; the Scots had numbers but the English had weight of shot and the first, bruising test had left the Islesmen in no doubt as to who would prevail if battle was resumed. Donald Macdonald promptly offered to change sides, expediency as ever being the driver. His offer was, however, declined, and he with most of his brigade was obliged to return home, leaving pledges and assurances for their good behaviour. Both sides would be fully aware of their worth. A couple of battalion-sized contingents, presumably not involved in the fight, did get through to Ireland unmolested. The Ulster patrol had, however, thoroughly proved its worth.

Such a battle would be fast and confusing; the capital ships would run out their guns at first sight of the galleys. That they were able to do so suggests they had the weather gauge but that the winds were not so strong as to spoil the gunners' aim. *Charles* we know was smaller, a mere 70 tons and 16 pieces. *Poppinjay* likely fired the heavier broadside. The guns, probably at this date brass or bronze muzzle-loaders, mounted on two-wheeled carriages and secured by tackle, might at best be 18-pounders. Gun captains would be ready with bags of powder ladled into the muzzle, shot and wadding thrust down and secured with the rammer, a fine trickle of priming powder poured down the quill placed in the touch-hole. The great gun sighted and aimed, then a vast, crashing roar as the linstock lighted the charge, the gun belching fire and death. A fast-moving galley would be no easy target, but the very press of the Hebridean craft would have aided their demise. Screaming round shot would punch through the planking, shearing limbs, unleashing a lethal blizzard of splinters, which could impale and mangle as sure as iron. Grape, fired from the deck-mounted swivels, would flense the waists, killing men so tightly packed by the dozen. Holed and mastless, galleys would swiftly founder leaving a spew of spars, cordage and a seaborne carpet of bobbing corpses.

If the Scots had experienced relatively little loss of life in the fight, perhaps 100 men or so killed, some, at least had learned a salutary lesson. In August, Thornton met Maclean of Duart on Mull. The chief offered 2,000 broadswords for the Queen's service, subject only to Argyll's acquiescence. In the last decade of the sixteenth century, Maclean was at odds with Clan Donald over the Rhinns of Islay, and English assistance would more than make up for the naval shortcomings of his Campbell allies. Maclean also enjoyed a significant windfall as the doomed Armada hastened to its destruction, salvaging a rich haul of invaluable ordnance. His offer to supply men to the Queen for service in Ireland was as much calculated to make friends of the English as to net the usual financial reward. Perhaps one of the best and most experienced masters to serve with the Ulster patrol, George Thornton died, still active, in 1601.

Such successes were relatively rare. In the majority of instances the Scots got through; the galleys were outdated and outclassed as men-of-war but they still possessed agility, speed and the handiness of the oars. When confronted, a fleet would simply scatter, depriving their opponents of a worthwhile catch. If the weather turned foul as it was frequently like to do, there was no sense in continuing to hazard a capital ship in the continuing pursuit of minnows. Efforts were made to prevent the Islesmen importing Irish timber supplies and the need to have some form of oared vessel added to the strength was recognised. In 1596 it was proposed to add a pair of light pinnaces of suitably shallow draft. Three years later the revised intention was to construct substantial oared vessels, 44 feet in the keel and with a beam of 14 feet, carrying 40 oars and armed with bow-chasers. Though they might cruise with relative impunity, galleys were vulnerable once beached and out of the water. Captain Norreys deployed three galleons against rebel-held Rathlin Island in 1575 and, in the ensuing action, not only destroyed the garrison but added a total of 11 beached galleys to the final tally.

Captain Plessington of *Tramontana* engaged an Irish galley in the summer of 1601. The English man-of-war succeeded in driving the galley inshore but was obliged to launch her boat close to contact. The Irish galley carried 30 oars and a well-armed complement of 100 or so, many of whom were equipped with firearms. For an hour, the two boats skirmished and sniped, using only small arms and the English were suffering the more heavily. Plessington ran out his great guns and, shooting over the heads of his longboat crew, made a swift conclusion. The vessel he destroyed was one of Grany O'Malleys, apparently skippered by one of her illegitimate offspring!

A legionary from the 1st Century AD, wearing the classic plate harness, *lorica segmentata*

Largs Bay, the site of the battle or extended skirmish of 1263 which brought to an end Norse claims of sovereignty in the west – the distinctive 'pencil' shaped monument faces over the bay towards the islands of Cumbrae and beyond to Arran. *Photography by Adamskii.com*

Facsimile of Viking vessel on display in Largs. *Photography by Adamskii.com*

wark Castle, located on the south side of the Clyde Estuary, was built by the Maxwells in
'8 as a classic tower house with surrounding wall or barnekin. It was much extended towards
end of the sixteenth century and then gradually subsumed in a slew of industrial devel-
nent, now largely cleared away. *Photography by Adamskii.com*

mbarton Castle. Set in a spectacular location on the volcanic plug of Dumbarton Rock, the
:le formed the chief hold of Dark Age Strathclyde and remained a functioning fortress till
5. It sits on the north bank of the Clyde. Most of the current structure is from the eighteenth
tury, combining utility with elegance. *Photography by Adamskii.com*

Opened to the public in 1989, Inveraray Gaol was a court and prison since the nineteenth century, a statement, like the castle, of the power of Campbell lairds.
Photography by Adamskii.com

A view looking up Loch Fyne into the heart of Campbell Country. *Photography by Adamskii.c*

unadd. The 'Fortress on the River Add', a magnificent almost Cyclopean hill top fortress and
incipal place of the Scots of Dalriada, the mysterious boar incision and kingly foot well crown
e summit with a long view all around. *Photography by Adamskii.com*

Kilmartin Churchyard. Some remarkable and revealing grave slabs – shows the fourteenth century dress of the highland warrior, pointed bascinet, and mail pisane, quilted aketon and 'lang swerd'. *Photography by Adamskii.com*

Dunstaffnage Castle. Another Dalriadic fortress, on a rocky outcrop some three miles north of Oban. The stone structure was constructed by the Macdougalls in the mid thirteenth century and captured by Bruce in 1309. Subsequently, it was granted to Colin Campbell 1st Earl of Arg (1479). Torched after the fiasco of 1685 and Argyll's failed rising it was garrisoned by the crown 1745 and later housed a captive Flora MacDonald. *Photography by Adamskii.com*

astle Stalker. Impossibly romantic, this soaring tower, 'the Castle of the Hunter' was built by
ewart of Appin in 1540, located at the mouth of diminutive Loch Laich a branch of Loch
nnhe. It sits astride the 'Rock of the Cormorants'. Abandoned by 1780 it was not restored until
e 1960s by the late Lieutenant Colonel Stewart Allward. *Photography by Adamskii.com*

poignant and mute testament to the Clearances, abandoned coastal settlement on the south
nk of Ardnamurchan Peninsula. *Photography by Adamskii.com*

Mingary. Impressively and strategically situated on the southern shores of Ardnamurchan, this ancient hexagonal bastion was the hold of MacDonald of Ardnamurchan, and covered the Sound of Mull. Most of what stands dates from the sixteenth century and, from here. Maclean of Duart, having gained possession, fought off the Armada galleon *Florida* in 1588. In the Civil Wars MacColla laid brief siege to the place which surrendered, virtually without a fight, so terrifying was the paladin's roar! Currently the interior is inaccessible.
Photography by Adamskii.com

Tioram. Magnificently situate on the small tidal island of Eilean Tioram this 'the Dry Castle' w the seat of Clanranald and the curtain wall dates from the thirteenth century. In the hands of government forces in 1715, Clanranald returned from exile to wrest back possession, slighting tl place when the rebellion failed, the location is quite magical. *Photography by Adamskii.com*

ntallon. A Douglas fortress, some 5km east of North Berwick facing out over the Firth of
rth, built by the First Earl in the mid fourteenth century, a dominating screen wall enclosing
: headland, traces of civil war works on the landward side, it overlooks another, even more
bidding bastion on the Bass Rock. *Photography by Adamskii.com*

nbar. Once mighty, ancient refuge of the Goddodin, this was a Northumbrian outpost in the
on era, granted to the exiled Earl Gospatric after he fled to Scotland to escape the wrath of
: Conqueror. It became the fortress of the earls of Dunbar and was slighted after the fiasco at
rberry Hill. *Photography by Adamskii.com*

Gunsgreen. A wonderful mid Georgian house, of most pleasing proportions, this impressive mansion was constructed by local entrepreneur John Nisbet in the 1750s. It was intended to showcase his wealth though much of this was derived from questionable sources! He lost possession in 1787 but the house has recently and lovingly been restored by the current trustee. *Photography by Adamskii.com*

Arisaig. It was here, in this most romantic of locations, that Prince Charles Edward landed in 1745 at the outset of his ill-conceived adventure, SOE trained agents here during the Second World War. *Photography by Adamskii.com*

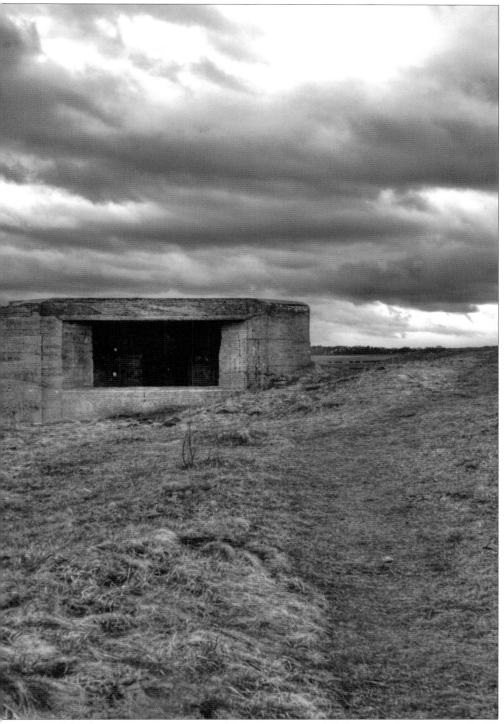

emerston. Of rather more recent vintage, this concrete coastal defence emplacement was built
r 1940 to guard the north-east coast against German invasion, happily it was never tested.
ily accessible, it would benefit from some conservation and interpretation.
tography by Adamskii.com

The monument at Glenfinnan with its wonderful views commemorates the raising of the Jacobite standard in 1745. *Photography by Adamskii.com*

Loch nan Uamh, the scene of the naval duel in 1746 between French frigates and English sloops o'war. *Photography by Adamskii.com*

e White sands of Morar in deepest winter. *Photography by Adamskii.com*

e Road to the Isles through Arisaig to Mallaig is one of the most romantic journeys in these nds. *Photography by Adamskii.com*

Originally a Comyn hold in the fourteenth century this fort featured in the two battles of Inverlochy, it lies by the loch side in the midst of a much decayed industrial area on the northern fringe of Fort William. *Photography by Adamskii.com*

Facsimile seventeenth century Locaber axe and hide covered targe – *Author's collection*

t George. Arguably the most substantial eighteenth century military construction in Britain,
ugh built after the Jacobite threat had been hammered into oblivion at Culloden. This is a
w of the outer face of the main fortifications and ditch below. The barrack piles are impressive
l house a series of first rate regimental collections.

Excellent facsimile of an early eighteenth century highland broadsword with full basket hilt – the flowering of the Scottish sword and hilt-makers art. Courtesy of *Armourclass*

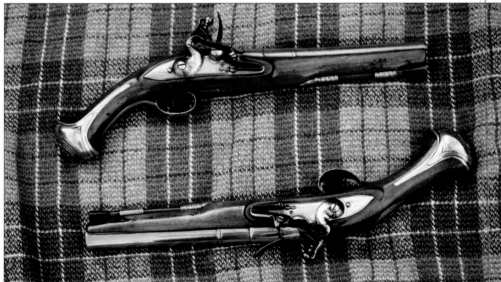

Pair of English made brass-barrelled flintlock officers pistols by Hudson, c.1740, English officers and indeed Jacobites would have carried similar weapons during the '45, it is not impossible th pair were used during the rebellion.

SIX

———◆———

Letters of Reprisal: The Privateers

27 March 1666, Edinburgh

About 14 days since, Captain Hamilton commander of a private man of war, went out and had a sharp fight with several vessels and had seven of his men killed, but yet came off successfully, bringing away with him his prize, a vessel of 200 tons laden with wine and brandy, and two others, one of 300 the other of 400 tons, with ballast, going northward about for Bordeaux.

Another privateer, Captain Murray, has taken four small vessels laden with fish, which he brought safe home.

The London Gazette

THE BOUNTY OF THE SEA could be harvested in a number of ways. Taking vessels and their cargoes as prizes was, while ostensibly reprehensible, a highly lucrative trade. Piracy in Scottish waters, as we have seen, was nothing novel; Provost Davidson, Sir Andrew Wood and the Bartons all grew rich on the trade. There was clear distinction between a pirate, an outlaw who made war on the world, and a privateer who sailed under the authority of a commission or 'letter of marque'. This was not a mere formality, akin to a modern fishing licence, but a detailed indenture, which spelt out in considerable detail the type of vessel the holder was entitled to take up. This had to fall within the stated definition of a 'just prize'. A target craft should, with her cargo, be owned wholly or at least in significant part by the specified enemy and normally a commission would only run for the duration of hostilities. In theory, each skipper received his commission from the king acting in the monarch's role as high admiral. In practice, the issuing body was usually the Privy Council.

THE PROVENANCE OF PRIVATEERING

'Privateer' was not an expression much used until the late sixteenth century. Captains cruised usually under the authority of an earlier commission or licence called the 'Letter of Reprisal'. This was issued by the court when a complainant could show he had been robbed by agents of a foreign power and had tried but failed to achieve redress through the courts. He was thus empowered by the court to seize property to make good his loss, rather akin to the 'Hot Trod' on land. A Letter of Reprisal was thus a specific legal remedy, and its award did not depend upon a state of hostilities being in existence.[1] In Scotland, this form of authority was a heritable asset; it could pass by will in the usual way; in 1561, Captain Patrick Blackadder was taking Portuguese prizes in reliance on a grant made in 1476! It has to be said that the process was open to fairly liberal interpretation, and the lure of prize money might certainly affect a court's findings. That the situation could lead to widespread abuse is recognised by the terms of a proclamation from 1525:

> Our Sovereign Lord [James V] and Lords of Council are sickerly informed that an certain [number] of his lieges, masters, owners and mariners of ships [dwell]ing in Leith is to depart in warfare, and by their robberies and spoils made upon friends, they have caused our Sovereign Lord and his lieges to have many enemies whilks were friends before, and presupposes that they shall do siclike in time to come . . .

Not only were the enemy's ships always fair game in time of war, neutrals carrying cargoes that contributed to his war effort were also legitimate targets. Once taken, the prize could be sailed back to a Scottish port or allowed to continue but subject to the payment of a ransom, secured by the taking of hostages. Before the privateer could realise gains by selling vessel and cargo, his right had to be validated and the prize 'condemned' by the court. In Scotland, this meant the Admiralty Court (Scottish High Court of Admiralty[2]), which sat in the Tolbooth either in Leith or Edinburgh. So brisk was the trade in prizes during the later Dutch wars that daily sessions were merited. Proceedings required the privateer to present his commission and to declare the prize. He then had to satisfy the evidential burden that his prize was a legitimate one, and, finally, the master of the enemy ship was allowed a hearing. This process initially involved a series of separate sittings though, latterly, the whole matter was dealt with in a single session.

A separate hearing might be required in order to deal with the often more contentious question of the prize's cargo. If this comprised war supplies, the matter might be quickly disposed of. If, however, as was often the case, it had to be proven that the cargo comprised materials that *could* facilitate the enemy's war effort, this was more difficult and thus likely to be protracted. In 1626, Watson of the *Blessing* took three merchantmen out of Hamburg (at that time under Spanish control) and argued in the court that the ships' cargoes of canvas, tar, wax, cloth, some muskets and a quantity of provisions were all war materials. As the haul included innocuous items such as 24 bags of cumin seed, there could legitimately have been some doubt. Nonetheless, Watson won his case!

He was one of the more successful captains in the war of 1626–1629; after netting the Hamburg ships, he took a further couple of prizes the following year and three in 1628. David Robertson of Dysart in *Grace of God* and, latterly, *Joans* was active, as were James Binning and David Alexander. These were the early days during which the privateering 'industry' was in its relative infancy. Specially constructed men-of-war were scarce, as were captains with the resources to put them to sea. Men like Watson were, most probably, established merchant skippers who 'diversified' into privateering as opportunities arose. Some captains hired out their vessels for troop transports. Robert Langlands of North Leith, master of *Blessing*, was hired to transport soldiers to Elsinore, though she was lost on the voyage, with only the guns being salvaged.

Charles I, in pursuance of his war aims, sought to resurrect a Scots Navy and, responding to royal command the Privy Council, in the summer of 1626, took on *Lion, Unicorn* and *Thistle*. Ready ships and crews were in short supply. *Unicorn* was found at Leith, but the other two had to be purchased in England. Cash, as ever, was hard to find. Even with ships available, suitable sailors were still wanting. Most who might be tempted found the greater lure of privateering more attractive. Recourse had to be had to a levy, and the squadron was not ready for sea until November. Archibald Douglas of *Lion* (300 tonnes) was appointed as Admiral. Murray of *Unicorn* (300 tonnes also) as Vice Admiral, while Auchmoutie of the diminutive *Thistle* (perhaps 50 tonnes) still qualified as Rear Admiral.

This squadron finally sailed from the Thames, but did not raise the Forth till early January 1627. Once in Scottish waters, the flotilla came under the orders of the Earl Marischal, except that he gave no orders and the winter months were spent in a blur of inactivity. This notwithstanding, merely keeping the ships ready, with the crews waged and victualled was an expensive business. Pay alone gobbled up some £1,100 per month. In the spring a use was found for the ships, which were to be converted as troop transports. Now, arrears of pay were substantial and crews much thinned by desertion, getting the exercise underway consumed time and more treasure. By the time they returned from their mission, it seemed likely all three would simply be sold off, but alarums and the threat of enemy action prompted a cruise along the North Sea coast and the ships were not, in fact, disposed off until the following year.

As the Scots Navy perennially comprised very few vessels, one who held a letter of reprisal or, subsequently of marque, was entitled to style himself as captain. Merchant skippers were not called captain until the following century. The heyday of privateering in Scotland was really the second half of the seventeenth century, the period of the Dutch wars (1652–1654, 1665–1667 and 1672–1674)[3], though Scottish captains had not been idle during the earlier wars with Spain, France and England (both Crown and Parliament). During the period of the Dutch wars, when the available English strength was fully committed, as many as 90 Scottish privateers were active, mainly out of Leith and the ports of Fife, with the North Sea as their principal stalking ground. As the Channel was likely too hot or too well guarded, Dutch merchantmen and fishing vessels preferred the wider sweep of the North Sea, and Scottish predators grew fat on the pickings.

Privateers were free of the obligations of naval officers in that they were concerned entirely with economic warfare, they did not cruise simply to pick a fight with an opposing vessel or squadron, sailing for profit, patriotic dividend purely incidental. These were wolves and merchantmen the sheep they preyed upon. James VI of Scotland, when he became also James I of England had, as part of his inheritance, acquired a world class navy. The race-built English galleon had emerged as the leading design of the sixteenth century, the Spanish had lost out by clinging to the grand carrack and the Dutch were just entering the race. Of the 42 vessels James now possessed, nearly two-thirds comprised capital ships but, once peace was concluded with Spain in the year following his accession, the fleet had scant opportunities for deployment.

INNOVATIONS IN DESIGN

There were, however, innovations in design with a swing back, in part, toward the earlier carrack of the towering superstructures. Hulls became larger and, while the length of the new vessels resembled that of the race-built galleon, the greater bulk would carry more above. True sons of the Elizabethan age, such as Sir Walter Raleigh, deprecated the trend, opining it arose from a desire for greater comfort aboard. To the old sea dog, this reeked of decadence! James VI took a keen interest in the construction of his great capital ship *Prince Royal* designed by the rather dubious naval architect, Phineas Pett. She was first of the great three-deckers and carried 55 guns when she first entered the water in 1610, a formidable instrument of war at sea. For nearly three decades, she had no peer until, in 1637, Pett designed an even mightier ship for Charles I, *Sovereign of the Seas*. Ships did play their part in the great Civil Wars and inflicted a serious reverse upon the Dutch during the first clash, and *Sovereign*, with some modifications, was still doing good service as late as the 1670s.[4]

Charles I, having embarked upon an attempt to rule without the sanction of Parliament, remained wedded to the notion of restoring England's naval power to the equivalent of the great days of the

Elizabethan sea dogs, though he continued to be hamstrung by a desperate cash shortage. One remedy, finally adopted in 1634, was the levying of Ship-Money, a form of naval taxation that further exacerbated the king's difficulties with his increasingly restless subjects. While the major engagements of the Bishops Wars and the the Great Civil Wars took place on land, sea power remained vital. Parliament in England retained control of the navy, and there was the constant fear of an invasion from Ireland, disgorging thousands of savage and Popish Irish into England. In Scotland, the Estates entered into terms with Parliament in England whereby, in January 1644, a Scottish army crossed the border and joined the fight, an intervention which led, in that year, to the decisive battle upon Marston Moor which saw the Royalist hegemony in the North of England destroyed.

Montrose's battles during 'The Year of Miracles' were fought out on land, and sea power did not play a significant role, though the wily Argyll cannily stayed aboard his galley in Loch Linnhe while his clansmen were decimated by the vengeful blades of Clan Donald in the fight at Inverlochy. English naval power aided Cromwell when he subsequently campaigned against the Scots, alienated by the regicide, but his great victories, Dunbar, and then Worcester, were won on land.

Large capital ships, such as the *Sovereign*, were clearly beyond the purse of a privateer captain, however successful, but, even as Pett was designing his great flagships, there was a perceived need for lighter, handier craft, intended to take on the Dunkirk privateers who were, themselves, most active during the French War of 1627–1629.[5] Ten 14-gun vessels, built to a standard pattern and called Whelps – the first to the tenth – were floated. 'Whelp' did not endure as the brand of a particular class; a European term 'frigate' came into use. It was this type of vessel that the Scottish privateers adopted, also referred to as capers; some were purpose built and others converted to purpose. The ship had to be a good sailor, of a size to accommodate a respectable weight of ordnance, anywhere from 6 to 30 guns of varying calibres – standardisation was still not fully established – but mainly demi-culverins or sakers. The frigate would be somewhere between 100 and 250 tons in the water, fast in the chase and equally handy if she had to outrun an enemy man-of-war. Crews needed to be large: sufficient sailors to man the guns in an action and to provide prize crews for captured vessels. All of which, for the owners, represented a significant capital outlay. The captain would not usually lack for volunteers: the work carried risk and discipline had to be enforced to naval standards, but the lure of prize-money was always a powerful incentive.

It is fair to assert that naval service in Scotland never quite acquired the same social cachet as it did in England, yet during the sixteenth century Scottish mariners, and privateers, were highly regarded, and rightly so, on account of their able seamanship. The connection with the French ports of Dieppe and Le Havre implied Scots mariners were well placed to benefit from the innovations directed by a Huguenot school of navigators based there. By 1547, often in partnership with the French, Scottish captains were already scenting the rich harvest to be gathered from the gold-rich Spanish colonies of the New World. Two decades later, the port of Burburata was taken up by a Franco-Scottish expedition. As mentioned, James Lindsay had, in 1540 acted as pilot to James V and guided the king's squadron through the waters of the Pentland Firth to the Western Isles where James was engaged in 'putting some stick about'. Lindsay compiled a navigational aid or pilot book, his famous 'Rutter'.

REWARDS OF PRIVATEERING

Susan Mowat, from whose detailed work on the subject much of what is written here has been drawn, has recorded the worth of numerous prizes. *Green Lyon*, a 300-ton Danziger, which a trio of Scots captured in 1628, was sold for nearly £13,000 Scots, exclusive of her cargo of masts and cordage. Prize money was apportioned 1/15th to the crown, a tenth of the residue to the Lord High Admiral, the remainder split into thirds, one each for the owner, the victuallers and the crew. The latter was then distributed on a sliding scale from the nine shares awarded to the captain to the single share given to the ship's boys! A successful cruise brought considerable reward: Captain Scott of *Blessing* out of Burntisland scooped four vessels in cruises during 1626, netting a cash gain of £372 Scots, plus a salary bonus of £80. One of his crew would earn something just under £42, the equal of over two years' pay. The ship's surgeon also netted some £400 in total. Small wonder privateering was proving such a popular occupation!

TRAINING

Even piracy had its recognised training manuals, and, in 1627, Captain John Smith published his *Sea Grammar*, which included some handy tips for aspiring captains on how to instigate and control a fight at sea: Once the prize is sighted, the hunter must judge how she sails, put on his own canvas for the chase, but shorten sail once contact becomes imminent to avoid damage during an exchange. Once the strange vessel is in hailing distance, she is challenged and a warning shot fired if she proves recalcitrant. Close directions are given for the seamanship and gunnery required to continue an action, the handling of the guns in tandem with use of the sails to achieve and maintain the advantage to deliver your broadsides while, hopefully, minimising the likely damage when the quarry responds:

> He pays us shot for shot. 'Well, we shall require him. What, are you ready again?' Yea, yea, edge in with him again. Begin with your bow-pieces, proceed with your broadside and let her fall off with the wind to give her also your full chase, your weather broadside, and bring her round that stern may also discharge and your tacks close board again.

The instructions continue as to how to patch holes punched by round shot, when to close and board, how to deal with the ultimate peril of fire on board. Lastly, the wounded are left to the tender care of the surgeon and his mates, while the dead are dispatched without undue ceremony: '. . . wind up the slain, with each a weight or bullet at their heads and feet to make them sink, and give them three guns for their funerals'.

If the chase continues, the breathing space, once the casualties are accounted for, is put to good use. Carpenters plug holes, gunners scourge their pieces, men snatch rest and victuals, then make ready for the next round. Smith sets out some high standards of gentlemanly behaviour when dealing with a captured prize and its crew, standards that might frequently have been more honoured in the breach than the observance!

WAR AGAINST THE DUTCH

The consequence for Scotland of her involvement in the Civil Wars was a decade of Cromwellian occupation, a yoke that was not lifted until the Restoration of Charles II in 1660. Scottish privateers were by no means out of business, merely resting; the outbreak of the Second Dutch War in March 1665 was to herald the dawn of a veritable golden age of plunder. Preparations had been underway in the preceding autumn, as tensions mounted and some 500 Scots had been conscripted for naval service, many of whom lost their lives when *London* blew up off Gravesend. From the outset, Dutch raiders were active in the North Sea and severely restricted free movement of merchantmen. A garrison was established on Shetland to maintain watch upon the Sound of Bressay, now assuming a greater strategic value with the Royal Navy in command of the Channel routes. As hostilities deepened, the Scottish privateers, abetted by a 'flexible' approach from the Admiralty courts, enjoyed a bonanza. Leith was crowded with prizes. Fat-bellied Dutch 'flyboats',[6] 'hukers' and merchantmen, the former hunted in the sea lanes off Norway where they loaded with timber.

One of the rising 'stars' of the privateering industry was William Hamilton of Dundee, master of the 22-gun *Rothes*. He scooped no fewer than 22 prizes, the most valuable of which, *Charity*, laden with furs, netted some £4,000 Scots, a very appreciable sum. Ironically, the outbreak of plague which affected London in the closing months of 1665 and closed the port, linked to a similar pestilence spreading through Flanders, sharpened the hunger of Scottish owners and masters. Hamilton began his first cruise in March 1666 and enjoyed an immediate run of successes. His second cruise began in June when he netted ten further prizes, including the recapture of a Scottish frigate *Morton* of Wemyss, which the enemy had taken previously. By late June or early July, *Rothes* was cruising as part of a squadron of four Scottish sail and became involved in a sharp action against a superior Dutch flotilla, four of which were captured and the rest seen off with loss. Hamilton was reported killed but, in fact, survived. Much aggrieved by the Scots' depredations, the Dutch sent three men-of-war to blockade the Forth. Hamilton was joined by John Brown of Leith and John Aitchison of Pittenweem, when he sailed out to mount a challenge. A further brisk action now ensued and, though the Scottish privateers gave a good account of themselves, the Dutch proved too strong to defeat.

This was but a beginning. The Dutch were badly stung by the boldness of the privateers and their trade was much affected. Accordingly, on 29/30 April 1667 they mounted a raid in force against the Forth. Some 30-odd sail entered Leith Road on the evening of the 30th; three English men-of-war were within two miles but remained inactive, '. . . the captains being pitifully drunk . . .' Burntisland was bombarded, but the forts returned a brisk fire and the attackers could gain no advantage. Locals flew to arms and Dalziell's regiment came up. The magistrates at Leith sank one of Hamilton's prizes as a block-ship and mounted guns around, sufficient to foil the enemy's attempt to send in a fireship. The attackers achieved nothing and, by the start of May, Hamilton was active again, cutting out a 30-gun man-of-war. *Rothes* was by no means the only active privateer. Gideon Murray, who captained the 16-gun *Thistle* of Leith, garnered 17 prizes; John Brown, also of Leith with *Lamb* (16 guns), scored up to ten. Others who notched up notable captures were James Bennet (*Barbara*), William Gedd (*Good Fortune*), James Alexander (*Lesley*), George Cheyne and Andrew Smeaton.

No sooner had the Dutch departed than a fresh alarum occurred, on 29 May, when the sound of naval gunfire spread alarm and the citizens of Leith again rushed to arms, a fresh block-ship was sunk and the guns manned. Happily, this was an entirely false panic. The newcomers were an English squadron under Sir Jeremy Smith, discharging their ordnance to keep station in fog. Smith's ships had already encountered an enemy convoy and taken 14 prizes and continued to ratchet their score most impressively. The boom in warship construction brought an additional benefit, creating a market for timber. The ubiquitous Pett purchased pine from Northern Scotland, and an enterprising Edinburgh businessman, Patrick Lyell, set up as a broker for timber and cordage taken as prize cargo. When the Treaty of Breda, sealed on 21 July 1667,[7] brought hostilities to a close, the bonanza was ended, but Scottish privateers were bringing in prizes until virtually the moment of signing. Captain Archer of the 6-gun *Joseph* from Newcastle upon Tyne, cruising under a Scottish commission, brought in a brace of hefty prizes, and Captain Wood from Berwick netted eight!

Peace proved but an interlude. Rivalry between England and the United Provinces was too compelling. By April 1672, drums were again sounding, and the king had need of Scottish mariners once more. The Duke of Lennox, in his capacity as Admiral of Scotland, was empowered to issue letters of marque. There was no shortage of takers and, within a week, a score of capers were being fitted out. So popular was the notion of privateering that many seamen from Newcastle were hurrying north to seek commissions out of Scotland. A fascinating record survives, detailing the acquisition and fitting out of *Lyon*, from Dundee, captained by Thomas Lyell and with the Earl of Kinghorn as principal shareholder. She was bought at Leith for some £2,700. Five of her great guns were then purchased for an additional consideration of £496, and the owners incurred the extra expense of fitting out, new canvas and studding sails, tackle and cordage, a new ship's boat and repairs to the pump. A crew had to be hired and victuals sourced: beef, pork, biscuit, dried fish, ale and salt. The captain enjoyed some additional supplies of liquor and tobacco. The master gunner, his needs more practical, needed powder and shot, paper for cartridges, sponges, a new copper ladle. Swivel guns were also purchased and a quantity of small arms. Total costs exceeded £6,000 Scots – a substantial outlay – and *Lyon* did not set off on her first cruise until 10 June.

As an investment, she soon proved her worth, returning with two handsome prizes, the cause for some celebration, even though the tortuous and costly business of the court proceedings lay ahead. War was the harbinger of a ripe harvest for the Admiralty court, and Susan Mowat calculates the returns during 1672 to have been handsome indeed, with the Judge Admiral picking up some £12,000

Scots, a very acceptable dividend for one who had ventured neither neck nor purse! For the *Lyon*'s owners her second cruise, which began on 11 September proved substantially less rewarding. She'd suffered some minor damage on her initial voyage, but was now riven by storm and driven aground off the coast of Scandinavia. Her salvage and repair were protracted, and she finally limped ingloriously home with nothing to show for her cruise other than significant costs. She was sold in the course of the following summer at a considerable loss. Privateering was, in every sense, a high risk venture.

Another investor in this high stakes game was Lennox himself. The Lord Admiral owned his own frigate, *Speedwell*, and his captain was the experienced Richard Borthwick, one who'd learnt his trade in the earlier conflict. We are fortunate in that a quantity of her lieutenant, Charles Whittington's, correspondence survives. *Speedwell* sailed from Harwich on 27 April, cruising with another frigate, *Portland*. The Duke of Lennox was aboard the other vessel, but the ships soon parted and *Speedwell* gave chase to a flotilla of flyboats. As Whittington records:

> We parted from them at the east end of the Dogger [Bank], chasing a dogger in the night, and next morning saw tow large flyboats, which we lost in a fog. Next day we saw ten flyboats from St Tuball which we gave chase to Thursday, Friday and Saturday, and took six . . .

This was a most encouraging beginning; while sailing from Leith in June the frigate scooped two more prizes. In late summer, she was active off the Dutch coast, taking a shoal of small craft and driving others ashore. This was after she'd caused some annoyance in Newcastle, where her press-gang had been active! Though she beat up the Dutch coast, causing much alarm and triggering the militia's impotent rage, worsening weather and the presence of several Dutch men-of-war denied her any worthwhile captures. *Speedwell* set out on a fresh cruise in the autumn, suffering badly in foul weather, as Whittington's letters reflect. While she was beating the harsh waters of the North Sea, she had lost her owner. Lennox had fallen overboard and drowned. *Speedwell*'s time as a Scottish privateer was at an end. The Duke's death caused something of a hiatus as the commissions he'd issued now lapsed and had to be temporarily validated by the Lord Chancellor. In March 1673, the king's brother, James, Duke of York, the future James II, was appointed High Admiral, though this did not immediately clear the backlog. Halcyon days were coming to an end. Many prizes were taken, but the accommodating ease of Scots law had been tightened to reflect the closer scrutiny of English practice. More and more cases were 'assoiled' – the captains failed to establish their case and captured vessels were not ajudged lawful prizes.

If the privateers, in the late seventeenth century, were enjoying something of a trade boom, the rest of the country was not. Times were hard; Scotland remained a small nation on the fringes of Europe. Restoration and the threat to religious independence had prompted a reaction from the more extremist members of the Kirk. Firstly, the abortive Pentland Rising of 1666,[8] then the series of disturbances and repression centred on the south-west and known as 'the Killing Time'.[9] After the further political upheavals of the 'Glorious Revolution', with a smaller economy and limited exports, disadvantages exacerbated by a string of poor harvests in the 1690s, a climate of recession and uncertainty prevailed in Scotland. Even the privateers found war with France after 1689 not much to their liking. Some prizes were to be had off the west coast, but the glory days were gone. One of the proposed solutions was that advocated by William Paterson, founder of the Bank of England: the creation of a trading colony on the Isthmus of Panama.

NEW CALEDONIA: THE DARIEN DISASTER
Previous attempts at establishing Scottish colonies had been muted. A venture in South Carolina was begun but as soon abandoned. The reasoning behind Paterson's plan for Darien was that the colony could become a major trading base linking to the Pacific and Far East. A trading corporation, the Company of Scotland, already existed and sought to raise, through subscription, sufficient monies to translate the dream into commercial reality. While domestic investors flocked to buy shares, contributing some £400,000 Scots, a vast sum, equal to almost 30 per cent of the nation's capital, pressure from the administration persuaded English shareholders

to withdraw. William III was aware Darien nominally fell within the Spanish sphere of influence and, being at war with France, he had no need to recklessly antagonise Spain. On 14 July 1698, the first Darien expedition – 1,200 souls crammed aboard *St Andrew, Caledonia, Unicorn, Dolphin* and *Endeavour* – set sail from Leith. By 2 November, by way of Madeira and the West Indies, the flotilla weighed anchor off 'New Caledonia'.

Despite the industry with which the settlers began their enterprise, it was doomed. The climate was hostile, fevers and tropical diseases endemic. Local natives, while by no means hostile, were unenthusiastic. The Williamite government, rigidly opposed, denied vital succour, and the colonists succumbed in droves. It was grand tragedy: all of the investment, the considerable industry, the aspirations and ideals were utterly wasted and, by midsummer 1699, evacuation the only remedy. Barely a quarter of the original settlers survived; one desperate party was turned away from Port Royal. Unwilling to concede that the scheme was fatally flawed, the tragedy was compounded by a further attempt, which led to yet greater losses of life and treasure. Darien was a disaster for the nation, its people and its economy.[10]

It was easy to blame the English. Had William not deterred investors, had the government not wilfully obstructed succour, it was argued the position could have been saved, but the plain fact was it was simply a bad plan: the wrong idea, in the wrong place at the wrong time. The crippling damage inflicted by the disaster on an already failing economy contributed to the level of acquiescence which obtained once the possibility of parliamentary union arose. The fact that the government undertook to make good these catastrophic losses of Scottish investors undoubtedly fuelled enthusiasm for union. When the draft terms were first made public, in October 1706, they were still greeted with horror in Tory and Jacobite circles but, on 16 January 1707, the Act of Union passed through the Scots Parliament, which thus voted itself out of existence. On 21 May, the Kingdom of Great Britain came formally into being. As was rightly observed at the time:

Now, there's an end to ane old song.

THE 'GOLDEN AGE OF PIRACY'

One of Orkney's more notorious sons was the pirate John Gow.[11] Probably born in 1698 in Wick, Gow moved with his family to Stromness as an infant and thus grew to manhood in Orkney. He may have gone to sea at a fairly early age but in the summer of 1724 he was in Amsterdam, where he became second mate on the *Caroline*, a trading vessel bound for Santa Cruz, where she was to take on a cargo of leather, wool and beeswax for Genoa. Discipline was poor on board, there was much grumbling over rations and conditions. Captain Ferneau kept his pistols loaded. On 3 November 1724, Gow led a well-organised mutiny. The first mate was silenced in his cabin. The surgeon, badly wounded, managed to make it as far as the deck, where Ferneau defended himself manfully until a ball from Gow ended his career. The latter's new career as a pirate had just begun.

John Gow swiftly made his mark as a ruthless buccaneer,[12] making war on the world from the quarterdeck of the renamed vessel, now sailing as *Revenge*. By the turn of the year, Gow and his cutthroats had returned to Orkney, where they planned to lay low. Their ship was renamed once again as the *George*, and Gow, somewhat unimaginatively, took the name 'Smith'. This deception didn't last long. Another skipper recognised the vessel, and a spate of desertions followed. One of the buccaneers, Robert Reid, gave himself up at Kirkwall, doubtless hoping for clemency after denouncing Gow and his other accomplices. On 10 February, Gow raided the home of Robert Honeyman of Graemsay, the Hall of Clestrain, stripping the place of valuables. He may have kidnapped two serving girls, but his next raid proved disastrous. Aiming to pillage the property of James Fea in Eday, he ran *Revenge* hopelessly aground and was eventually obliged to strike his colours.

Transferred to England, Gow at first refused to plead, but once the penalty for such recalcitrance was pointed out – a slow death, being pressed under great weights and left either to starve or asphyxiate – he opted for a not guilty plea. Inevitably he and his confederates were speedily convicted and sentenced to die by hanging at Execution Dock on 11 June. It was not uncommon for the hangman, for a consideration, to administer a sharp jerk to the victim's flailing legs, thus snapping his neck and offering a release from further suffering. Gow's man botched the job and the rope snapped. The condemned pirate was forced to mount the scaffold a second time and swing from the gallows as the life was choked out of him.

Piracy is most commonly associated with more glamorous or certainly warmer waters, such as the Caribbean or off the Carolinas. Certainly one of the more celebrated exponents of buccaneering, William Kidd, was of Scottish birth. Kidd, born in 1645, was the son of a minister and began his career at sea hunting other pirates. Despite marrying and having two daughters, Kidd returned to sea and, at some point, made the transition from gamekeeper to poacher. His career as a pirate was neither particularly fruitful, nor glorious, and he was subsequently tried for the murder of William Moore, whom he'd killed in a heated dispute over leadership and the captaincy of his vessel *Adventure Galley*. Convicted of the crime, Kidd ended his career dancing at a rope's end at New York on 23 May 1701.[13]

Numerous Scots, like Kidd and Gow, became embroiled in the Golden Age of Piracy. James Browne was hanged by Lord Vaughan, Governor of Port Royal in Jamaica, in 1676. John Alexander sailed with the notorious Bartholomew Sharp but died ingloriously when a longboat, loaded with spoil, capsized. A quartet of Scottish buccaneers was hanged at Charlestown on 8 November 1718: George Dunkin and George Ross, both Glaswegians, with William Eddy and Neal Patterson from Aberdeen. John Hincher, physician and graduate of Edinburgh, was press-ganged into service beneath the Jolly Roger when the vessel on which he was sailing was taken. Another surgeon, James Ferguson, drowned when the pirate ship he had willingly joined sank off Cape Cod in 1717.

One of the most colourful and successful Scottish pirates was the corsair Peter Lisle. He was captured in 1796 by the notorious Muslim galleys from Tripoli on board an American schooner *Betsy*. Lisle found conversion to Islam an easy choice and swiftly rose to distinction in the Bashaw's squadron. Now in command of the *Betsy*, re-named, up-gunned to 28 pieces of ordnance and with a crew of over 300, Murad Reis as he now styled himself carved out a formidable reputation; taking the 44-gun US frigate *Philadelphia* after she'd grounded on a sand bar. Soon he had married the Bashaw's daughter and reached the rank of Grand Admiral of Tripoli. Of a violent and quarrelsome disposition, even the Bashaw felt constrained to send his son-in-law into, albeit temporary, exile following a savage attack on the US Consul in 1816. Sixteen years later, his remarkable career came to a fittingly violent end when he was fatally struck down by round shot in the course of internal strife.

———◆———

EIGHT

Ships of the White Cockade

And it is further enacted. That from and after the 1st August 1747 no man or boy within Scotland, other than such as shall be employed as officers and soldiers in the King's forces, shall on any pretence whatsoever, wear or put on the cloaths commonly called highland cloaths, that is to say, the plaid, philabeg or little kilt, trowse, shoulder-belts, or any part whatsoever of what peculiarly belongs to the highland garb; and that no tartan or party-coloured plaids or stuff shall be used for great-coats, or for upper coats; and if any such persons shall, after said 1st August, wear or put on the aforesaid garments, or any part of them, every such person so offending, being convicted thereof by the mouth of one or more witnesses, before any court of judiciary, or any one or more Justices of the Peace for the shire or stewartry, or judge ordinary of the place where such offence shall be committed, shall suffer imprisonment, without bail, during six months and no longer; and being convicted of a second offence, before the court of judiciary or the circuits, shall be liable to be transported to any of his Majesty's plantations beyond the sea, for seven years.'

The Act of Prescription, 1745

'JACOBITE', DERIVING FROM THE LATIN *Jacobus* (James), was the name given to the supporters of the exiled James II after the 'Glorious Revolution' of 1688. When Queen Anne, last of James II's daughters died, the Stewart dynasty was replaced by dour Hanoverians who were, if little else, at least Protestant.

Though the series of land battles which occurred in the course of the abortive risings of 1715, 1719 and 1745–1746[1] have come to define popular understanding of the doomed crusade that was the Jacobite cause, naval power and events at sea are equally important. It was never expected that a rebellion in Scotland, relying to a very large extent upon the broadswords of the Tory clans,[2] could unseat a Whig dominated Hanoverian government in London. It was rather intended that raising the standard north of the border would trigger a series of uprisings south of it and that the whole would be supported by the French landing quantities of arms and men. Though support from Versailles remained often as fickle as the weather cock and was at all times subject to the expediencies of the greater game in Europe, serious attempts at major French intervention did occur. These, inevitably, were opposed by the British Royal Navy.

THE FRIGATES

By the end of the War of the Spanish Succession in 1713, the Royal Navy had established its place as the world's most powerful fleet, having, in 1714, some 131 'ships of the line' in service. This description came into being as a consequence of evolving naval tactics, whereby the opposing fleets manoeuvred in line against each other. By mid century, the British fleet had a total of 339 vessels under sail, though most of the recent additions were of smaller 'rates'. The Georgian Navy was its country's largest employer and its largest undertaking. The vast dockyards of Deptford, Woolwich, Chatham, Portsmouth and Plymouth were teeming with armies of shipwrights, artisans and labourers. By the time of the Forty-Five, the 'rates' were defined as follows:

- First-rate: a three-decker with a poop-royal, 100 guns, 178 feet on the gun deck and an individual figurehead
- Second-rate: a three-decker with 90 guns, 170 feet on the gun deck, individual figurehead
- Third-rate of 80 guns: three-decker, 165 feet on the gun deck, lion figurehead (in common with all the lesser rates below
- Third-rate of 70 guns: two-decker, 160 feet on the gun deck
- Third-rate of 60 guns: two-decker, 150 feet on the gun deck
- Fourth-rate: two-decker with 50 guns, 144 feet on the gun deck
- Fifth-rate: two-decker with 40 guns, 133 feet on the gun deck
- Sixth-rate: two-decker with 24 guns with most of the ordnance on the upper deck and oars on the gun deck; 113 feet in length.

Blockade work and patrolling the sea lochs and islands of the west coast was not work for ships of the line. Fourth-rates with 50 guns were being phased out, no longer able to take their place in the line and were mostly gone by 1760. Fifth-rates, the forties, forty-fours and large frigates (frigate being now a ship of two decks which carried between 20 and 50 guns on the upper deck, quarterdeck and fo'c'sle) began to encounter heavy French frigates during the 'War of Jenkins' Ear' (1739), and the weakness of this smallest class of two-deckers became apparent. It was difficult, if not impossible to work the lower gun decks in heavy seas and they made heavy sailers when contrasted with similar ships that had all of their main armament on the one deck. French vessels were of superior design. *Embuscade*, taken by the RN in 1746, mounted 28 12-pounders on her top deck, ten 6-pounders on the quarterdeck and two in the fo'c'sle. As she had no gun ports on the lower deck, this could ride on or below the waterline, while the upper deck had a freeboard of around 8 feet. Despite the weight of the great guns she sailed well, having a length of 132 feet 6 inches and being 36 feet in the beam.[3]

SLOOPS-OF-WAR

For the demanding task of patrolling long sea lochs and the myriad islands of the west, sloops were an ideal choice. Such vessels encompassed all that mounted a score of guns or fewer, the larger being ship-rigged and frigate-built. Those constructed in the opening years of the eighteenth century were of a type with stepped deck in ships and brig-rigged. Later craft carried their ordnance on an open deck with platforms for stowage in the hold. Some of these gun-vessels were of a similar length to a small frigate, nearly 120 feet in length, and latterly might have 'carronades' – on-board howitzers invented in 1752 by the Scots firm Carron (see following chapter) – to augment their firepower.

Day to day the work of the sloop or gun-vessel was undramatic and unglamorous, the routine of patrolling and landing. Some masters, like the notorious Captain Fergusson, behaved like privateers, treating Islesmen and their women as cattle. Rarely was the tedium enlivened by action. Battles such as that which took place in Loch nan Uamh were very rare. This does not, however, diminish the importance of vigilant sea power during the Jacobite Wars. All French or Spanish aid, be this men and/or materiel, had to come by sea. Any bridgehead the Tory clans might purchase for an invader would have to be backed up by amphibious operation. In 1745–1746 an early naval encounter, that between HMS *Lyon* and *L'Elisabeth*, was to severely damage Prince Charles Edward's ability to raise his standard. Throughout the period of his rebellion, the ships of the Royal Navy maintained an effective blockade. Naval action denied him men, money and equipment.

Early Jacobite Attempts

In 1708, the French sponsored a serious intervention on behalf of 'James III', son of deposed James II, known as the 'Chevalier St George' or, by his enemies, 'The Old Pretender'. This coincided with the ebb of French fortunes in the War of Spanish Succession, having been battered by Marlborough's repeated and bloodily successful assaults. French Admiral Forbin was appointed to lead an invasion fleet with 5,000 troops crammed into transports. Despite an active British naval presence maintained by Byng, James urged the Frenchman to hazard the blockade, and the flotilla slipped out of Dunkirk unchallenged under the cover of a providential fog. A landing of sorts was made along the Firth of Forth, but Forbin's fears of an RN presence struck deep. The expedition slunk back across the Channel without firing a shot.

Seven years later, the Fifteen proceeded without direct French intervention; John Erskine, Earl of Mar, dubbed 'Bobbing John' by his innumerable opponents raised the 'Restoration' standard on 6 September. On 13 November, his forces, the strongest the Jacobites were to field, clashed with Argyll's inferior numbers at Sheriffmuir. The battle proved both confused and indecisive, but Mar could ill afford a draw and a subsidiary rising of Northumbrian Jacobites ended in ignominy at Preston. His rising, which had swelled mighty dangerous at the outset, again faded into failure. Four years later, James's supporters were ready for another try. It was anticipated that the Duke of Ormonde would lead a descent upon the south-west of England, while George Keith, tenth Earl Marischal, would command a Highland diversion. The affair was sponsored not by the French but by Spain, smarting from the hurt of Byng's victory off Cape Passaro. Ormonde's volunteers were to be conveyed in an impressive armada, which did set sail from Cadiz but was shattered and dispersed by storms before even reaching Corunna, where the duke and his battalions awaited.

Keith's far less impressive squadron, which transported scarcely more than 300 Spanish foot, did make landfall at Eilean Donan Castle, by the mouth of Loch Duich, on 2 April 1719. It was not an auspicious beginning, marred by uncertainties and the bickering of Jacobite officers. Though the Royal Navy had failed to intercept the landing, the garrison of Eilean Donan was compelled under threat of naval bombardment to surrender, and these together with the Jacobites' supplies fell into government hands. As a stark warning, ships then pounded the ancient tower into rubble. On land, matters were scarcely more promising. An extended and untidy skirmish was fought at Glenshiel on 10 June.[4] In consequence, this brief flickering of the Stewart flame was again soon extinguished. After this it would have seemed to most that the Jacobite cause was now relegated to a historical footnote, but its final, dramatic and quixotic flourish was yet to occur. As before, it was the shifting chiaroscuro of European alliances and conflicts that was to provide a final opportunity:

We are, in this instant, alarmed with the old ministerial cry of France and the Pretender; of armies and transports, incog. At Dunkirk; of invincible armadas from Brest . . . either true or false. If true; how will our all sufficient statesman excuse himself from having treated France as a contemptible power, from which so little was to be feared, that we had nothing to do, but to draw the sword, and carve out his dominions into what shreds and fritters we pleased? Where was the intelligence which ought to be the fruit of all those mighty sums, which are said to be annually expended in secret service? How can he keep himself in countenance for having embroiled us in his rash and ridiculous measures abroad and thereby draw upon us this shocking insult at home? That the French were able to put a formidable squadron of ships to sea is now self-evident; that till the very instant, almost of their sailing, we were ignorant alike of their strength and their preparations, seems to be highly probable . . . the affair of Dettingen might have convinced us that she would not stand upon ceremonies when revenge was in her power.

Old England (the opposition London newspaper)

This extract from the anti-Whig paper *Old England* reflects a reaction to the crisis of 1744, calling for the recall of British troops from Flanders. Jacobite bogeymen, as the foil of France, continued to exert considerable influence. The last, desperately flawed champion of the cause was poised in the wings, ready to make his dramatic entrance. Charles Edward Louis John Casimir Silvester Severino Maria Stuart had been born, amidst rejoicing, in Rome on 31 December 1720 and grew to young manhood in those arid, despairing years of exile. His mother, Clementina Sobieski, was descended from the great Jan Sobieski whose magnificent Polish Winged Hussars had driven off the Turkish besiegers of Vienna in 1683. It was said that, on the night of his birth, a new bright star appeared in the firmament, and certainly the guns of Fort St Angelo roared a celebratory cannonade.

His mother died young, at only 33, and was buried in St Peter's, where her tomb became something of a shrine. The prince had been brought up in the sure conviction he was, after his father, the rightful king of both England and Scotland but the empty years gave little hint of any prospect of restoration. The defeat at Dettingen in 1743 humiliated Louis XV to the degree he was prepared to dust off the faded relic of Jacobitism and reconsider its worth as a medium of revenge. His minister, Fleury, habitually a paragon of caution, had died and reports from French spies appeared to be encouraging. By November, the king was writing to both James and Philip V of Spain advising of his renewed support. In this he appeared most earnest.

THE FORTY-FOUR

The expedition was to be commanded by no lesser general than Marshall de Saxe, who would lead just over 10,000 bayonets. This invasion force would target the south coast (Maldon was the preferred landing) and then march directly on London. Initially, the English Jacobites requested a second, lesser expedition to bolster the Tory clans, who would rise simultaneously. This element did not proceed, but Saxe's 10,000, should they succeed in crossing the Channel, would almost have parity of numbers with the troops the Hanoverians could muster in the south of England. The Scottish military establishment, fewer than 3,000 strong, was minuscule. There was a suggestion that the invaders rely on small boats, but the Marshal wanted men-o'-war as ushers for his vulnerable transports.

The naval aspect would involve the Brest squadron taking station by the Isle of Wight to block the inevitable British riposte. Sir John Norris commanded the home fleet, at anchor in Spithead. If he got past their blockade, the French were to engage while a handful of warships shepherded transports towards the Thames Estuary. Winter weather delayed the fleet's embarkation during January 1744, and it was not until early the next month that the ships raised anchor. By now, British intelligence had divined that Charles Edward had slipped out of Italy and was believed to be in France. The threat of imminent invasion hung in the air and yet the government was clearly confident the Royal Navy could see off any attempt. Nonetheless, a further 6,000 Dutch troops were to be put on standby. Some confusion now arose as to the destination of the supposed invasion fleet. Was there to be an attempt on Ireland? Charles Edward had arrived safely, despite the Navy's best efforts, in Paris by 8 February. His intermeddling was, at this stage, in fact unsolicited, perhaps even unwelcome. The French were aware that his presence would only serve as a banner advertisement for any forthcoming attempt.

British agents had meanwhile disbursed a hefty bribe to gain sight of French plans; additional army units from Holland were now requested. The upshot of this security leak was that the French blamed the failure, unfairly, upon Charles Edward, on account of his precipitate action, which served to ensure they would think twice before involving him too deeply in their future counsels. Parliament was quick to affirm the members' undying loyalty to George – the old spectre of Popish Plot and rising was paraded. Despite this, there was no vast outpouring of pro-Hanoverian sentiment in the country.

By late February, the two fleets were in sight of each other off

Dungeness, but strong winds scattered both before battle could be joined and the French tacked back towards Brest. More bad weather struck at Dunkirk, damaging transports and ruining supplies. Saxe began to fret, as he had neither warships nor pilots (the latter promised by the English sympathisers). Once again, the weather showed a strongly Hanoverian shift: early in March a further great storm did yet more damage to the transports riding at Dunkirk. Saxe now wrote to Charles advising the invasion had been cancelled. The Forty-Four was over before it began, and the government in Britain scented deliverance. Largely forgotten by his French hosts after the abandonment of the expedition, Charles had resided for a while in Gravelines, maintained if ignored by Louis XV, who would not grant him an audience. In the spring, he moved to the outskirts of Paris, from where he wrote to his father:

> The situation I am in is very particular, for nobody nose where I am or what is become of me, so that I am entirely burried as to the publick, and can't but say that it is a very great constrent upon me, for I am obliged very often not to stur out of my room for fier of some bodys noing my face. I very often think that you would laugh very hartily if you saw me going about with a single servant bying fish and other things and squabling for a peney more or less. I hope your Majesty will be thoroughly persuaded, that no constrent or trouble whatsoever either of minde or body, wil ever stoppe me in going on with my duty, in doing any thing that I think can tend to your service or your Glory.

It is only natural that such a frustrating relegation to pensioner status on the sidelines would jibe with a young man of dash and fire, especially when he has been keyed up for great events. Charles certainly had charm and charisma, physical courage and stamina. He lacked experience, any real knowledge of the military art and the ability to cope with adversity. If the projected invasion had proved a fiasco, this did not diminish its value to France in terms of diverting British attention from the European theatre and in creating a scare that might promote a redistribution of resources. In the bigger game the Forty-Four thereby served a purpose. This was of no value to the Jacobites, though a definite gain for France and her allies. Robert Trevor, British ambassador at The Hague felt that:

> . . . perhaps this uneasiness is all that France at present aims at; and that if she could augment it enough to make us weaken Flanders, she would strike a home blow on that side . . . I have no idea of an invasion, though the news from Dunkirk and all along that coast are suspicious.

For the French, it could be argued that their success in diverting British attention allowed them to seize, and thereafter to retain, the strategic initiative in Flanders. This they did not relinquish for the remainder of the war, and their gains placed them in a strong position when the time came to negotiate peace terms. Most eighteenth-century military operations tended to be relatively limited in their objectives. France was not at home with the hazards of amphibious operations. As the century progressed it would be the British who became masters of the combined operation. France's involvement with the Jacobites, therefore, could be viewed as both cynical and opportunistic. However, the shades of Jacobite hopes for an actual landing would inform thinking during the Forty-Five, would influence the decisions of men of large estate in throwing in their lot with Charles Edward and would lead to their utter ruin in his cause.

Louis was certainly not overly impressed by his royal guest. Prince Charles Edward's request for 3,000 foot to support a bid for Scotland, lodged in October 1744, produced no response. Undeterred, he went ahead seeking to finance his war chest from private sources. In this he enjoyed some success. He was able to tap into the web of finance and banking contacts managed by a band of Scottish and Irish expatriate entrepreneurs. Some of these had shipping interests in Nantes and St Malo. Their willingness was not entirely philanthropic. Obviously if the great gamble now being planned came off, rewards would be substantial. Probably the most influential of this affluent clique of émigrés was Antoine Walsh of Nantes.[5] A former officer in the French service, grown wealthy on the proceeds of slavery, he had been introduced to the prince by Lord Clare, commanding the Irish Brigade. The French administration was, outwardly, keeping its distance from Charles Edward while, at the same time, opening doors and greasing wheels.

THE FORTY-FIVE

In the spring and summer of 1745, Britain faced a growing crisis in Flanders. On 11 May, Saxe defeated Cumberland in the long, bloody duel of Fontenoy.[6] Ghent and Bruges were lost in July, and Ostend capitulated on 23 August. This was very bad indeed and distracted British attention away from the plans of Charles Edward who appeared to be a very small player in the midst of such grand manoeuvres. However, on 22 June, the prince boarded the frigate *Le du Teillay* and sailed from St Nazaire. He was about to take centre stage. Nearly three weeks before his departure, the prince had written to Louis XV, whom he addressed as 'uncle' intimating that he had resolved single-handedly to make himself known by his deeds. To embark on an enterprise to which even a very moderate amount of help would ensure success, and being so bold as to think that the King of France would not refuse this:

> I would certainly not have come to France if the expedition which was planned to take place last year [1744] had not shewn me that your Majesty wished me well . . . and so I go to seek my destiny which, apart from being in the hands of God, is in those of your Majesty.

This would clearly seem to indicate Charles had confidence in the eventual certainty of French aid, once his expedition should be seen to stimulate results. What he had not taken into account was the fact that Fontenoy and the gains in Flanders had conferred the strategic initiative on France. There was no real need for any sideshow, other than it might sow further confusion. Certainly, the French could not pretend they were unaware of what was afoot. One of the vessels the Prince's entrepreneurial friends had chartered was the 64-gun *L'Elisabeth*. It was quite customary for the French Navy to grant charters with letters of marque to enterprising merchant raiders, who might seek a profit from the wars. It appears unlikely that *L'Elisabeth* could have been hired for the expedition to Scotland without the direct authority of the minister concerned.

The ship carried a naval complement, and large stores of arms, accoutrement, powder and shot had been amassed, which required ministerial authorisation. From the French perspective, the expedition was a low cost extension to the war which had the potential to increase the pressure on Britain, with whom France was tentatively seeking to negotiate. Charles had, on 12 June, written to his father to explain the desperate venture on which, without James's commission, he was about to embark:

> I believe your Majesty little expected a courier at this time, and much less from me; to tell you a thing that will be a great surprise to you. I have been, above six months ago, invited by our friends to go to Scotland, and to carry what money and arms I could conveniently get; this being, they are fully persuaded, the only way of restoring you to the Crown, and them to their liberties . . . After such scandalous usage as I have received from the French Court, had I not given my word to do so, or got so many encouragements from time to time as I have had, I should have been obliged, in honour and for my own reputation, to have flung myself into the arms of my friends, and die with them, rather than live longer in such a miserable way here, or be obliged to return to Rome, which would be just giving up all hopes . . . Your Majesty cannot disapprove a son's following the example of his father. You yourself did the like in the year '15; but the circumstances now are indeed very different, by being much more encouraging, there being a certainty of succeeding with the least help. . . . I have tried all possible means and stratagems to get access to the King of France, or his Minister, without the least effect . . . Now I have been obliged to steal off, without letting the King of France so much as suspect it for which I make a proper excuse in my letter to him; by saying it was a great mortification to me never to have been able to speak and open my heart to him. Let what will happen, the stroke is struck, and I have taken a firm resolution to conquer or to die . . .

Brave words, appropriate in the romantic, if not the pragmatic, sense, Charles, in this apologia to his father, suggests he has been drawn to the Scottish venture by the assurance and entreaty of sympathisers there, but his initial reception in the Highlands would indicate otherwise. On the other hand, the expedition may be seen to represent the final throw of the despairing gambler, determined to risk all on a last roll of the dice. The fact that the fount of overt French support had dried up should have indicated to a wiser man how the land lay in that direction. Hubris is a poor reason for campaigning without some more substantive bedfellows. On 2 July, the sleek *du Teillay* was joined by the heavier and ageing *L'Elisabeth* off Belle Isle, and the pair sailed north-west until, with typical misfortune, they ran foul of HMS *Lyon* (58 guns). The English man-o'-war, if under-gunned, was faster, having just been refitted. Captain Dan of *L'Elisabeth* ran out his guns to make a fight of it. The French ship cleared for action, exchanged token shot and hoisted her colours. The Englishman gave chase and presently the two warships were exchanging broadsides. No subtlety here, but a grinding, yardarm to yardarm, attrition of screaming round shot.

At one point in the action, *Lyon* was able to rake her opponent,[7] causing fearful loss, yet she certainly did not have matters all her own way, and the Frenchman shot away her rigging and partly dismasted her. The battle raged until darkness when *L'Elisabeth* limped back towards Brest with 57 dead, including her gallant skipper, and nearly twice as many wounded. Though she was neither sunk nor taken, her priceless cargo of supplies and quota of volunteers was lost to Charles Edward. Diminutive *du Teillay*, with the prince's equally modest entourage on board, sailed on alone. Despite the continued vigilance of the Royal Navy, Captain Durbe steered his ship north and west, around the treacherous coast, past the bastion of Cape Wrath and, on 23 July, sighted the Outer Hebrides. The vessel made landfall off Barra, where the steep hills crowd down to the anchorage. The Highlander turned financier, Aeneas MacDonald, went ashore to establish contact with his brother-in-law and staunch Jacobite, Macneil of Barra: The Forty-Five had begun.

It did not begin particularly well for the prince. Macneil was away and it was feared the government had rumbled the whole affair. Undeterred, Charles was for pressing on. There was a further fright when what appeared to be a large man-o'-war was sighted and *du Teillay* took shelter among the necklace of islands. More alarums followed. Charles and his tiny band received a taste of the fury of a West Coast summer storm. The laird of Boisdale was the first man of consequence the prince spoke to on the barren strand of Eriskay. His advice was as harsh as the wind, but the Jacobite counsels were disturbed by the renewed attentions of supposed British warships.

On 25 July the swift French frigate nosed into Loch nan Uamh and the prince, with his tiny entourage, stepped ashore at Arisaig.[8] Charles was now upon his native land, the arms and stores were unloaded and local gentlemen consulted. Having revictualled, *du Teillay* made ready to put out to sea. If Prince Charles Edward was having any second thoughts, now was definitely the time. If he lacked wisdom and judgement, he lacked for neither courage nor energy. Durbe and Walsh, who had accompanied the voyage, said their farewells, the latter departing with a letter of commendation from the prince in his pocket. It was time for business.

Whether the prince possessed sufficient intellectual wherewithal to contemplate the wider, European picture, must remain doubtful. That he first allowed himself to be deceived before proceeding, in turn, to deceive others may be quite likely. The Forty-Five, therefore, was born out of false optimism and launched on pious hopes, presented as sure. In short, it was founded on an entirely false premise that the Highlands had but to show the white cockade and the French would be sufficiently enthused to intervene, as had been so tantalisingly close the previous year. None of those chiefs, seduced by the prince's easy charm and charisma, which would hold only as long as he was seen to be winning, seriously envisaged that the clans must bear the weight of the whole campaign unaided.

Monday 19 August saw the prince with his following at Glenfinnan, where the high hills crowd the loch. Apart from a pair of local shepherds, the tranquillity was undisturbed by the tramp of marching feet. After what must have been an increasingly anxious wait, a small MacDonald contingent, no more than 150 broadswords, came in and, with them, James Mor MacGregor, son of the celebrated Rob Roy and as much a rogue.[9] It was not until around four in the afternoon that Cameron of Lochiel finally made an appearance, bringing in perhaps 700 of his affinity, to be followed by Keppoch with, at best, half as many. It was scarcely an army, hardly sufficient for two weak battalions.

What followed was a formidable feat of arms. Charles's ragged forces defeated Cope at Prestonpans. Despite the chiefs' misgivings, the army was soon tramping in good order down the western spine of England. They took, firstly Carlisle, then, on 27 November, Preston. Despite a remarkable dearth of recruits, the clan regiments pressed on initially to Manchester and, finally, on 4 December attained Derby. Whether the decision forced upon Charles by his officers to withdraw was the correct one remains open to debate.[10] But the prince, his brittle personality bruised by this reverse, took more and more counsel with his Irish cronies, and a widening chasm opened with his Highland commanders, particularly Lord George Murray. If Charles had significantly misrepresented the actual level of likely French support, his core belief that victories won by the Highland army might stimulate their enthusiasm to the point of significant military intervention was not so wide of the mark. Even as the rebel army was setting its face towards north and beginning a long retreat from the high-water mark of Derby, some modest French reinforcements succeeded in eluding the Royal Navy blockade and entering Montrose.

This was not an army; the Royal Ecossais was merely a weak composite battalion of companies drawn from the regiments in the Irish Brigade. Nonetheless, as far back as 13 October, Louis had taken a decision to support Charles with a force of several thousands. By mid November, the ubiquitous Walsh was instructed to assemble transports and the Irish were moved up to Dunkirk. Any chances of the expedition setting sail were hampered by adverse winds, while the RN waited in the Downs. A landing either on the south coast or further west seemed the likeliest option. So heightened was the tension in England that on 10 December a French descent was announced – somewhat prematurely – the supposed invaders were nothing more than local smugglers plying their illicit trade off Beachy Head! As ever, the RN took the fight to the enemy, the French shipping constantly subjected to enterprising cutting-out raids, which relieved the French of a score and more of vessels.

On land, the Duke of Cumberland and his officers were determined that this affair, which had seemed to shake the very roots of his family's dynasty, should not peter out with the clans melting back, unscathed, into the heather. It was time for a final and decisive reckoning. On 17 January, a further battle was fought at Falkirk, a confused and untidy fight in which the government forces, led by General 'Hangman' Hawley, were again worsted.[11] Almost three months later, on 16 April, the last great battle to be fought on British soil erupted at Culloden. The Jacobites, depleted, hungry, exhausted and footsore, confronted the larger Hanoverian army, well-formed, well-drilled and competently led. In the driving sleet, the clans charged for the last time, winnowed by round shot, grape and musketry. They fell by companies, by mid afternoon it was all over, and the Stuart cause was in ruins. Charles, who had commanded in person, fled the field, and his corpulent cousin, Cumberland, enjoyed the only victory of an otherwise failed military career.

A few weeks before the battle, a French sloop, aptly named *The Prince Charles*, formerly HMS *Hazard*, which the Jacobites had taken in Montrose harbour less than six months before, had attempted to land additional detachments from the Irish Picquets. These reinforcements would have been welcome. Even more welcome would have been the quantity of gold coin on board; that the prince's war chest was empty may have been a spur to his accepting battle on Culloden Moor. Captain Talbot, who had attempted to run the blockade and make landfall at Portsoy on the Moray Firth, came up against a quartet of British men-of-war: the 40-gun *Eltham*, *Sheerness* (24 guns) and the fast sloops *Hawk* and *Hound*. The odds were unfortunate, and Talbot crowded sail to run northwards along the coast. Pursuit was relentless and, as a fitful wind dropped, the fine sailing qualities of *Le Prince Charles* were of little advantage. Only by taking to the oars and rowing for their lives did the ship's company escape into the darkness. By dawn, she was off Caithness preparing to run the Pentland Firth, when her pursuer once again hove into view. This was a classic sea chase of the age of sail. The sloop had to try and outrun her tormentor. If the frigate closed, the ship was lost, for *Le Prince Charles* was heavily outgunned. Worse, Talbot's Jacobite pilots were all Islesmen, unfamiliar with these waters. As she now fled westwards, the Frenchman was moving ever further away from the HQ of Charles's cash-strapped army at Inverness.

Talbot encountered a small fishing smack and took the crew as unwitting and unwilling guides. Knowing he could probably not now outrun the frigate, he sought any haven where his shallow draft would confound the pursuit. As the tide ebbed, the French captain ran his small vessel into the shallows of the sands of Melness at the western opening of the Kyle of Tongue. O'Brien of *Sheerness* took the risk of fouling as he swept in behind. A standoff now ensued, both ships riding at anchor, guns run out. Talbot could not match his adversary's broadside, six-pounders against nines, but he was game and full of fight, his crew perhaps less so. For three hours battle raged, the smaller ship maintaining a gallant but ultimately one-sided fight. *Sheerness*'s gunners dismounted her deck guns and riddled *Le Prince Charles*'s masts and rigging; the decks a mess of tumbled yards and cordage, garnished with blood and entrails. With *Le Prince Charles* crippled, O'Brien stood off to finish the job at longer range. Talbot's surviving crew had by now had quite enough and bolted for temporary sanctuary in the hold. Undismayed, Talbot drew his sword to beat them back to their posts, using the Picquets as marines. Despite such near-fanatical gallantry, there was no remedy for the fact his ship was badly holed and sinking. Cutting the cables, he allowed her to drift inshore and come aground.

Lugging their sacks of coin, the Irish soldiers, led by Captain Brown of Lally's regiment, climbed down from the shattered hulk, disembarking all of their arms and powder, while still under intense fire. Talbot, remarkably unscathed, spat defiance at *Sheerness* and literally nailed his colours to the stump of the mast. The French-man's wounded had to be left on the shot-scoured deck, while the fit survivors followed the Irish on to the beach. O'Brien had sent a commanded party of marines to cut off the landward exits. To escape they had now to move inland, over rough terrain, of which they knew nothing. A providential encounter with one of the few Jacobites in the vicinity, William Mackay of Melness, was encouraging, but his news was not. These French and Irish were in a hostile land. Lord Reay was a Whig and had raised two companies of militia to fight for King George. Mackay provided horses to carry the gold and his son as a guide. He could do no more. O'Brien had by dawn inspected the damaged vessel to see if she could be salvaged.

Lord Reay's people too were not inactive. A forlorn hope of seven locals, led by his factor Daniel Forbes, were stalking the French column while the militia was mustering. Talbot had his own survivors from *Le Prince Charles*, many of the wounded left on board had succumbed during the night, six officers and three score other ranks from Berwick's with a motley of volunteers from Clare's, Royal Ecossais, the French Guards and some from Spanish service. Forbes, undeterred by the odds, kept up a steady harassing fire in the course of which his marksmen dropped eleven Irish, three of them fatalities. The fight spilled along the Jacobites' intended line of march towards a high pass skirting the flank of Ben Loyal. Here 50 militia arrived to bolster Forbes seven. More potent than their numbers were their drums, a great rolling, dolorous tumult reverberated around the cockpit of the pass. The Jacobites, now cornered in the narrow arena, decided enough was enough and prepared to lay down their arms, first dumping their coin into Loch Hacoin. Factor Forbes, or so the story goes, salvaged 1,000 guineas as compensation for his efforts; not a bad morning's work. As for the Jacobites, a vital resource was denied them. The Royal Navy, despite a most spirited and gallant opponent, had once again performed its role.

Final cannonades and the death rattle of the execution squads were not the final echoes of the Forty-Five. On 30 April 1746, two French privateers, *Mars* and *Bellone* had anchored in Loch nan Uamh, where it had all begun the previous year. The Frenchmen were initially sniped at by Jacobites onshore who believed them to be Royal Navy. These Highlanders, including Perth, Lord John Drummond and Lord Elcho, quickly acquainted their newly arrived allies with tidings of the disaster. The visitors were able to provide much needed supplies and took time to come ashore and marvel at the desperate poverty and general wretchedness of their hosts.

Captain Noel RN, on board the sloop *Greyhound*, was stationed barely 30 miles from Loch nan Uamh and was aware of the privateers' presence. The rest of the captain's small flotilla was widely dispersed but, by dawn on 2 May, both *Greyhound* and another sloop, *Baltimore*, were under sail and were later joined by a third, *Terror*. At first light, a little after three in the morning, these three small British vessels crept into the still waters of the loch.

John Daniel, a Jacobite volunteer, was, that night, sleeping among the other fugitives on the shore, and the sight of the British men-o'-war provided a most unwelcome jolt. The French, however, alerted by the sighting of an earlier patrol boat, were ready to fight. Captain Rouillee of *Mars* remained, unwisely, at anchor while Lory of *Bellone* got underway. To receive *Greyhound*'s broadside while thus immured was very nearly fatal, and *Mars* took a substantial pounding. Nearly a score of the privateers were killed, her decks, according to an eyewitness, awash with blood. One of the Jacobite refugees, Major Hales, was among the dead: having been bidden to throw himself to the deck to avoid injury, he preferred the upright pose of quixotic contempt, which, in his case, proved lethal. *Baltimore* now bore down on *Mars*, while *Greyhound* attacked *Bellone*. The two smaller British vessels were heavily outgunned and began, in turn, to suffer some serious punishment. Both suffered damage to their rigging, and Lory was manoeuvring to board. He failed, but the respite enabled Rouillee to slice cables and get his battered ship underway. The tiny *Terror* weighed into the fray, but was seen off by a broadside from *Bellone*. The two Frenchmen were now under sail, heading up the narrow confines of the loch with *Mars* taking shelter in a small bay, the three English ships, like terriers, snapping at *Bellone*.

For a good three hours the Jacobites on the shore were treated to the spectacle of a fierce little battle raging on the normally placid waters. It seemed as though *Mars* was crippled and could be picked off at leisure while the sloops directed their attention towards *Bellone*. Noel was not blind to the scurrying Highlanders on the shore, busily removing inland cargoes of arms and cash, the latter amounting to some £35,000 in bullion. Such a sum would have very possibly enabled the prince to stave off the defeat at Culloden and guaranteed the continuance of rebellion. Flying round shot from *Greyhound* added urgency to the work. Having managed to jury-rig repairs to his damaged sails, Captain Howe of *Baltimore* once more brought his vessel to the attack. Both his sloop and the gallant little *Terror* suffered grievously, *Baltimore*'s rigging and sails cut up, Howe himself among the wounded. After some six hours of battle, the fight petered out. All of the English ships had suffered damage, if relatively few casualties. *Bellone* unleashed a final broadside to speed the retreating ships on their way. *Mars* was by now in a bad state, hit repeatedly below the waterline, and with 29 dead and 85 wounded littering the decks, slippery with their spilled blood.

The French, knowing that other British ships could soon be expected to enable Noel to renew the assault, worked feverishly to ensure their badly holed vessel was seaworthy. Jacobites onshore meanwhile enjoyed the plentiful liquor their guests had left them. MacDonald of Barisdale, whose regiment had missed the fight, had by now appeared and began by appropriating a portion of cash before departing. The remaining Macleans too, dispersed, while one of the inebriated rebels unwisely elected to smoke his pipe in close proximity to a barrel of powder and succeeded in blowing himself to bits, his befuddled comrades mistaking the noise for a fresh alarum! As the privateers nursed battered ships back towards their Breton lairs, they took off the fugitive Duke of Perth, his brother and Lord Elcho.

John Fergusson[12] was skipper of *Furnace* and, in April, before Culloden, his marines had engaged in a drink-fuelled foray against hapless MacDonald womenfolk on the island of Canna. Having finished with Canna, Fergusson moved his attentions to Eigg, where the business of rounding up rebels was leavened with additional pillage and rape. Captain Felix O'Neill, of Lally's regiment, in the French service, was one of his victims, captured and about to be tortured until an officer of the Royals intervened and faced the brutal captain down. In their hunt for the prince, the soldiers and sailors of the crown even descended in force upon St Kilda, the most remote and westerly of the isles, whose terrified inhabitants must have seen these swarming redcoats as a vision of Hell. Needless to say, the prince was not to be found.

It would have been far better for Prince Charles Edward Stuart had he died on the field at Culloden, so history might remember a handsome, if flawed, young man, whose army came within an ace of unseating the House of Hanover. Better by far than the long years of an embittered, wasted life, his cause in ruins, increasingly an unwelcome anachronism, whose only succour came from a bottle; he died, also forgotten, in Rome in 1788.[13]

———◆———

NINE

Band of Brothers

My strength is failing fast
(Said the sea-king to his men).
I shall never sail the seas
Like a conqueror again,
But while yet a drop remains
Of the life-blood in my veins
Raise, oh raise me from my bed,
Put the crown upon my head,
Put my good sword in my hand,
And so lead me to the strand,
Where my ship at anchor rides
Steadily:
If I cannot end my life
In the crimsoned battle-strife
Let me die as I have lived
On the sea.
Charles Mackay, 'Sea-King's Burial'

D ESPITE THE WIDESPREAD OPPOSITION which the Act of Union had engendered, Scotland, after 1707, was able to harvest the manifold benefits of free trade within the burgeoning empire, an empire of which she was now very much a part. Scottish teachers, thinkers, philosophers and artists did not merely blossom at this time, they soared. Edinburgh, with the metropolis of the New Town as the very epitome of Georgian elegance,[1] became the new Athens. Well might as eminent an observer as Voltaire exclaim, 'We look to Scotland for all our ideas of civilisation.' Titans such as Hutcheson, Hume and Adam Smith developed the 'science of man', a blend of historical patterns of behaviour linked to the decisive forces of a modern, enlightened world. Smith's seminal work *The Wealth of Nations* (1776) remains an influential politico-economic polemic even today.

By one of history's particular ironies, as the old ways of the clans were suppressed, Pitt the Elder, with a brilliant flourish, found new employment for the young men of the glens. From now on, their martial skills would be harnessed toward the service of the crown; they would swap the plaid for the red coat, and their loyalties would be channelled towards the regimental rather than the tribal or factional. Recruits were not wanting and the Highland regiments became one of the British army's prime assets, entering service just as the demands of global warfare guaranteed their military skills and natural hardiness would be at a premium.

DEVELOPMENTS IN NAVAL TECHNOLOGY

Although the eighteenth century witnessed some innovations in terms of fighting ship design, naval architects of the calibre of the Petts or Anthony Deane, who created the blueprint, were less in evidence. British designers, such as Ward, Stacy, Hayward, Locke, Allen and Slade, were active, but confined their labours to improving and streamlining the earlier models. As a net result, ships were able to stay at sea longer and defy winter conditions, a necessary feature of blockade work.[2] This additional seaworthiness could serve to force an enemy into a fleet action; Hawke's great victory at Quiberon Bay in 1759 was won in tempestuous November seas.[3] In terms of pure design, the French tended to be viewed as superior and many of the perceived best sailors in the English fleet were prizes, notwithstanding the fact that their standards of construction were viewed as markedly inferior. An example was the great capital ship *Commerce du Marseilles* taken at Toulon in 1793. So weak was her build that she was deemed unfit to bear the weight of her ordnance and of no more service than as a troop transport! The French Revolutionary Wars were the longest and most bitterly contested naval conflicts in history. In that whole time, the RN lost only four capital ships as prizes and none sunk; the French lost 131 captured and 29 sent to the bottom.

Naval gunnery had taken a number of significant steps forward. Ordnances dating from 1716, 1740, 1757, 1762 and 1792 specified the number and weight of guns appropriate to each of the rates. During the eighteenth century, weight of shot was also increasing; techniques for milling powder and casting of barrels had improved considerably. The industrial revolution had allowed Britain to maintain and indeed extend her technological advantage. Guns were now cast in the solid and then bored out, infinitely stronger than the earlier bronze and a shade more accurate. If gun barrels were improving in design and quality, the basic timber carriage remained unchanged, secured against the slamming recoil by tackle, bolted to the solid timbers, each side of the gun-port. This system tended to inhibit firing on the traverse, though certain ameliorating refinements were pioneered by Captain Sir Charles Douglas in the 1770s. His ideas included the introduction of a flintlock firing mechanism.

At the forefront of the new firepower was the Scots firm of Carron,[4] noted as a leading manufacturer even before 1752, when General Robert Melville produced a different type of shipboard ordnance, the carronade. This was a form of naval howitzer, a weapon having a short barrel but wide bore, throwing a ball from 32lb to twice that weight. Its lower muzzle velocity actually meant that, at close ranges, the shot caused greater destruction. Though initially mounted on carriages, the carronades were later furnished with a slide and worm screw to effect elevation, as the slide was pivoted on a vertical bolt, traversing was entirely feasible. Carronades had the added and not inconsiderable advantage of only needing a two-man crew. The guns first came into widespread use during the American War of Independence and did good service throughout that and the later conflicts with France. Despite their numerous advantages, the French were slow to pick up on this concept. Their style of gunnery was to stand off and direct much of their fire against rigging, seeking to disable rather than sink.

JOHN PAUL JONES

One of Scotland's more colourful sons of this era, born near Kirkbean, Kirkcudbrightshire on 6 July 1747, was John Paul Jones, though his fame would not rest upon service to his native land. On the contrary, he was destined to become famous as a commercial raider in the service of newborn America. His parents were in service, and the young man went to sea at an early age, quickly demonstrating a ready wit and aptitude for learning. His early career was aboard merchantmen and, when times grew hard, included employment in the slave trade. His life was never uneventful and, as a result of a dispute with a well-connected ship's carpenter, whom he'd had occasion to flog, he found himself under something of a cloud. He was on hand, an experienced and capable sailor, when Congress established the fledgling US Navy, and he was offered a commission, serving under Commodore Hopkins. His first taste of action occurred in a fight between the US squadron and HMS *Glasgow*, a 20-gun frigate. The action was indecisive; the English vessel, despite being both outnumbered and outgunned, gave a good account of herself and got safely off. In the acrimony which followed, several of the American officers were discharged, and Jones stepped neatly into the void.

As a commercial raider, he enjoyed considerable success, latterly being given *Ranger*, a fast 26-gun frigate. He now received his orders from none other than Benjamin Franklin, then the American commissioner to France. *Ranger* ran the British blockade with French assistance and embarked on a highly productive cruise, taking prizes off Kintyre and in the Irish Sea and launching a daring cutting-out expedition against the packed shipping at anchor in Whitehaven harbour. That same evening. he struck across the Solway at his native shore, anchoring off Kirkcudbright and landing a commanded party in a bold attempt to seize the Earl of Selkirk, whose illustrious person could then be exchanged for a selection of rebels. Only the family silver proved to be to hand, and the sailors gladly carried this off. Jones bought the treasure back and returned it with a note of apology. Off Carrickfergus, *Ranger* took on HMS *Drake*, the latter more than game even though she was significantly outgunned. Jones wisely declined giving his opponent a chance to board, when her superior complement would tell, but kept her at a distance, shooting up her rigging while his marksmen played havoc on the crowded deck. With her master and first mate dead, *Drake* hauled down her colours after an hour's battle.

Now something of a celebrity, Jones was promoted to the rank of commodore and was enabled to convert a fast East Indiaman into a heavy 40-gun frigate. His rise was facilitated by having Franklin as patron, and he judiciously named his new ship *Le Bonhomme Richard* (Franklin's nom de plume was 'Poor Richard'). She was a fine vessel, but securing a worthy crew proved challenging and the motley hands he was able to bring aboard included French, Portuguese, English, Scots and Irish. Fewer than half were American. Discipline proved a constant headache, not just on board *Le Bonhomme Richard* but throughout the five sail he was to command. In his flotilla he had the US *Alliance* and a trio of French frigates. Though the latter were nominally under his command, they received their orders from France, an unhappy arrangement.

On 4 August 1779, the squadron slipped out of Lorient and cruised the west of Ireland. Prizes were scant and desertions rife. One of the Frenchmen defected, and Captain Landais of *Alliance* was detached to spread the net. Off Cape Wrath, Jones secured his first substantial prize and took several more as he sailed down the east coast. By the middle part of September he was off the Forth with his truncated squadron and, despite the faintheartedness of his remaining allies, mounted a demonstration. Beating down the length of Northumbria's 'Lordly Strand', he sailed as far south as Flamborough Head without picking up any scent. Then his luck changed as a fat British convoy of 41 sail hove into view. Here were prizes indeed, but the Americans would take none without a fight, HMS *Serapis* (54 guns) and the sloop HMS *Countess of Scarborough* were shepherding the merchantmen and ran out their guns.

Jones had been rejoined by *Alliance* and the Frenchmen were game, but *Serapis* carried a heavier broadside. *Le Bonhomme Richard* was sailing under British colours, a not unusual tactic; she need only declare her true identity in the moments before the guns began to roar. Raising his US colours, Jones closed for the fight. HMS *Countess of Scarborough* received the full attentions of both Frenchmen and soon struck, while *Alliance* proved of no particular assistance. Drums were rattling out the summons to clear for action: partitions were struck, livestock and the boats cast overboard, netting and hammocks rigged to afford some minimal protection. The two big ships now closed and exchanged broadsides. French sharpshooters deluged the Britisher's waist with small arms fire and grenades. On the gun decks, the sailors sweated and heaved in the filthy, choking miasma, senses battered by the concussion, sponging, loading and ramming, each salvo sending the great guns hurtling back, tons of hot, angry iron and timber, jerking savagely on the lines.

Powder monkeys scurried like hares to deliver charges. The heat would be terrific. When a screaming round shot punched through the planking, it would loose a lethal blizzard of oaken shards, as dangerous to man as the ball itself. Men would be struck down by these, impaled or studded. If a gun was struck, the carriage would rear up as though tossed by a giant's hand, crushing luckless crew. As men fell, writhing, shorn of limb or eviscerated, the more lightly wounded would be taken below for the tender ministrations of the surgeon, while those beyond salvation and those already dead would be unceremoniously heaved out of gun ports. On the quarterdeck, captain and officers would don their dress uniforms – the etiquette of slaughter demanded formality, even though the brightness of their attire marked them as high-value targets.

A grenade from the American dropped down an open hatch and caused both explosion and fire, but the British frigate never slackened her shooting, her heavier broadside taking fearful toll, punching though the hull and holing her opponent in several places. Jones's efforts to close and board were frustrated, his gun deck a mangled, blood-spattered shambles and the ship taking in more water than the pumps could handle. As darkness fell and the British sensed victory, Captain Pearson of *Serapis* called upon Jones to strike his colours, to which he received the immortal response, 'I have not yet begun to fight!' Captain Pearson was to discover this was not mere bravado, for Jones had, at last, succeeded in getting his badly damaged vessel alongside, *Serapis*'s anchor caught in the American's shrouds. Jones's boarders sprang away, marksmen still firing into the smoke. Now *Le Bonhomme Richard* was sinking and was only kept barely afloat, lashed to her opponent. William Hamilton, one of Jones's rebel Scots, managed to slither along a yardarm and neatly drop a grenade onto a heap of exposed cartridges. The blast caused heavy loss. At the same time, one of Jones's master-gunners lost his nerve and screamed for quarter, only to be knocked senseless by his captain. This fight was to be to the finish.

The duel between *Serapis* and *Le Bonhomme Richard* became the stuff of legend, an epic single-ship engagement with extreme valour amply demonstrated by both sides. Captain Pearson, virtually the only officer surviving unwounded, finally hauled down what remained of his colours, 117 of his crew dead or injured. Though he had finally lost the battle, he'd inflicted 150 casualties on his opponent. It was none too soon, for the American ship was sinking fast, despite a press of volunteers and prisoners working feverishly through the smoke-shrouded darkness. *Le Bonhomme Richard* went down next morning. She had given good service. Though he had taken both British men-of-war, the greater prize of the convoy had long sailed clear. Nevertheless, Jones was extensively feted in France. This action proved the high-water mark of his career. His remaining service under Congress was undistinguished and, in 1787, he accepted an invitation to join the navy of Catherine the Great of Russia. This proved a disadvantageous move, and his career entered the downward spiral. He died in Paris on 18 July 1792, at the early age of 45,[5] but by then attentions had shifted to other, even more momentous happenings.

SCOTS IN THE ROYAL NAVY

John Paul Jones was not the only Scot to make his reputation in the late eighteenth century. Others included Admiral Sir James Douglas, who took part in Wolfe's expedition against Quebec in 1759 and subsequently captured Dominica, rounding off a distinguished career serving as MP for Orkney. Vice Admiral John Campbell sailed with George Anson on his epic circumnavigation and served as flag captain under Hawke at Quiberon Bay, his final posting was as governor of Newfoundland. Nor was Jones the only Scot to take service in Russia; Admiral Sir James Greig was widely regarded as the founder of her navy, after acting as admiral of the Baltic Fleet. Others who enjoyed outstanding career success at sea were Sir James Athol Wood, Sir Richard John Strachan, Sir Pulteney Malcolm, Sir Patrick Campbell, Sir George Cockburn and Sir

Charles Napier. Described as arrogant and boastful, somewhat addicted to strong liquor, Napier came from a naval family and his early career was spent in mounting patrols along the east coast to detect and deter would-be French invaders. Temporarily laid up, he volunteered for service with the army and saw action in the Peninsula campaigns. Subsequently, as captain of the frigate HMS *Thames*, he put the lessons learnt on Spanish soil to good effect, sending many French gunboats and inshore craft to the bottom of the Iberian Sea, while finding ample employment in coastal raids and cutting-out expeditions.

After 1789, France and then Europe was traumatized and transformed by the events of the French Revolution. The *Ancien Regime*, with its support for the American colonists, had opened the floodgates to political notions of liberty and free citizenship that would combine with the rising tide of dissent to topple the Bourbons and plunge the country into a bloody maelstrom. The wars which ensued and the further wars of Napoleon Bonaparte (1804–1815) transformed the face of armed conflict. New tactics and his own towering genius empowered Napoleon to conquer most of Europe.

Throughout the darkest days of this great struggle, when Britain seemed isolated and vulnerable to invasion, it was the Royal Navy which defied the entire might of France and her allies – 'I do not say they will not come I only say they will not come by sea.'[6] This was to be perhaps the Navy's finest era, with actions fought across the globe and fought by a brilliant cadre of officers, Nelson and his 'Band of Brothers', whose crowning achievement was the victory off Cape Trafalgar in October 1805, one of the most significant in European history. The Navy disrupted French trade relentlessly, blockaded harbours and picked off her remaining colonies. Freedom of the seas and Britain's unchallenged industrial dominance placed her in an inexpugnable position. Naval strength dominated British military thinking with interventions, prior to the Peninsula, consisting mainly of extended guerrilla-type operations through amphibious raids. Of these, the largest, the Walcheren Expedition of 1809,[7] intended to relieve pressure on Austria, proved an expensive fiasco. Though the Royal Navy performed its part well, poor support from land-based allies could frustrate the most careful planning. At Corunna,[8] the

Navy was called upon to conduct a Dunkirk-style evacuation that saved the near-frozen remnant of Sir John Moore's force from destruction.

Nelson's 'Band of Brothers' was a maritime fellowship of Homeric standing. It was they who lifted the proud boast of the song 'Britannia Rules the Waves' from jingoistic hubris to reality. The victory won at Trafalgar in October 1805 guaranteed the safety of Britain from invasion by Napoleon's armies and left her mistress of the world's oceans. A number of Scots served with dash and distinction in this revered fraternity or at least on its margins as a degree of anti-Scots bias appeared to prevail. One of these was Admiral Adam Duncan of Camperdown. Literally a giant of a man, born in 1731, he joined the RN at the age of 15, serving on frigates. He took part in a number of actions including the capture of Belle Isle and also of Havana during the Seven Years War. After 1778, he commanded *Monarch* and saw considerable action under Rodney during the latter's relief of Gibraltar, a successful expedition which also resulted in a number of sharp actions and garnering of prizes. Duncan was once again engaged in providing much needed succour to the besieged garrison of the 'Rock' under Howe in 1782 when he captained 90-gun *Blenheim*. Rapid advancement followed: rear admiral in September 1787, vice admiral on 1 February 1793 and, two years later, he was commanding the fleet in the North Sea, engaged in the vital if unglamorous business of blockade.

Not only was the blockade of the Dutch Coast a singularly thankless chore, but appalling conditions and generous application of the lash had greatly soured morale. There was, by 1797, more than a whiff of mutiny in the air. That the rot was contained was due, in no small part, to Duncan's charisma and qualities of leadership. These uncertainties prompted the Dutch to venture out, Admiral de Winter, carrying soldiers for a projected descent upon Ireland, England's Achilles Heel. On 11 October, battle was joined at Camperdown. Duncan, facing a skilful foe, adopted a novel tactic: with no time to form line as tradition dictated, he gave the order, 'pass through the enemy's line and engage to leeward', which became the blueprint for 'the Nelson Touch'. The battle was no walk-over; the Dutch fought long, hard and well, but the day went to

Duncan, taking 9 of 16 enemy sail. The butcher's bill was high on both sides, but the Dutch were broken and dreams of invasion utterly ruined. As a reward for this signal triumph, he was elevated to the peerage as Baron Duncan of Lundie, dying at Cornhill in August 1804.

Admiral George Keith Elphinstone, Viscount Keith, was one of those whose career, though distinguished, was always overshadowed by Nelson's comet. As has been suggested, the RN, or certain senior officers within it, exhibited a strong bias against the sons of Alba, and none more virulent than Lord St Vincent, under whom the young Elphinstone learnt the profession of arms. His rise was steady if unremarkable; a post captain by 1780, he led the naval landing party that took Charleston in a well-executed amphibious attack, winning a considerable haul of prisoners and prizes. The following year, he took a 50-gun Dutch frigate and went on to add a 40-gun Frenchman to the haul. Despite this exemplary record, Keith was left on the shelf for a decade after the Treaty of Versailles, when he transferred his energies into politics. The outbreak of the French Revolutionary Wars revitalised his career, and he was given a ship of the line, 74-gun *Rebus*. His experience of combined operations, gained in the American War, stood him in good stead and he fought a number of successful encounters when the RN, at the invitation of Royalist supporters, beat up Toulon. He took and held the fort at La Malgue, assisted in the destruction of the Arsenal and the burning of ten ships of the line. Others defected or were cut out. He was promoted rear admiral in time to command an expedition against the Dutch in Cape Colony, where he again demonstrated a genius for amphibious operations, leading to the defeat of superior Dutch and local forces.

His next mission, to help quell the naval mutinies, required great tact and understanding, and his clear achievement should rank alongside his martial accomplishments. In the closing months of 1798, he was appointed as C-in-C Mediterranean Fleet, a veritable plum, succeeding his former mentor. Vincent, with typical surliness, proved reluctant to relinquish, placing Elphinstone in the invidious position of having his predecessor, who enjoyed seniority, still exercising command. This duality proved unfortunate when the French were able to avoid the blockade and, with the Spanish, slip clear from Cadiz. The anti-Scots faction was quick to point a finger: 'This undetermined method of acting convinces me [*Captain Troutbridge, one of the 'Band'*] he [*Elphinstone*] is no great thing and a true Scot.'

Though Vincent did finally hand over the baton, Elphinstone experienced continued frustration as the French fleet eluded him and refused battle, despite the odds being heavily in their favour. Successful operations against Massena in Genoa followed. An amphibious operation landing Turkish troops at Aboukir was also undertaken, but the Scot was denied his Trafalgar and appears to have remained excluded, despite, or perhaps because of, his seniority, from the brilliant cadre clustering around Nelson's flame. A further and more ambitious attempt on Cadiz was wisely averted as plague was stalking the city, but partnership with fellow Scot, General Abercrombie, proved more fruitful when the latter's troops were successfully disembarked in Aboukir Bay. A resounding victory was won, but at the cost of the general's life.[9] Honours were heaped on Elphinstone after the French surrender in Egypt, and his career continued with a series of important if unglamorous roles. In spring 1803, he was appointed to command the North Sea Fleet and, for three crucial years after 1812, led the Channel squadron. His was, despite the shadow cast by Nelson, a brilliant career which mixed success on land and sea and demonstrated his mastery of amphibious operations, an area wherein the paladin himself was not always victorious. Lord Keith retired to his estate at Tullyallan and died in 1823.

THE SEA WOLF

Nelson is regarded as Britain's finest fighting admiral. Undoubtedly, this is deserved, yet the distinguished maritime novelist Patrick O'Brien did not, when seeking factual inspiration for his fictional hero Jack Aubrey, look to Nelson. Rather he drew upon the career of Thomas, Admiral Lord Cochrane. If the latter is not the most famous of British captains, he is perhaps the most remarkable. Napoleon himself christened this charismatic Scot, 'The Sea Wolf', an epithet that was hard won and richly deserved. His life was tempestuous. Like his fictional alter ego he suffered financial ruin and imprisonment following accusations of fiscal irregularities. These proved utterly false, and he spent near a score of arduous years clearing his name in which time he fought for the revolutionary governments of Chile, Brazil and Greece. Not until 1848 and at the grand age of 73 was rehabilitation complete, with his appointment as rear admiral in command of the American squadron. Unlike the other sea dogs of his age, his longevity meant his image was captured by photography. Even in old age, the bulldog resolution that carried him through so many long years of shame and exile is evident; a hero from the waning era of sail, he glares out at the modern and unfamiliar industrial age.

Born in Lanarkshire in 1775, he came from a family with strong naval antecedents. His grandfather, Captain James Gilchrist, had fought a notable single ship action 17 years before when he had matched his frigate *Southampton* (32 guns) against the 40-gun *Danae*. After an epic and sanguinary duel lasting six hours, the Frenchman was boarded and taken. In 1800, Thomas Cochrane was appointed to command *Speedy*, a diminutive sloop whose armament comprised only 14 four-pounders; the officers and crew, crammed into the tiny quarters amounted to 90 souls. *Speedy* quickly became a veritable terror, her master's prizes swelling the harbour at Port Mahon. On 6 May 1801, she was being pursued by the Spanish frigate *El Gamo* – 32 guns and a full complement of 319 – Cochrane, having detached prize crews, could muster barely a sixth of that number and was massively outgunned.

'They ain't shy lad – they just ain't ready,' a fictional assessment from Jack Aubrey who, in *Master and Commander*,[10] re-fights Cochrane's historic action. *Speedy* made straight for her heavier opponent, who hoisted colours and delivered a warning shot. Cochrane was maintaining a fiction of the American flag and tacked about so he faced the Spaniard bows front. *El Gamo* fired her broadside, but the shot went high while the nimble *Speedy* ran in under her lee, entangling rigging. Having elevated his aim, Cochrane unleashed his less potent but infinitely more effective salvo, which flensed the enemy's main deck, killing her captain. Locked in what seemed an unequal embrace, the Spaniard, with her higher profile, fired impotently into air, while every round from the

British sloop took dreadful toll. For the Spaniards, the only and obvious recourse was to board and use weight of numbers to win the day. Cochrane had, of course, anticipated this. As the boarders mustered, he pulled off just sufficient distance to refuse, then hosed them with fire. Twice the Spaniards swarmed in the waist, cutlasses at the ready, but both times the riposte succeeded, though by now the smaller ship's yards and rigging were fearfully shot up.

The fight continued in this way for an hour. *Speedy* had two killed and twice as many injured, but stalemate could not continue. The sloop could never sink her opponent, but if she broke off the heavier guns of the Spaniard would soon find the range. With the ship's doctor at the helm, Cochrane prepared to board, to scramble up onto the Spaniard's blood-spattered decks and take the fight to her diminished but still formidable complement. Inspired by their captain's ardour the Speedies swarmed onto *El Gamo*, the fight moving to handstrokes. This was not a test of seamanship, but a hacking, clawing, stabbing melee, clash of steel, crack of pistols, curses and screams of men locked in mortal combat, fought across decks already smeared with blood. When it was over and *El Gamo* a British prize, Cochrane had lost 3 dead and 18 wounded. The butcher's bill was remarkably light in the circumstances; 14 Spaniards had died, including the captain and two score more would bear the scars. All in all, a remarkable victory, one of the finest single-ship actions ever fought.

THE VICTORIAN AGE

With the fall of Napoleon, Britain was left as the world's only superpower. Her naval supremacy was now untouchable, the vast, great spread of her mercantile and maritime empire reaching out over the globe: Pax Britannica. Industry boomed as never before. A network of railways sprang up across the land, revolutionising the movement of people and goods. The shipyards of the Clyde were among the busiest in the world. Until the outbreak of the Russo-Japanese war of 1904–1905, there were no significant naval battles. An Anglo-Russian-French squadron severely chastised the Turks in Navarino Bay in 1827, a victory of Nelsonian quality but politically unwelcome. Despite the relative lack of major fleet actions, the nineteenth century witnessed a veritable revolution in warship design, extending to propulsion, armament and construction. Steam, as a means of propulsion, was an engineering innovation which affected all branches of shipbuilding. The increased speed and force which steam power implied even revived the possibility of ramming as a tactic. The Royal Navy witnessed an unfortunate demonstration of these possibilities in the accidental melee and collisions involving HMS *Vanguard* and *Iron Duke*, *Victoria* and *Camperdown*.

With the introduction of high explosive shells, the science of naval gunnery was utterly transformed and wooden-hulled ships were rendered hopelessly vulnerable. Improvements in gunnery spurred the practice of encasing warships in an iron carapace: the Ironclad. These, and the ungainly inshore gun vessels, known as Monitors, were employed extensively during the American Civil War of 1861–1864. An ironclad, USS *Kearsarge*, demolished the Confederate raider *Alabama* in a dramatic single-ship action off the coast of France, which amply heralded the winds of change. Heavier, more accurate, rifled guns throwing a high explosive shell were not the only innovation in firepower. By the end of the nineteenth century, navies had, in their swelling arsenals, another new engine of destruction, the torpedo. This weapon operated as a swiftly moving mine, capable of being aimed and striking below the waterline with devastating effect. Torpedoes could be delivered by a small, fast-moving vessel, which could nonetheless, sink a far larger capital ship, thus threatening the battleship with redundancy at the very time the capability of big ships was increasing exponentially.

By the close of the century, the shape of modern battlecruisers had begun to emerge; steam-powered, steel-plated, mounting a relatively small number of heavy guns, typically carried in rotating turrets, arranged in linear formation along the main deck. At Tsushima in 1905, the Japanese completely outfought their opponents from the Russian Baltic Fleet, inflicting great loss in men and ships.[11] Torpedoes were employed with some success, as were mines – the Russian flagship *Petropavlovsk* and the Japanese battlecruisers *Yashima* and *Hatsuse* were all lost to the latter – but it was the big guns of the battleships that decided the day.

TEN

———◆———

First Battle of the Atlantic

Admiral Jellicoe is the only commander on either side capable of losing the war in a single afternoon.
Winston Churchill

O N 2 8 J U N E 1 9 1 4 , I N the Bosnian capital of Sarajevo, the official car carrying Archduke Franz Ferdinand, heir to the Habsburg throne, and his wife took a wrong turning. This was to prove something more than a temporary inconvenience for it placed the royal couple firmly in the sights of a tubercular young assassin, Gavrilo Princip. Fatal shots fired that afternoon were to ignite a conflagration more terrible than any which had gone before, and the flames would consume not only the Austrian empire, but those of Turkey, Russia and Germany. It would severely damage the British and French empires and lead to colossal loss of life. The First World War was about to ignite, and Scotland, like many smaller nations, would be sucked in. It was not dragged in protestingly, but on a wave of popular acclaim and unbridled patriotism as nearly a million young men of both kingdoms swelled to respond to Kitchener's famous challenge. Many would not return, and many of those who did would be irrevocably broken in body or mind.

In terms of events at sea, Scotland was very much the front line, as the strength of the Royal Navy was concentrated at Rosyth, Cromarty and Scapa Flow. The prime mission of the North Sea command was to prevent the German Navy – The High Seas Fleet – from penetrating into the Atlantic, where it could wreak havoc among Allied merchant shipping. Though both nations had previously embarked upon a naval arms race, the war at sea would witness only one major fleet action: the Battle of Jutland in 1916. Nonetheless, a more sustained campaign, known as the First Battle of the Atlantic, would rage for the entire duration of hostilities. While the British blockade caused serious hardship and shortages, Germany sought to counter by striking at Britain's vulnerable and extended lines of seaborne supply which stretched across the Atlantic and upon whose continuance successful prosecution of the war depended.

DREADNOUGHTS

When she entered service in December 1906, HMS *Dreadnought* represented a revolution in warship design as profound as any that had gone before.[1] The mere fact of her existence, and that of the class of capital ships to which she gave her name, rendered all existing battleships obsolete. Furthermore, the technological advance she marked was a material factor in inspiring the naval arms race with Germany. She was the first to be equipped with a uniform main battery, rather than, as previously, a handful of very heavy guns, bolstered by a complement of lesser ordnance. Parsons's invention of the steam turbine was a major factor in the technological 'edge' which *Dreadnought* enjoyed. Her turbines gave her a top speed of 21 knots, fast enough to outrun anything with a comparable broadside, and her armament allowed her to outfight any ship that might match her speed. She mounted five two-gun turrets, three of which were constructed in a row along the centre line, one fore and two aft, a further brace of wing turrets were built on both sides of the main bridge superstructure. Despite the huge weight of shot she could dispose, it was not possible to direct fire from all of her ten 12-inch guns upon a single target. Admiral Fisher,[2] who was closely associated with the design of *Dreadnought*, remained convinced that 'end-on' fire was more crucial than broadside. To add to her potency, fire control systems were considerably more sophisticated. In her day, she defined 'state of the art' warship design.

That Britain and Germany possessed such powerful fleets implied that any major engagement between capital ships would result in a sea battle infinitely more destructive than any which had taken place previously. Warfare on both land and sea had moved firmly into the industrial age. Britain had maintained an absolute dominion of the seas since Nelson's day, and few doubted the Royal Navy's ability to see off the High Seas Fleet,[3] though, at the outset, no titanic trial of strength loomed. There were a number of small actions off Heligoland and Dogger Bank. In the South Atlantic an ageing squadron was badly beaten by the Germans at the Battle of Coronel, though the RN took swift and sure revenge, destroying the Germans in turn in a subsequent fight off the Falklands. In home waters, it was thought likely that the High Seas Fleet would choose to operate in the North Sea rather than in the dangerous confines of the Channel. By 1916, the British naval blockade was starting to bite and, when the High Seas Fleet was given a new commander, the capable and aggressive Von Scheer, he immediately adopted a policy of actively seeking confrontation.

JUTLAND

Towards the end of April 1916, German warships provided provocation by shelling Lowestoft and Yarmouth. At the start of May, Von Hipper was at sea off Denmark with 40 capital ships. Scheer planned to win the coming showdown with the RN by harnessing the big guns of his battleships to the stalking capability of submarines – the German *Untersee* or U-boat. British Admiral Jellicoe, from Rosyth, ordered the inevitable riposte, and by 31 May both sides were squaring up for a major fight. For all that the RN had ruled the seas for over a century and still commanded a more powerful force than the High Seas Fleet, this would be a very different action from those fought in the days of sail. The British had not fought a major battle at sea since trouncing the Turks in Navarino Bay in 1827.[4] Scouting in the cold and wide expanses of the North Sea was undertaken by fast cruisers, the light horse of navies. By the time the position of the Germans was confirmed, Jellicoe had been reinforced by Beatty's battle squadron out of Scapa Flow. In terms of numbers, the British had the edge with an additional dozen big ships. From a distance of 10 miles – something that would have been inconceivable in

Nelson's day – the heavy guns began to boom. Battle had been joined.

In the opening salvoes, as Beatty's squadron closed with Hipper, the Germans established an initial ascendancy. *Indefatigable* and then *Queen Mary* were sunk, the former ripped apart by a magazine exploding. Hipper was joined by Scheer as the bulk of the High Seas Fleet pitched into the spreading battle. Before Jellicoe could come up, Beatty suffered further, grievous loss when *Invincible* went down. As the two fleets collided, Hipper veered north, a move Jellicoe interpreted as the precursor to a carefully laid ambush. Refusing to oblige, he instead made steam to the south in an attempt to drive between the Germans and their home bases. In the further fight which ensued, Hipper lost *Lutzow* with *Seydlitz* and *Derfflinger* crippled. The battle, as its last echoes receded across the grey waters, was, in tactical terms, something of a rather bloody draw, though the RN (14 ships and 6,000 lives lost) suffered more damage than the High Seas Fleet (9 ships and 2,500 dead). In strategic terms, however, Jutland must count as a win for the British. The High Seas Fleet scrambled back to port from whence it refused to budge. As a potential war winning arm, the German Navy was effectively corralled and impotent. But, if the battle of Jutland was over and the contest of battle fleets decided, the Battle of the Atlantic was far from won.

THE U-BOAT MENACE

Submarines had been in development during the nineteenth century, but the pace of innovation began to accelerate dramatically at the beginning of the twentieth, sufficient for the submarine to rate as a very significant weapon in the deadly arsenal of industrialised warfare. The invention of diesel-electric propulsion after 1895 and the use of the periscope were major steps. In June 1900, the French vessel *Narwal*, using steam and electric propulsion, also featured a double-hull design (which comprised a pressurised hull inside an outer, light carapace). *Narwal* weighed 200 tons and could cruise for 100 miles on the surface and for a tenth of that distance submerged. In 1914, Germany was to field a significant fleet of submarines – U-boats – essentially surface raiders, moving under engine propulsion, but submerging, reliant upon batteries, to deliver an attack with torpedoes. Silent, deadly and far ranging, these raiders were to become notorious with and feared by Allied merchant sailors.

As early as 6 August 1914, ten U-boats slipped out of pens in Heligoland, their targets, British warships in the North Sea. In fact, this first patrol came badly unstuck. One succumbed to mines, another, *U-15*, managed to fire a number of torpedoes but without effect and was finally rammed by HMS *Birmingham*, while a third was disabled by mechanical failure. On 5 September, however, *U-21* launched torpedoes against HMS *Pathfinder*, which went down with the loss of 259 lives. Worse was to follow. On 22 September, a trio of ageing RN Cruisers *Aboukir*, *Cressy* and *Hogue* were hammered by torpedoes from *U-9*, and all three foundered with the loss of 1,460 men. A mere three weeks later, *U-9* added HMS *Hawke* to the score. The U-boat had now fully arrived.

For the RN, these losses were a clear and unmistakable warning. Everywhere, including the vast lagoon of Scapa Flow was vulnerable. *U-9* was in reality a rather elderly and under-armed craft; what might the much newer, faster and better-armed boats achieve? Mines were another hazard, with two capital ships lost, including HMS *Audacious* sunk in the Irish Sea. Scapa Flow was temporarily evacuated. In October, the U-boats scored their first merchantman, though the sinking was accomplished without loss of life, the crew being permitted to take to the boats before torpedoes were launched. This gentlemanly conduct did not endure long. Presently the Admiralty was forced into the realisation that the submarine threat to Britain's economic lifeline was exceptionally potent. The blockade might strangle Germany, but the U-boats could bring the British Empire to its knees. The Atlantic was now the new battleground.

In recognition of the deadly conflict being waged, on 4 February 1915, the Kaiser declared British coastal waters to be included in the war zone. This was effectively a declaration that all Allied shipping could be attacked without warning. Gloves in the U-boat war were very definitively off. Possession of the Channel ports, particularly Ostend, had furnished the Germans with submarine bases that greatly facilitated their U-boat offensive. By August 1915, over 168,000 tonnes of shipping had been sunk. Fast destroyer escorts had helped to screen the larger, slower moving warships, though on 18 March 1915, HMS *Dreadnought* herself rammed and sank *U-29*. At this point in the fine balance of superiority between the surface ship and the submarine, the latter, while submerged, enjoyed a degree of invulnerability, though unrestricted sinkings added fuel to anti-German propaganda. This last received a major boost when, on 7 May 1915, *U-20* torpedoed the Cunarder *Lusitania* off Kinsale. The stricken liner, struck beneath the bridge, sank in just 18 minutes. This strike caused or led to a second, catastrophic blast from within, possibly as on-board munitions exploded. In the horror which ensued, nearly 1,200 people were killed, virtually all civilians, many children, and 128 of them US citizens. So loud was the outcry that, on 18 September, Wilhelm II abandoned the contentious policy of unrestricted attacks.[5]

Q-Ships

The Admiralty was obliged to find an effective response to the U-boat menace. This form of economic warfare was proving highly effective with these silent predators being free to strike undetected and at will. It was impossible to provide sufficient warships to patrol the coasts constantly, and even swift destroyers had a limited range of weapons and tactics to deploy. One possible remedy was to find a mongoose to take on the U-boat cobra, and the response was the 'Q' ship.[6] Quite simply, this was a trawler or small merchantman, ostensibly too puny to merit the cost of a torpedo, best dealt with by gunfire from the U-boats' deck-mounted weapons. But this target would not be as defenceless as it appeared. As the submarine surfaced and closed in for the kill, the victim would suddenly sprout an arsenal of its own and take the predator on in a surface gun duel, hunter thus becoming hunted. By the spring and then summer of 1915, a number of such vessels were in operation but without scoring any significant hits. However the armed collier *Prince Charles* was destined to do rather better.

Prince Charles was part of the vital collier fleet, which performed the necessary but unglamorous role of maintaining coal supplies to the fleet at anchor in Scapa Flow. Lieutenant Mark Wardlaw RN commanded a ten-man naval detachment on the small vessel, armed with a brace of concealed, small calibre guns. On the evening of 24 July 1915, one of those endless days in the Orcadian summer, *U-36* had stopped the Danish vessel *Louise* but decided the collier offered a more tempting prize. As the chase developed, the U-boat opened fire at extreme range with her deck guns. Wardlaw then responded by ordering the civilian crew to heave to and abandon ship as though in panic. *U-36* slid in to a range of 600 feet, confident of the kill. She was simply not ready when Wardlaw unmasked his two guns to commence a steady and accurate fire. This vital element of surprise proved crucial. The Germans were badly shot up and, as they attempted to dive, Warlaw's gunners finished the job, sending *U-36* to the bottom and taking 15 survivors prisoner.

This neat little action showed the worth of the Q-ship, and northern waters became a frequent hunting ground. These were, by definition, never proud men-of-war. In fact, the more down-at-heel the Q-ship appeared, the more likely she was to successfully tempt a U-boat into a surface attack. Occasionally, such a craft might carry torpedoes but more typically a number of smaller guns which could be easily hidden, along with machine guns and small arms. Deception was the key; naval crew had to blend perfectly into the less formal regime of a tramp merchantman. A U-boat would stalk her potential victim long before she surfaced, so the sailors had to look scruffy and unmilitary. This façade had to be maintained in port lest enemy agents be vigilant. Such men were in the mould of Drake and Raleigh. One could imagine Sir Andrew Wood or Cochrane fitting into such a role with gusto. The ship itself was an integral part of the ruse. She would be camouflaged and repainted lest her former lines become too familiar and thus suspect.

When a U-boat surfaced and rode in for the kill, deception reached its final theatrical denouement. A portion of the crew, equal in size to what might be expected of a merchant vessel of this class, would run around the decks, giving ample signs of incipient panic. After a decent interval, they would abandon ship with the captain or someone who looked like a captain, ostensibly clutching the tempting lure of her papers. This finely judged performance (as indeed it might be, as the sailors' lives depended on the reactions of the predator) was intended not only to maintain the deception but to draw the U-boat on, till the range had closed and the Q-ship's guns were suddenly unmasked.

Memories of the slaughter of *Lusitania*'s hapless passengers as a consequence of German action were still fresh, when the Q-ship *Baralong* steamed to the aid of another liner, *Nicosian*, attacked in the Channel by *U-27*. The German decided to punish the shabby tramp steamer for her impudence, but suddenly found herself under fire from the Q-ship's 12-pounders. Lt Commander Herbert, having crippled his opponent, showed no mercy to the desperate survivors. Numbers were shot in the water or as they sought to climb aboard the liner; total war was by no means a one-sided business. As pressure on Germany mounted, the attraction of unrestricted submarine warfare re-emerged as strategic doctrine; the U-boat fleet could put over 130 craft into the water, with technical capability being continuously enhanced.

Typically, a hunter type U-boat now had four tubes forward with two aft and either a pair of 86-mm, or a single 105-mm, deck-mounted guns. These formidable predators had, by the end of 1916, accounted for a staggering 443,000 tonnes of Allied merchantmen. Jellicoe cautioned that, with this rate of loss, Britain would be hard-pressed to maintain the war effort through the following year and on her knees by the summer. It was small wonder that Haig's plan for a summer offensive in Flanders included the notion of an amphibious assault on the U-boat pens located within the German-held Channel ports.[7] Sensing that the U-boats might yet achieve what German armies had not and break the will of the British Empire, Wilhelm II agreed to the resumption of totally unrestricted submarine warfare. Losses of allied merchantmen continued to spiral.

Beating the U-Boats

One response to the U-boat menace was the convoy system. This was a tried and tested expedient, but one which the Admiralty had, initially, resisted, fearing that to concentrate ships in large numbers would provide nothing more than a submarine feeding frenzy as the 'wolf packs' circled. It was not until May 1917 that a system was put in place, though convoy sailing was not obligatory for merchantmen. Losses, however, did begin to decline. The new system was complemented by the introduction and laying of improved mines and, critically, by a significant innovation, the D Pattern Mark III depth charge. These ungainly, underwater explosive devices, little more than a container filled with high explosive and set to detonate at a fixed depth, were used first in action during July 1916, though it wasn't until December of the following year that depth charges sank *UC-19*.

Improved means of launching projectiles and the hydrophone system of underwater detection, combined with maritime air patrols, began to turn the tide, to nibble at the U-boat's supremacy and finally chew it to pieces. In May 1918, some 16 U-boats were sunk. Operational life-expectancy of a submarine crew reduced to six weeks, leading to an even greater savagery on the part of U-boat commanders as time ran out. And time was indeed running out. On 22 October 1918, U-boats were ordered to refrain from further attacks on merchantmen, and it was German sailors who responded to Bolshevik calls for an armed revolution. When it was all over, time to count the cost: 5,000 Allied ships had been lost and with them 15,000 lives; the U-boat service had lost 178 craft and almost half its complement of 13,000 sailors. This First Battle of the Atlantic had been a very close run thing indeed.

CAPTAIN CAMPBELL

For all their swashbuckling, the Q-ships proved the least effective of the Allies' responses. Depth charges and hydrophones, linked to more and more effective mines, and the shepherding of the convoy system, combined to defeat the U-boats. Of the 180 Q-ships deployed, only 10 managed to destroy German submarines, 14 in all. One of the most successful captains was Gordon Campbell who, commanding *Farnborough* in March 1916, sank *U-68*. Then, just less than a year later, accounted for *U-83*, losing his ship in the process but winning a Victoria Cross. On 8 August 1917, he was master of *Dunraven*, a converted merchantman, which refined the Q-ship concept by carrying some minor but visible armament, her additional firepower concealed. On that summer's morning, she was engaged by *UC-71* and a rather desultory exchange of fire resulted in no damage or loss to either hunter or hunted.

When this opening exchange had spluttered on for half an hour or so, *UC-71* motored in for the kill. Her guns were now striking the superstructure, starting a fire in the poop-shack that threatened to spread to a small magazine. It was now 12.10 p.m. and the action had continued for nearly an hour. The 'panic crew' had already played their part, but one of the gun crews was horribly exposed if the magazine ignited. Nearly 50 minutes later the inevitable explosion occurred, wreaking carnage on the after decks and killing one of the gunners. Amazingly, the rest survived, though by no means unscathed. An injured lieutenant apologised to Campbell for leaving his post without orders! The captain had already issued instructions for his remaining guns to open fire, but the U-boat dived unscathed. She was still the hunter and the badly damaged *Dunraven* still the prey. A torpedo struck at 1.30 pm, blowing out a section of hull. The master ordered all but the remaining gunners to abandon ship, but the German commander, Leutnant Saltzwedel, was not disposed to take chances. Over an hour later, as the Q-ship was already settling, *UC-71* surfaced astern to conclude matters with gunfire. Campbell described the ensuing bombardment as extremely unpleasant – in the circumstances, something of an understatement!

Dunraven was wallowing, without sufficient power to turn and return fire upon her tormentor, who now dived once more and circled, like a hungry shark. Campbell promptly loosed two torpedoes of his own, but only one came close and that not close enough. *Dunraven* was clearly doomed. Campbell stayed aboard with only a single volunteer gun crew. But time was also running out for the Germans: *UC-71* could not afford to hang around indefinitely to finish the dying ship and most of her ammunition – shells and torpedoes – was now expended. She withdrew, and Campbell might at least claim the fight as a draw. A destroyer took the crippled *Dunraven* in tow; she eventually foundered, though without further loss of life. The lieutenant and petty officer who'd stuck to their gun even as the magazine smouldered beneath their feet each won a Victoria Cross. If the Q-ships were not a successful measure in terms of the strategy of the Battle for the Atlantic, this was no reflection of the extreme gallantry of their officers and crews.

SCAPA FLOW

Scapa Flow, Orkney is a lagoon-like stretch of water, a mere 24 km by 13 km, girded by the islands of Mainland, Graemsay, Burray, South Ronaldsay and Hoy. A superb natural anchorage, it has been a haven for battle fleets, certainly from the Viking epoch. Lyness on Hoy was the HQ for the British fleets that utilised Scapa Flow during the twentieth century and throughout the course of both world wars. Thus this desolate shelter has housed some of the mightiest assemblies of warships ever seen at a time when British naval power was both unprecedented and largely unrivalled. Slab-walled hulls and the vast, gleaming ordnance of dreadnoughts riding in the swell. It was from here that fleet ventured out to do battle with the Kaiser's navy at Jutland, and Scapa Flow remained the British navy's northern haven for the whole duration of the struggle. After an impudent U-boat penetrated the defences as early as November 1914,[8] over a score of blockships were sunk to act as a protective screen augmented with anti-submarine nets. During the following year, these measures were further improved with the laying of a cordon of minefields.

Despite being undefeated in battle, the German High Seas Fleet, by Article XXIII of the Armistice Agreement, was to be 'interned' – a total of some 74 vessels. This clause in the surrender called for the German ships to be sailed to an Allied or neutral port or ports. That Scapa Flow should be nominated implied a fate somewhat more certain than mere internment. It suggested that Britain had already decided upon the elimination of the High Seas Fleet as a matter of policy, clearing the oceans of its main and almost only rival. For both officers and crew, this represented an unbearable level of humiliation. Rear Admiral von Reuter, his flag on the battleship *Friedrich der Grosse*, took charge of the assembled warships, which comprised 11 battleships, 5 battlecruisers, 8 light cruisers with 50 destroyers. This fleet arrived off the Forth from Wilhelmhaven on the morning of the 21 November, a mere ten days after the Armistice. Admiral Beatty had assembled a vast armada of 250 British ships, lest the Germans be in any doubt as to who were the victors. At 3.57 p.m., the proud warships of the High Seas Fleet formally hauled down their colours and were duly inspected by the British. Within a week, all had been escorted to the cold haven of Scapa Flow.

Whatever the northern anchorage's attraction as a naval base, its amenities were never such as would excite generations of sailors. This was truly the ends of the earth. Kirkwall on Mainland was no Portsmouth, Valetta or Kiel, and, for the Germans, this cold northern harbour must have seemed the very epitome of Germany's shame. The Kaiser's mighty battle fleet was entombed within the cold and barren heart of the enemy's northern waters. As darkening autumn slid into winter, the crews were thinned to skeleton proportions, no more than 200 for a capital ship and barely a score per destroyer: a total of 250 officers and 4,565 ratings. It was not a posting to be relished, and indiscipline spread like contagion. Reuter, shifting his flag to *Emden*, did his best to maintain some form of order. By the time spring had crept over the northern rim and the long spring days had arrived, remaining crews totalled no more than 1,700 souls.

Orcadians had become used to the sight of Royal Navy ships crowding the islands, but never before had they witnessed such a concentration of naval power and might. For Reuter and his officers, the sight of his country's navy reduced to a tourist attraction for gawping islanders was intolerable. 'We were disarmed and dishonoured', he wrote, shamed and reduced, without ever having been bested in the fight. For a man of such punctilious honour, the notion that the British would simply acquire his ships was anathema. The only means of denying the victors their prize was to do themselves what the Royal Navy had failed to do in four years of conflict: send the entire fleet to the bottom!

No sailor can readily accept the notion of scuttling his own ship, destroying that which has defined him as a naval officer and which represents the very essence of his nation's pride and her greatest resource in war, now fully in his custodianship. Nonetheless, by the third week in June it was obvious the final negotiations that would lead to the Treaty of Versailles were stalling and British patience was running thin. To add to his frustrations, von Reuter's only source of intelligence was provided by back copies of the *Times* – at least four days old by the time they reached the distant north. On 21 June, the British, as he read, had issued an ultimatum; that his own government then gave way was something he could not immediately perceive.

That day – 21 June 1919 – was destined to be a day of epic high drama in the annals of Scottish waters. Most of the British ships had steamed out to participate in exercises, leaving the rusting German vessels riding in continued impotence. Von Reuter would have gazed out from *Emden*'s bridge, looked across at the serried pride of the Kaiser's empire, a sight he had decided he should never witness again. At 10.30 a.m. he gave the fateful order. This was not unexpected; watertight doors had already been removed to permit the onrush of engulfing waters once sea cocks were opened; bulkheads were stripped or weakened.

At 12.16 p.m. *Friedrich der Grosse*, Reuter's former flagship and the pride of the High Seas Fleet, slid below the grey waters. In a spectacle of Wagnerian finality, the *Götterdämmerung* was played out. Vessel after vessel went down, clouds of escaping steam and darkening palls of oil marking each separate demise. Some went straight down; others heeled over, borne by the weight of ordnance. Spilled oil and debris cluttered the anchorages as crews pulled for safety in the boats. Alerted to the unfolding drama by remaining destroyers *Vespa* and *Vega*, the Navy hastened to return, and by early afternoon British ships were fully engaged in desperate attempts at salvage.

Once a ship begins to sink in these circumstances, the only hope for salvage is to get a line aboard as quickly as possible then try and beach the stricken vessel before she goes under. Only four capital ships, including *Emden*, were successfully beached. The rest, with a final flourish of Teutonic efficiency, went to the bottom. All the crews got safely off, though, in the wrack and confusion, driven by frustration, the British shot dead nine German ratings – the last servicemen to die in the Great War. By 5.00 p.m. on that first day of summer 1919, as *Hindenburg* sank, it was all over. Germany's High Seas Fleet no longer existed. One of history's most powerful navies, born of a vast outpouring of the nation's treasure, the sum of her imperial pride, sunk in the very heart of the enemy but without a shot being fired. Some 400,000 tons of shipping went down, the largest loss on any single day in recorded history.

A youthful eyewitness, James Taylor, recorded his experience, conveying the compelling mix of tragedy and melodrama which unfolded before the awestruck passengers on the pleasure boat *Flying Kestrel* that Saturday morning:

> On Saturday June 21st 1919, I rose very early, as it would never do to be late for a school treat which was to take the form of a cruise on the 'Flying Kestrel' to visit the surrendered German Fleet. The thought of sailing up to them made us boys almost sick with excitement! At long last we came face to face with the Fleet. Their decks were lined with German sailors . . . who did not seem too pleased to see us. Suddenly without any warning and almost simultaneously these huge vessels began to list over to port or starboard; some heeled over and plunged headlong, their sterns lifted high out of the water. Out of the vents rushed steam and oil and air with a dreadful roaring hiss. And as we watched, awestruck and silent, the sea became littered for miles around with boats and hammocks, life belts and chests . . . and among it all hundreds of men struggling for their lives. As we drew away from this nightmare scene we watched the last great battleship slide down with keel upturned like some monstrous whale.

High drama was followed by entrepreneurial innovation. These wrecks represented a considerable investment in scrap metal, and salvage operations began in the early 1920s, continuing right through into the post Second World War era. As ever, tragedy and high drama offered a boost to modern tourism, and the scuttling has proved a long term boon for the island, exciting holidaymakers and diving enthusiasts alike.

A distant echo of this long and sanguinary battle was heard in 2006 when the wreck believed to be of a British submarine the *H-11* was located by divers, lying in deep water off Eyemouth.[9] The wreck is in good condition and lying on her port side with all the main features distinguishable. She was built in the USA and leased to Britain in 1917, sinking not as a result of enemy action but due to accident when her tow snapped as she was on her final voyage to the breaker's yard in 1920. A clear resonance of the bitter struggle now called the First Battle of the Atlantic. Titanic as this had been, an even more savage conflagration was to follow within a generation. The Great War was not after all 'the war to end all wars', merely the curtain-raiser for a yet more calamitous conflict.

———◆———

ELEVEN

Wolf Packs

The Battle of the Atlantic was the struggle between the Allied and Axis powers
for control of the sea routes between the Americas and Europe and Africa. It
began on the first day of the war in Europe in September 1939 and continued
until May 1945. It was the longest campaign of the Second World War, an
extremely bloody one, and the single battle on which the whole outcome of
the war depended . . .

War Museum of Canada

WHEN WAR BROKE OUT AGAIN in 1939, Great Britain was
quite simply not ready. The French, despite a huge
investment in fortresses and the seemingly invincible Maginot line,
were even less so. Germany had had six years to re-arm. Defeat in
1918 had forced her strategists to rethink offensive concepts and
'lightning war' or *Blitzkrieg* was the result. The Nazi war machine
firstly overran Poland, having gobbled up the truncated rump of
Czechoslovakia, then next proceeded to invade Norway, Denmark,
Holland and Belgium. Those men and women of the occupied
territories who refused to be ground beneath the jackboot began to
lay the foundations for resistance networks or escaped to join Allied
regular forces in Britain.

On 30/31 August 1939, three Polish warships survived the dash
to Leith, the beginnings of a fine bond between these brave Poles
and their adopted country. After Dunkirk, a further 17,000 Poles
joined the exodus. By the early months of 1942, the infant Polish
Independent Parachute Brigade and the 1st Polish Armoured
Division were forming and training in Scotland. As were others: on
1 May 1940, the first of a number of special forces' training areas

was established, and on 4 March the following year, commandos struck for the first time with a raid on the Lofoten Islands.[1] While not strategically significant, this pinprick so enraged Hitler that he strengthened the occupying garrison, thus committing more German troops to a purely reactive role. By the start of the following year, the legendary commando training centre at Achnacarry was established, and a mere half-dozen Norwegian special forces trainees, who'd learnt their skills at Aviemore, undertook the famous Telemark raid,[2] neutralising Nazi manufacture of heavy water on 20 February 1943. Two years later, as the Nazi tide was finally and inexorably rolled back, the liberation of Norway was, fittingly, planned in Scotland.

Scotland was very quickly in the war, *Royal Oak* was sunk with the loss of 800 hands on 14 October 1939, while at anchor in the seemingly impregnable haven of Scapa Flow.[3] A vast defensive undertaking, the Churchill barriers, was devised to make good the deficiencies with construction beginning in May 1940. Over 1,200 Italian POWs were used as labour. The battleship was not the first maritime casualty: SS *Athenia* out of the Clyde was torpedoed and lost with the lives of 93 passengers on 3 September, first of a long and dismal catalogue of such tragedies. It was on 1 July 1940 that the first of the Atlantic convoys also steamed from the Clyde and the level of marine activity invited the attentions of the Luftwaffe. They struck twice in 1941, on 13/14 March and again on 6 May, killing, in total, over 1,200 people. On 30 August, scars of the raids on Glasgow and Clydebank still smouldering, a very peculiar naval campaign mounted from the far north got underway: the very remarkable story of the 'Shetland Bus'.

THE SHETLAND BUS

In March 1943, Leif Larsen, master of the *Bergholm*, a trawler from Shetland, was undertaking a most dangerous mission against Hitler's *Festung Europa*. His vessel was bound for Traena in the Nordland delivering arms and equipment to resistance fighters based there. In all, Larsen and his crew were to make over 50 trips, missions fraught with risk from the fury of the elements and the vigilance of the Luftwaffe. This time luck ran out. They made their delivery of vital supplies safely but, motoring back towards Shetland, two cruising ME110s dived and strafed the boat mercilessly. Of the eight-man crew, six were hit, and one – a young lad named Nils Vika – died of his wounds. With the ship sinking, the survivors, mostly injured, took to the lifeboat and for four days rowed through harsh and unforgiving Atlantic waters. Mercifully, they were rescued off Alesund by a motor torpedo boat (MTB) from Shetland.

Larsen was already something of a legend. He'd escaped from occupied Norway in February 1941 in the fishing smack *Motig 1* and, after initial training, became a skipper on what was to become known as the 'Shetland Bus'. This was largely unsung but highly dangerous work, scratching at the flanks of Fortress Europe. Such brave men in small boats undertook a constant series of daring missions, contesting the worst of the elements and the fury of the Nazis. The German invasion and subsequent occupation of Norway in 1940 is chiefly remembered for the fiasco of attempted Allied intervention. Thousands of Norwegians, finding the yoke of Nazi tyranny intolerable, escaped in fishing craft and other small boats, many landing in Shetland. Those who remained, in many instances, formed the core of a nascent resistance movement. By summer the following year, a base had been established at Lunna on the north-east flank of Shetland mainland and civilian craft pressed into service as transports for supplies and agents being infiltrated into Norway. Thus the Shetlanders were in the forefront of a small but steady assault on Hitler's Europe.

Many of those who fled this grim oppression did so in conditions of extreme peril. Kare Iversen, a fisherman, who'd joined the Norwegian resistance in 1940, pressed his father's craft *Villa 1* a 13m-long fishing vessel into service when he and several companions, hunted by the Germans, sought refuge in Shetland. Their passage was eventful:

The first two days passed in perfect weather conditions. But at 3.10 on our third day trouble arrived. I was coming out of the engine room when I saw through the wheelhouse door that a German flying boat was coming straight for us. At the time two of us were down in the engine room, two in the forward cabin. After the first burst of gunfire, I went out on deck and released all the halyards to let the sails drop to the deck, then we went back down to the engine room. The Germans continued shooting at us for twenty minutes. Their gunfire riddled the wheelhouse and holed the boat just above the water line with their shelling. Whenever we rolled, a big rush of water now came into the hold. The flying boat tried to land but the sea was too rough, so they gave up the attempt.

After a fraught passage in high seas, his vessel damaged by Axis gunfire, Kare reached Shetland, anchoring at Sandwick. After initial debriefing, he trained with fellow Norwegian exiles and then returned to Lunna where he sailed with Leif Larsen on *Arthur, Feie, Siglaos* and *Heland*. In December 1943, after many adventures, he became part of the crew of MTB *Hessa* and served until the end of the war, though he found time to court and marry local girl, Cissie Slater.

Lunna was a reasonable beginning, but the place lacked adequate facilities, so, by 1942, efforts were switched to Scalloway where a local concern, William Moore and Sons, acted as engineers and repairers to the growing fleet of small boats. This was the very stuff of derring-do, a channel for the frustrated exiles, with local assistance to strike back at the occupier. It was not undertaken without cost; *Sjo, Aksel, Feioy, Bergholm* and *Brattholm* were all lost with the lives of over 30 men. As unit strength was never more than double that number, such losses were dismal indeed. When it was suggested that this was unacceptable and that the sailors could be more effectively employed in a conventional naval role, they simply replied 'Give us better boats and we will continue the fight.' This proved a turning point; the Shetland Bus service was re-equipped with three fast US motor launches: *Hitra, Hessa* and *Vigra*. These sleek craft were built entirely for war, 100 feet in length and powered by twin 1,200 hp General Motors engines. Cruising at 17 knots with a further five in reserve at full throttle and bristling with machine guns, they could give a good account of themselves against marauding Messerschmitts. From November 1943, these replaced the ad hoc conversions to carry out many further operations. None was lost, nor did the crews sustain any fatal casualties.

CLOSING THE BACK DOOR

Shetland had been in the front line since November 1939 when half a dozen Heinkels came in low over Lerwick, aiming to attack vessels in the harbour. Eight bombs were dropped to no effect, but strafing attacks wrecked a flying boat, though all the crew were rescued by a brace of haddock boats. Happily, three trawlers each heavily loaded with marine munitions, in this case depth charges – *Northern Foam*, *Northern Isles* and *Northern Princess* – were spared. Once Norway fell, there was a looming possibility that Shetland could form the target beachhead for an invasion of Britain. As a result, a large garrison – at its height, some 20,000 strong – was drafted in, and hutted camps sprang up by Scalloway, Sumburgh and Sullom Voe. Sandbagged anti-aircraft (AA) batteries were positioned around Lerwick, and new airstrips were levelled at Sumburgh and Scatsta. Sullom Voe also played host to a squadron of flying boats. Shetland became a militarised frontier with access strictly controlled, locals acting as Home Guard. During the war years, Scotland became an embattled landscape; over 28,000 pillboxes, 414 roadblocks and 296 coastal battery positions were constructed, making it the most heavily defended part of Britain.

ANDREW CUNNINGHAM

One of Scotland's more distinguished sons who served in both world wars was Andrew Browne Cunningham (later Admiral of the Fleet Lord Cunningham of Hyndehope). Like many famous sailors, he came from clerical stock and first joined the RN as a cadet in 1897. He gained experience in commanding destroyers and served with considerable distinction throughout the First World War as captain of HMS *Scorpion*. By 1936 he had risen to vice admiral, his flag briefly featuring on the ill-fated HMS *Hood*.[4] When war came in 1939, he held the position of C-in-C Mediterranean, based primarily at Alexandria. His task was an unenviable one and obfuscated by frequent interference from Churchill in London. In spite of this pernicious intermeddling and the considerable superiority of Axis forces, particularly in aircraft, he inflicted several major defeats upon the Italians both in the sea battle off Cape Matapan[5] and the subsequent daring attack on Taranto.[6]

Like General Archibald Wavell, C-in-C Middle East, he entertained grave doubts over the wisdom of the Allied intervention in Greece, which, as feared, proved a costly debacle. The situation was only prevented from becoming total catastrophe by the timely intervention of Cunningham's ships. Actions off Crete in late May 1941 were to illustrate how completely the dominance of the airborne arm had changed the nature of war at sea. Ships, like infantry on land, could not function without adequate air cover. Often the bombs struck before the bomber was seen: 'The fleet AA could only fire barrages into the sun [and] hope for hits . . . In some cases of major damage or sinking the air attack had been of such intensity and duration . . . that the vessels were out of ammunition long before the bombing ceased.'

A German aviator, hungry for victory, described the exhilaration of the chase and that moment when he moved in for an attempted kill:

I had the vessel [in my bombsight] . . . From bows to stern she filled the circle, and then with decreasing distance she seemed to grow fast . . . this was a cruiser and now I saw two more of them in line ahead. This was something I had never seen before . . . My cruiser . . . shot at mew with every gun barrel and her speed was so fast that she forced me to flatten my dive . . . I pushed the button immediately turning to starboard and the bombs dropped. I was now within easy reach of the light guns and the tracers . . . were everywhere . . . I would have given a fortune for more speed to get out of the range of those gunners. All of a sudden there were cascades of water coming up my way. They shot at me with heavy artillery planting water trees right in my course . . . I began to dance . . . 'The AA Waltz', turn and turn upwards and downwards . . . It was not fun, however. I felt that there were professionals firing at me . . . This was my first encounter with British cruisers, and I am still alive, still flying . . . home to Eleusis. The bombs had hit the wake.

If the attempt to seize Crete by aerial envelopment represented a significant tactical innovation, the concurrent battle at sea would see a major air force take on a dominant battle fleet in a savage and sustained fight, ships utterly unprotected from the air other than by the weight of their own AA barrage. The experience would, for the British Navy, be both chastening and costly. By May 1941, Admiral Cunningham's ships carried an onerous burden, or series of burdens, shadowing the more numerous Italians, shielding Malta, blockading Libya, supplying the outlying bastion of Tobruk and, most recently, shipping the army to and rescuing it from Greece, all at a time when the RAF was least able to provide supporting air cover. Before the battle for Crete began, Cunningham was noting that his ships and crews were worn out; vessels needed servicing and refit; men needed rest from the constant strain of action. Ammunition, particularly for the AA guns, was running at dangerously low levels.

During the course of the forced evacuation of the army from the small ports and beaches of the Peloponnese, the strain had increased significantly and 22 ships had been lost. None of these went down in ship-to-ship engagements. All were sunk by marauding German bombers or dive bombers, and it was clear that the main danger came from the skies. Italian ships, rarely sighted, now declined to engage and the Axis had no fleet other than theirs available, but the Luftwaffe more than compensated for the deficiency. The cardinal lesson learnt from the Greek fiasco was that naval operations could now only proceed safely under the cover of darkness. To be exposed at sea in daylight hours was to court disaster.

Despite the great burden he carried, Andrew Cunningham fought a highly successful naval campaign in the Eastern Mediterranean at a time when Britain's fortunes were at dangerously low ebb. He was, in every way, a worthy addition to the proud pantheon of Scottish admirals. On land, some 20,000 Scots were to take part in the D-Day landings. By the end of the war, the nation would have cause to mourn 58,000 of her sons and daughters.

SECOND BATTLE OF THE ATLANTIC

Running in tandem with the great land battles was the grinding attrition of the Battle of the Atlantic, the second to be waged in the twentieth century. Like that of 1914–1918, it pitted German U-boats and surface raiders against Allied merchant shipping and their naval escorts. It was difficult, dangerous and unendingly grim. Final Allied victory, as in the previous war, was won at huge cost. Scotland, by virtue of its strategic location, was, once again, in the front line throughout. Germany had, in terms of its naval arm, been rendered impotent by the crushing terms of the Treaty of Versailles in 1919. She had only begun rebuilding her surface fleet in the late 1930s during the run-up to war. U-boats offered a cheaper alternative. Though Germany could still not hope, in 1939, to match the Royal Navy in terms of warships, she could use her U-boats to effect victory by destroying the shipping which provided Britain's lifeline.[7] To keep in the war, Britain needed to import something of the order of 1 million tons of supplies per week. This enormous total included foodstuffs and materials. The Battle of the Atlantic was a *Materielschlacht*.[8] U-boats had to sink ships faster than the Allies could build them. Latterly, they sought to interdict supplies for the vast build-up necessary to mount a Second Front, the invasion of Europe.

THE TECHNOLOGICAL CONTEST

In terms of interwar technical developments, these related primarily to the vital field of communications, now encrypted by the Enigma cipher machine.[9] This significant innovation heralded the adoption of new tactics. No longer would the U-boats stalk their prey in the classic mould of the hunter and the hunted; they would now hunt in packs, appropriately named 'wolf packs' (*Rudeltaktik*). The battle to be won would stretch over a very broad canvas, thousands of miles of barren, unforgiving ocean, from the frozen, wind-lashed coasts of Scandinavia to and beyond the Arctic Circle to the South Atlantic. Over a hundred convoy battles would be fought and ten times that number of single ship encounters. On the outcome hung the success or failure of the war effort; had Britain lost then the war too would have been lost. The cost to both sides would be very high indeed. Some 3,500 ships with a gross tonnage of 14.5 million went down; 175 warships were sunk, over 30,000 sailors died. Germany lost 783 U-boats and 28,000 crewmen.

Despite the signal successes of German U-boats during the First Battle of the Atlantic, the Royal Navy had not paid particular attention to the threat since 1919. The Treaty of Versailles, by outlawing unrestricted submarine warfare, appeared to have marginalised the threat. That Germany would repudiate these restrictions on submarine warfare had not raised any alarm bells, with the dire consequence that British naval tactical doctrine had not evolved accordingly. Submarines were regarded initially as the rather poor relations of surface raiders. The main counter-measure until 1939 was nothing more than inshore patrol craft equipped with hydrophones and depth charges.

As the concept of radar detection was to prove crucial to air battles, the technology of ASDIC (possibly for British Anti-Submarine Detection Investigation Committee) had a similar impact on anti-submarine warfare. ASDIC was an extension of the hydrophone system developed during the earlier war, featuring a transducer fitted into a dome-like pod located on the underside of a surface ship's hull. This sent out a beam of sound in a series of pulses to a maximum range of around 3,000 yards. The resultant sound echo would produce an image of any submerged object. It was far from foolproof: temperature variations, currents and even concentrations of fish and marine life could confuse. Highly trained operators were thus essential, and detection was only possible at relatively slow speeds, (15 knots or less), else the sound of the vessel's passage through the water excluded the echoes. Nonetheless, this had the potential to prove a very effective tool for the hunter-killer.[10]

A prevailing weakness, during the pre-war period, was that U-boats could dive both deeper and faster than their British counterparts; below the effective range for depth charges. Furthermore, the operator did not have a 'view' directly beneath the surface ship, so he would lose contact with the target in the vital stages of the hunt. Pre-war strategic thinking, straitjacketed by budgetary restrictions, chose to regard Asdic as the entire and perfect solution. Necessary parallel investment in long-distance destroyer escorts, sufficient to provide security for convoys, was lacking. The dire economic circumstances affecting Britain during the hungry 1930s had produced swingeing defence cuts. The great days of Empire were already sinking into the haze of memory, and the straitened circumstances facing the armed forces had eroded capabilities. Matters declined to such an extent that mutiny over proposed pay cuts had erupted at

Invergordon in September 1931.[11]

When war came, the Royal Navy was primarily concerned with the likely effectiveness of German surface raiders, though in 1939 an ageing and outgunned squadron encompassed the ruin of *Graf Spee* at the conclusion of the Battle of the River Plate. Any respite was short-lived. On 5 November 1940, Convoy HX-84 was set upon by pocket battleship *Admiral Scheer* with the loss of five vessels. In February 1941, *Admiral Hipper* sank 7 out of 19 ships making up Convoy SLS-64. One month earlier, a formidable pairing of *Scharnhorst* and *Gneisenau* had been unleashed. It was only the Germans' odd reluctance to try conclusions with often hopelessly outdated or outgunned escorts that saved a number of convoys. In May 1941, the most potent threat of all arose from the cruise of *Bismarck* and *Prinz Eugen*. This time, thanks to good intelligence, the Royal Navy was able to intercept them, but the ensuing Battle of the Denmark Strait was a disaster. HMS *Hood* was destroyed by an explosion and sank with the loss of virtually all hands. Massive retribution followed, and *Bismarck*, at the conclusion of an epic chase, was hunted to extinction. For Germany, the loss of this great capital ship seemed to take the heart from the surface raiders, which for Britain was providential. Though the raiders had sunk relatively few ships, disruption of the war effort had been extensive. The battlecruisers had also engaged British warships in a singularly one-sided encounter.

LOSS OF HMS GLORIOUS
In northern waters *Scharnhorst* and *Gneisenau* had, on 8 June 1940, attacked the aircraft carrier HMS *Glorious* with her escorting destroyers *Ardent* and *Acasta*. This proved, for the British, a disastrous engagement, distinguished by the extreme gallantry of the destroyers and the cardinal folly of leaving a carrier so hopelessly exposed. *Glorious* had been taking part in Operation Alphabet, the evacuation of Norway and, early on the 8th, had requested and been granted permission to proceed directly to Scapa Flow, accompanied only by two shadowing destroyers. The flotilla sliced through the waters at 22 knots, slowing only to adopt the zigzag pattern designed to confuse lurking wolf packs. None of the carrier's aircraft was

prepared for take-off. None of the ships possessed radar, and lookouts do not appear to have been posted. First sightings of a potential enemy occurred at around 4.00 p.m. The German ships, instantly alert, increased their speed to 30 knots. *Scharnhorst* was the slightly slower of the two as she was experiencing some trouble with her boilers.

Just after 4.30 p.m. the German warships found their range and opened fire on *Glorious*. Pressing her attack with cool daring, *Ardent* surged forwards loosing torpedoes. Her puny 4.7-inch guns could not match the range and hitting power of the German batteries, which fired on her from 16,000 yards. Both destroyers made smoke, which brought some respite to their precious charge, but *Ardent* paid a fearful price for her audacity and sank just before 5.30 p.m. *Scharnhorst* had also scored a hit on *Glorious*: one heavy shell bursting through the flight deck, starting fires below. Secondary damage to her boilers caused the ship to lose speed. Any respite provided by smoke was short-lived. At 5.20 p.m. she was hit again, and one shell found the bridge, killing her captain and other key personnel. Next the engine room was wrecked, and she began to slow dramatically. *Acasta* now made her own suicidal run against *Scharnhorst*, her torpedoes inflicting not inconsiderable damage as did her gunnery. The end, however, was never really in doubt. Valiant *Acasta* was crippled by the battlecruisers' secondary armament and sank around 6.20 p.m. Perhaps ten minutes before she went down, *Glorious* too slid beneath the waves. There were very few survivors.

If the menace posed by the German surface raiders proved to be of relatively and indeed mercifully short duration, that created by the U-boats was both sustained and terrible. As early as 22 January 1940, the destroyer *Exmouth* was torpedoed by *U-22* off Wick and lost with all hands. On 16 March, Scapa Flow was bombed, receiving a second visit on 2 April. Churchill, who in 1939 was acting as First Lord of the Admiralty, typically favoured an energetic and aggressive response to the U-boats, consisting of the deployment of anti-submarine hunting groups, but the fox these hunters sought would always sight the hounds first and slip beneath the waves. Carrier-based aircraft, though ideal for observation, did not, at this stage, possess adequate weaponry to engage. *Ark Royal* only narrowly missed becoming the quarry when *U-39* launched three torpedoes. Happily these proved defective. Those of *U-29* did not, and the carrier *Courageous* was sunk on 17 September 1939. Providentially for the Allies, Germany's standard magnetic torpedo was deficient, prone to exploding prematurely, and, as a result, many British ships escaped damage during the Norwegian fiasco.

WINNING THE BATTLE

This Second Battle for the Atlantic was to rage for the entire duration of the war, but can be divided into several distinct phases. The first of these – June 1940 to February 1941 – has been dubbed the 'Happy' time; happy that is for the wolf packs. With France out of the war and Britain's naval commitments considerably extended, the U-boats also gained the inestimable advantage of being able to operate from French bases, Brest, Lorient, La Pallice and St Nazaire.[12] The British were reduced to mendacity and begging obsolete 'lease-lend' destroyers from the US, while U-boats and their 'ace' commanders enjoyed halcyon cruising. Between June and October 1940 the Allies lost over 270 merchantmen. Hunting in packs and with British naval codes broken, the predators struck again and again. On 21 September, Convoy HX-72, comprising a flock of 42 vessels, lost 11 to U-boat attack. Next month, Convoy SC-7 fared worse, nearly two-thirds being sunk. Despite the best efforts of escorting warships in every case, British technologies and tactics were found sadly wanting. At this desperate time in the war, Britain appeared at imminent risk of being starved into submission.

In the spring of 1941, with more destroyers available and the formation of permanent escort groups, the odds began to shorten. Introduction of 'Flower' Class corvettes, a British-designed vessel, also contributed considerably to the fight back, as did the emergence and expansion of the Royal Canadian Navy, which operated many of its own corvettes. Although the Flower Class was by no means ideal for convoy escort, not particularly fast, rather short in length for the open seas and under-gunned, they were cheap and easy to build, a necessary expedient in a very dark hour. Latterly, they were superseded by the improved 'Castle' Class and then almost completely by frigates. Vice Admiral G.O. Stephenson was placed in command of a new escort base and training facility located at Tobermory on Mull. Typically, the escort groups would comprise a pair of destroyers and handful of corvettes. Their deployment rapidly demonstrated some headline successes. Three of the leading German aces found this out to their cost: *U-47*, *U-99* and *U-100* were all accounted for. A major breakthrough came on 9 May 1941, when HMS *Bulldog* succeeded in recovering an intact naval Enigma machine from *U-110*. This astonishing coup facilitated the cracking of Enigma by the resident geniuses at Bletchley Park, a major step in the march to Allied victory. Breaking Enigma had a pronounced effect upon the grim struggle being waged in the Atlantic. Germany never realised her seemingly invincible security had been breached. Even after the war, Admiral Dönitz refused to accept this unpalatable truth.

Both sides were striving to expand their respective technologies. New and improved craft began to swell wolf packs, the Type VIIC. To counter this, the Allies, increasingly assisted by the US, even though the defining attack on Pearl Harbor had not taken place, were experimenting with on-board catapults. The idea was to hurtle a fighter into the air, very much a one-shot weapon as the plane had to ditch. High-Frequency Direction-Finding (HF/DF or 'Huff-Duff') enabled operators to home in on the direction of a radio broadcast. U-boats needed to surface in order to transmit and, when two or more escort vessels were present, they could obtain an accurate 'fix' on the submarine's position. Final entry of the USA into the war in December 1941 added a new dimension to the struggle, prompting Dönitz to mount an offensive against shipping along the eastern seaboard. US Admiral King, a noted Anglophobe, disdained advice from the Admiralty and thus handed wolf packs a golden opportunity, one upon which they were not slow to capitalise. In just six months, some 2 million tons of shipping was lost.

From the middle of 1942, after the Americans had reluctantly instituted a convoy system, the main action shifted back towards the North Atlantic, wolf packs again dogging Allied convoys. U-boats were numerous and active, striking in waves, battering beleaguered convoys with repeated and costly blows. Admiral Horton, newly appointed as C-in-C Western Approaches, devised a strategy for countering this renewed threat. He created independent battle groups that could range unfettered by escort duty and hunt down the U-boats without being tied to a primary responsibility for merchantmen under their care. In attacking their prey, hunter-killers now had a new and formidable weapon in their expanding arsenal, the 'Hedgehog'. This was a mortar-like device which hurled a salvo of two dozen contact-fused projectiles ahead of the attacking warship, rather than, as before, sowing a line of depth charges behind. Such improved technology increased the kill ratio in contacts from 7 per cent to 25 per cent.

Aircraft effectiveness was also greatly enhanced by the introduction of the Leigh light, a powerful beam aligned in sync with the plane's radar to illuminate the target U-boat for the attack run. Hitherto, German commanders had thought themselves largely safe at night, but centimetric radar could not be detected and the first a U-boat would know of its peril was when it was suddenly lit up by the Leigh light. Reaction time was only a matter of mere seconds before aircraft released depth charges. Faced with the challenge of these new technologies, U-boat kills began a steep decline. But, by August 1942, wolf packs were receiving Metox radar detectors, which enabled the boats to pick up signals from older types of radar, particularly those sets still used by US and Canadian escorts.

Despite these technical advances, which greatly aided the Allies, spring 1943 was to witness a terrible apogee of the wolf packs' offensive when convoys took a most fearful hammering. In March 1943 alone, some 260,000 tonnes of shipping was lost to U-boats, which swarmed the vast reaches of the North Atlantic like schools of hungry sharks, devouring all in their path. For Britain, a pervasive smell of defeat hung in the air. Dönitz and his wolf packs were winning. Though it was very likely far from obvious to the combatants, the battle for Convoy ONS-5 has been considered a turning point. This convoy comprised a slow-moving flock of 43 merchantmen guarded by a modest escort of two destroyers, a frigate and a handful of corvettes. Battle dragged on through the last days of April, and a swarm of 30 U-boats circled the laden ships, striking at will. In the running, ragged and desperate fight, U-boats claimed 13 kills, but lost 6 of their number in the taking. Exhausted Allied survivors, hunted by the wolves and battered by a ferocious storm, would count themselves lucky to reach safe haven, but, for the wolf packs, Convoy ONS-5 marked the beginning of an end.

A number of factors combined to swing the final balance in the Allies' favour. The advent of long-range planes, such as the B-24 Liberator, closed gaps in available air-cover. Even better, sea-scanning centimetric radar could be fitted into the aircraft. This negated the value of the Germans' Metox gear. Merchant aircraft carriers (MAC) were being introduced, flying US Grumman Wildcats. Success with North African landings (Operation 'Torch') released numbers of escort ships. Frigates were proving a most effective compromise between destroyers and the cheaply built but otherwise very limited corvettes. This provided not only more and better escorts but more aggressive hunter-killer squadrons. A more effective Allied response added enhanced value to Ultra decrypts. With the USA now harnessing its vast industrial base and producing merchantmen, including the crude but robust 'Liberty' class ships, new vessels were going into the water at a faster rate than the wolf packs could hope to destroy them. Thus the Allies were winning not just sea fights, but the battle of logistics. For the U-boats, their glory days were over. It was they who were now the hunted. Losses spiralled as kills plummeted. It was defeat.

Even in decline, the Kriegsmarine remained formidable and, despite the mounting odds, continued to fight. U-boat crews displayed outstanding bravery and dedication, their losses among the highest for any branch of German or Allied service. Submarines were up-gunned to provide better AA cover, given improved radar for beneath the immediate surface. Torpedo design also kept pace. The German Navy Acoustic Torpedo ('GNAT') could home in on propeller noise. Yet the ingenious Canadians had, within days of this type being deployed, invented a simple and effective counter-measure – a motley of scrap iron and pipes towed behind, like 'chaff' from a modern jet fighter, which confused the torpedo. Declining German morale, as hammer blows resounded against Fortress Europe and the Fatherland itself, delivered from both east and west, was cheered by the hope that new and secret weapons might yet tip the balance. One such concept was the Type XXI *Elektroboot*. This had a top speed underwater of 17 knots, fast enough to outrun most of the hunters above, but, fortuitously, the new variant could not be built in sufficient numbers to affect the outcome.

Scotland, as a maritime nation, remained in the forefront, build-ing ships, manning them and fighting in them. One incident, which typifies many in the Battle for the North Atlantic occurred on 27 December 1942, when the 7,000-tonne tanker *Scottish Heather* was sailing as part of Convoy ONS-154 – 45 merchantmen and their escorts with an average speed of only 8 knots. *Scottish Heather*, classed for the purposes of the operation as an oiler was tasked to refuel escorts at sea. Winter weather in the North Atlantic that season was ferocious, even by local standards, one of the harshest winters on record. In the small hours of 27 December, U-boats began to bite. Soon four ships were torpedoed and sunk by *U-356* before the escorts accounted for her with depth charges. In the short, cold glare of the winter's afternoon, *Scottish Heather* was attacked by *U-225* as she wallowed some 15 miles behind the flock, but the fire from her deck-mounted gun was sufficient to cause the raider to break contact.

When the tanker received a signal from one of the corvettes, *Chilliwack*, she abandoned her cautious but slow zigzag motion and steamed towards the escort, which swiftly came up. Undeterred, Kapitan Leimkuhler remained patient, a true hunter stalking his prey. A chance came when the corvette was masked by the bulk of the tanker and he loosed a torpedo, which struck home with deadly effect, blasting a great rent in the oiler's side. It was 8.40 p.m. and, though *Chilliwack* gave chase, *U-225* showed a clean pair of heels. The stricken ship now began to list, and an order to abandon ship was given. Survivors took to the boats. For them, the prospect of being adrift in an open boat in the chilling wind of the North Atlantic was dire. The second mate did, however, succeed in re-boarding the ship, which had not gone down, and managed to bring her under power. With a skeleton crew, he set about combing the dark waters for his friends and managed to rescue them all. The badly damaged ship somehow staggered back to harbour. In the course of the next few days, however, 15 ships were sunk with 1,077 sailors on board. Of these, just rather more than half were rescued. The Second Battle of the Atlantic, like the first, ended in an Allied victory, but it was victory achieved only at the conclusion of what must have seemed a never-ending battle against a ferocious and determined foe, fought out in the harshest and most merciless of conditions.

———◆———

Cold Warriors: The Nuclear Age

Peace is but a cessation of hostilities in a war that is never-ending.

Thucydides

Why does the establishment of the Scottish parliament and Executive have implications for the UK nuclear deterrent? The main reason is that the UK nuclear force has been entirely located in Scotland since 1998, when free-fall nuclear bombs previously deployed by the Royal Air Force were scrapped. The four Vanguard submarines with their Trident missiles, which operate out of the complex of rivers, estuaries and sea lochs known as the Firth of Clyde, then became the only UK nuclear delivery system.

Malcolm Chalmers and William Walker, 'The United Kingdom, Nuclear Weapons and the Scottish Question'

'WARSHIPS WILL BE ATTACKED BY "terrorists" on water scooters as they move up the Clyde': a chilling scenario, though it comes with the reassuring rider 'in a major exercise'. 'Neptune Warrior' or NW063[1] ran from 23 October to 2 November 2006 as a perceived response to the growing threat of terrorist action resulting from British involvement in Iraq. It was an altogether massive affair involving 4,000 service personnel drawn from 11 countries, including: UK, USA, Germany, Greece, Turkey, Italy, Norway, Belgium, Canada, France and Denmark. A squadron of five capital ships, four destroyers, eight frigates, seven mine hunters and three submarines was deployed. The declared objective was to permit the participating countries to test systems and response times. Eleven helicopters and fifty aircraft were also engaged. Scottish Greens were outraged. They objected to the live firing off Cape Wrath and the spread of action which encompassed much of the west coast, Argyll, Sutherland and the Clyde. Stornoway Airport was the principal helicopter base and would be subjected to mock air attack. Civilian vessels would be hailed and boarded. Training in amphibious operations would be conducted at Loch Eriboll and Durness.

In the half century following the end of the Second World War, Scotland's coast was regarded as a potential front line in the Cold War.[2] This was the war that never was, a state of tension between two ideologically opposed superpowers. One as potent and threatening as any that had ever been seen in history before, where weapons of such fearful portent were ranged from east to west and vice versa. It was a war that was contained not by moral responsibility, but by the certainty of 'Mutually Assured Destruction' (MAD). The consequences of an all-out war between the major powers were the inevitable destruction of both. So the conflict was played out in a myriad of vicarious wars: Korea, Vietnam, in Africa and the Middle East. As that threat diminished, the risk of terrorist attack increased. The events of September 11 in New York, the ill-judged invasion of Iraq in 2003 and the London bombings of July 2005 raised the constant spectre of a long and deadly struggle with a largely invisible but fanatical foe.

An early manifestation of the Cold War was a form of early warning system or 'ROTOR', and this resulted in the construction of a chain of radar stations studding the entire east coast of mainland Britain.[3] Where the threat was perceived to be greatest, these were placed underground and that at Troywood in Fife (1951)[4] is the largest survivor, now restored and open as a museum. These bunkers were massive affairs. An initial excavation was sunk to a depth of 150 feet (45m), and a bed or lining of aggregate was topped by a reinforced concrete structure, some 10 feet (3m) thick, the reinforcement in the form of 1-inch (25mm) tungsten steel rods. An outer skin or casing of brick was revetted with netting soaked in pitch. Spoil from the excavation was used to form a mound, laced with additional concrete blocks, to provide 'burster caps'. From the surface, the landscape remained innocuous, a typical Fife farm steading.

Despite this enormous outlay in sweat, ingenuity and taxpayers' cash, the site was run down in the late 1950s but enjoyed a new lease of life after 1958 when it was re-designated as a civil defence bunker, suitable for use as a Regional Seat of Government (RGS). This new role endured for a decade till the wind-down of Civil Defence, when it was again re-designated and refitted as the Central Government HQ for Scotland in the event of a nuclear conflict (RGHQ). Preparing the site as an emergency location for the Scottish administration necessitated a considerable rebuild, and the place was due to be refurbished again in 1992 but the demise of the perceived threat from the Soviet bloc overtook the rebuilding and it was officially mothballed in 1993. On 1 April 1994 it opened again, this time not as a top secret establishment but as a major visitor attraction.

The North Atlantic Treaty Organisation (NATO) came formally into being on 4 April 1949 as a planned response to perceived Russian aggression. In reality, the confrontation had begun when Allied and Russian forces joined hands on the Elbe in May 1945. No sooner was the Second World War over than the foundations and battle lines of the next were being laid down. The Soviet riposte came on 14 May 1955 with the formation of the Warsaw Pact, with Northern Germany being viewed as the likely battleground. Both sides, at the outset, believed an armed confrontation was inevitable, and this dark shadow of doomsday hung over the world for nearly two generations. Sea power was expressed not only by surface fleets but in the form, sinister and deadly, of the nuclear-powered and nuclear-armed submarine, carrying its frightful payload of submarine-launched ballistic missiles (SLBMs). Britain had entered the first rank of nuclear powers, albeit as a poor relation and with the deterrent initially focusing on a force of medium-range 'V' bombers. A shift to sea power came during the 1960s and thrust Scotland even further into the front line.

Organised and large-scale anti-war movements are, as far as we may surmise, a peculiarly twentieth-century phenomenon, beginning with groups such as the Peace Pledge Union (PPU) after the Great War. The nuclear threat, awesome in its destructive potency, produced a reaction in the form of the Campaign for Nuclear

Disarmament (CND), which after 1958 quickly established an autonomous organisation in Scotland. The overall situation is further clouded by the emergence of the Scottish Nationalist movement and its increasing electoral success.

As Professors Chalmers and Walker point out in their paper of 2002, 'The United Kingdom, Nuclear Weapons and the Scottish Question', establishment of a separate political authority in Scotland creates a raft of complications over any potential deployment of nuclear weapons. With the concentration of the UK nuclear arsenal in the four Vanguard class submarines based on the Clyde, Scotland houses the most deadly naval force in the British deployment, one of the most powerful in the world. This is essentially a book about battles and encounters at sea in Scottish waters. The Cold War produced no such engagements. It was not that the possibility was lacking but the consequences were very likely so dire. Battles during the Cold War were shadow fights, they never assumed the mantle of deadly earnest, for which we must all be thankful.

From now on, the management of Trident assumes a changed character. Overall, the UK nuclear deterrent and its deployment remain solely the responsibility of central government, though a considerable amount of multi-agency working is involved. The Scottish National Party (SNP) is committed to the removal of nuclear weapons from Scottish soil. As a result of the May 2007 local government elections in Scotland, the SNP emerged as the largest single party, overtaking Labour. Questions therefore arise as to the continuance of the present policy and operational deployment should a fully devolved form of government come into being.

Scotland first assumed this front-line role in the relatively early days of the Cold War. In the 1960s, the USA, as the leading partner in NATO, was seeking bases from which missiles, launched from Polaris submarines, could hit targets in the Soviet Bloc. Holy Loch in the Clyde met all of the (then) current operational requirements: 'a sheltered anchorage with access to deep water and situated near a transatlantic airfield and a centre of population in which the American service personnel and their families could be absorbed'. At the same time, Britain was trying to adapt to the post-imperial age with decreased resources and international 'clout'. Attempts at producing a domestic nuclear deterrent ('Blue Streak') had foundered in expensive ignominy. In 1962, Prime Minister Harold Macmillan bowed to the realities of post-war power structures and bought in Polaris from the Americans. From February 1963, in the grip of a singularly bitter winter, one of the worst to affect Britain in the twentieth century, and thus perhaps an appropriate clime in which to consider the implications of nuclear war, a working group was established. The brief was to examine a range of sites and produce an options appraisal scored against fixed criteria.

Of these, the key determinants were identified as operational suitability, safety and, as ever, cost. Approaches would have to be easily navigable and with adequate space for the extensive establishment required. The Royal Naval Armament Depot (RNAD) had to be a minimum of 4,400 feet distant from the other installations and possessed of its own berthing facilities. Conversely, these sites all needed to be reasonably proximate to maximise efficiencies of servicing, rearming and maintenance. In due course the group recommended a shortlist of only ten sites throughout the UK, of which six were located in Scotland: Loch Ryan, Gare Loch, Loch Alsh, Fort William, Invergordon and Rosyth. The final choice lay between Rosyth in the east on the Forth or Faslane on Gare Loch. The latter became the favoured choice, with nearby Coulport nominated as an RNAD site. When Polaris docked at Faslane for the first time in 1968, this became the UK first major naval harbour to be established since Rosyth itself became operational nearly six decades before. The four Polaris submarines were HMS *Resolution, Repulse, Renown* and *Revenge*, all of which were based at Faslane. Twelve years after Polaris, the decision was taken to replace this ageing system with firstly Trident C4 and then C5. Even though the devolution debate was very much alive at this point, removal of nuclear weapons always a key tenet of SNP policy, the further extension of Faslane and Coulport went ahead regardless.

The Faslane/Coulport complex, with ancillary facilities, now forms the whole of Her Majesty's Naval Base (HMNB) Clyde. Faslane is located on the Gare Loch some 25 miles from Glasgow, and its sister site RNAD Coulport is sited on Loch Long, some 8 miles distant. The base at Faslane existed prior to the Cold War, established during the Second World War, and forms the home base for Vanguard Class nuclear-powered and nuclear-armed submarines. These are not the sole complement, being joined by conventionally armed nuclear-powered submarines, together with a Royal Marines detachment, a number of senior naval postings, all served by 3,000 personnel and a further 4,000 civilian workers. Given the long-standing opposition from peace groups to the UK nuclear deterrent, Faslane, like Greenham Common, became a focus for protesters and a 'Peace Camp' has sprawled untidily outside since 1982. The 'Big Blockade' has become, since 1999, an annual event, a firm fixture in the peace activists' calendar, attracting several thousands every year. The aim is to cause a blockade and closure of the base for a period of 24 hours.

RNAD Coulport on Loch Long acts as the arsenal for Faslane, housing both nuclear and conventional weapons systems. Storage bunkers are dug into the ridge line above the base, and it is within these that the nuclear warheads (British) are fitted to the body of the Trident missiles (US manufacture – Lockheed Martin). In terms of ownership, these missiles do not belong to the Royal Navy. Rather the Navy has a licence to draw from a pool of those available, usually fewer than 60, which is shared with the Americans. The actual missiles are not serviced and maintained on site. This work is undertaken in the USA at the US Navy base in Kings Bay, Georgia. At present, the Ministry of Defence (MoD) is reviewing the future of the three main UK naval establishments, (the other two are HMNB Devonport and HMNB Portsmouth) and while, at the time of writing, no firm decisions have been taken it does not appear likely that the axe will fall on HMNB Clyde.

When, in the 1950s, nuclear power began to replace diesel-electric propulsion in submarines, a new age in naval warfare dawned. This development, allied to other technology which permitted the extraction of oxygen from seawater, enabled the submarine to remain under water for weeks or months. Epic voyages, such as the passage of USS *Nautilus* beneath the ice sheet of the North Pole in 1958, left the realms of science fiction. Only the organic limitations of human crew remain a barrier: the need for resupply and submariners' morale. During the fraught decades of the Cold War, Britain, the USA and the USSR developed a major strategic role for their undersea fleets. While no battles were fought and weapons systems, providentially, were never used in earnest, losses did occur. At least four Russian vessels were lost at sea (*K-129*, *K-8*, *K-219* and *Komsomolets*) and others were damaged by on-board blazes or radiation leaks. Two US submarines, *Thresher* and *Scorpion*, also went down. When HMS *Conqueror* launched a conventional torpedo attack on the Argentine cruiser *General Belgrano* in the early stages of the Falklands War in 1982, she became the only nuclear-powered submarine to sink an enemy vessel in time of war. Scottish MP Tam Dalyell has been fatuously vociferous in condemning the action ever since.

Organisations such as the Celtic League have blamed NATO submarines for the sinking, through unreported collisions, of a number of fishing vessels, including the MFV *Mhairi L*, a scallop trawler out of Kirkcudbright on the coast of Galloway, lost in 1985 with all hands. The League, an inter-Celtic organisation which lobbies for the various rights of Celtic nations, avers that 'in the period between 1979–1989 there were scores of accidents at sea caused by NATO and Warsaw Pact submarines, with a significant number of such incidents occurring within British coastal waters'. This is the conspiracy-theorists' heaven, which is not to say it's necessarily fanciful. Any collision with a nuclear submarine would be fatal to a small fishing vessel. What is sure is that when, in November 1970, a blaze broke out on board the submarine tender USS *Canopus* in Holy Loch, the stricken vessel was carrying several 'nukes' and a brace of nuclear-armed submarines was moored in close proximity. It took four hours to bring the fire under control, and three lives were lost. On 8 November 2002, the *Daily Telegraph* reported that HMS *Trafalgar* had struck rocks off Skye. No serious damage or casualties resulted, but the spectre of the 'near-miss' always shouts louder when the vessel concerned is a nuclear submarine!

Faslane, as mentioned, is home to four Vanguard class nuclear-powered, nuclear-armed (SSBN) submarines: HMS *Vanguard*, *Victorious*, *Vigilant* and *Vengeance*. At the same time, it also accommodates 'Swiftsure' class, nuclear-powered, conventionally armed (SSN) craft, of which only HMS *Sceptre* remains. In the future, it is likely that Faslane will be home to three 'Astute' class SSN vessels, and the facilities currently also maintain the 1st Mine Countermeasure (MCM) Squadron. Prior to its decommissioning in 2005, the Northern Ireland Squadron (shades of the Ulster Patrol) was also based there. The extensive port facilities include a floating jetty and a large ship-lift, engineering workshops, an internal electricity generating plant and capacity for six Trident crews. In the 1990s, the RN experimented with a two-crew rota, reduced to a single, enlarged complement in 1998 (a measure since put aside and the dual crew pattern reinstated).

HMS *Vanguard* first carried fully armed nuclear weapons, 16 Trident D5 types, after the US missiles were fitted with warheads at RNAD Coulport in December 1994. When, as mentioned, she'd first sailed into Scottish waters in October 1992, she received a less than rapturous welcome from a motley flotilla of seaborne protesters. Vanguard class is fitted with pump-jet propulsors rather than conventional propellers. Despite these being heavier, more expensive and generally less efficient, they run more silently, a tactical consideration which outweighs design disadvantages.

> Scotland is usually seen as being a peripheral country, stuck out on the north-west fringes of Europe. To the military planners things look rather different. Scotland sits in a commanding position overlooking the vast expanses of the north-east Atlantic. It lies on the shortest routes by air, sea and telecommunications from the USA to Europe, and it has large expanses of sparsely populated terrain suitable for military training.[5]

'Ownership' of the nuclear deterrent was clearly a thorny matter in the negotiations over devolution and in the drafting of the Scotland Act of 1998. The statute clearly and unequivocally reserves matters of defence to the UK government, including, inter alia, 'the naval military or air forces of the Crown including reserve forces'. To reinforce this continuing monopoly, the Scottish Assembly conceded the UK government's right to exercise a veto and prevent putative legislation from the devolved assembly becoming law if 'it has reasonable grounds to believe [*that it*] would be incompatible with any international obligations or the interests of defence or national security'. This ring-fencing of the nuclear bases thus appears watertight but, in terms of day-to-day working of relationships between the MoD and the Assembly together with the relevant local authorities, the situation is more complex. Matters such as planning, health and safety, the environment, highways, disaster planning, etc. are taken care of at local level.[6]

At present, this web of relationships is covered by a memorandum of understanding, the Defence Concordat. How the present balance would be tilted should Scotland seek and attain full autonomy is unclear. The SNP, likely to be the majority party in a fully devolved government, is, as we have seen, committed to an anti-nuclear policy, and the continuing existence of Faslane would become an anathema. It is difficult, nigh on impossible, to look into the future on such difficult and complex issues. Nonetheless, the view put forward by Professors Chalmers and Walker seems to be an entirely reasonable one:

> It seems quite likely – some would say highly probable – that the UK government will operate Trident out of Faslane and Coulport until the end of its operational life, or until it decides to dispense with it, without being seriously disturbed by the 'Scottish Question'.

For five decades, Scotland remained part of the front line of NATO defences. Some 200-odd installations dotted the map, radar stations, training camps, ranges, airfields, defence bunkers and large-scale air and naval bases. The Cold War came at a time when Scotland was suffering from a pervasive decline of her traditional manufacturing, mining and industrial base, and the extent to which investment in defence either alleviated or deepened this decline remains open to debate. The everyday lives of Scots living in proximity to such installations were clearly affected. The writer, as a boy, was frequently offered a stark reminder of the perils of what are now fashionably termed 'weapons of mass destruction' (WMD), when the family motored past Gruinard Island by Laide on the west coast,[7] a grim legacy of wartime experiments with deadly anthrax.

With the collapse of the Soviet Bloc in the 1990s, it seemed that the nuclear threat, Armageddon as promised by the underlying threat of Cold War, immediately retreated into history. None, at that time, could necessarily have foreseen the events which occurred in New York on 11 September 2001 – '9/11'. With the destruction of the Twin Towers and the monstrous loss of life, a vision of almost biblical fury, which immediately assumed iconic status, our whole perception of the nature and direction of the current threat veered dramatically. These fears were found to be fully justified when London suffered attack on 7 July 2005. Such random acts of terror delivered against urban targets by small groups of fanatics and fundamentalists create an entirely new raft of defence consid-erations. Inevitably, they also pose questions as to the vulnerability of large, sprawling installations such as Faslane, precisely the scenario envisaged for exercise Neptune Warrior. The notion that suicide bombers might strike at HMNB Clyde, using fast inflatables, was based upon a real incident which occurred in Morocco when a trio of suspected terrorists were arrested, accused of planning such an attack on British and US vessels.

We have never believed that the terrorism threat is confined to London – this affects the entire country and everyone should be aware of that.

Charles Clarke, former Home Secretary
(as reported in The Scotsman, 21 September 2005)

The article quoted above notes that Scotland is firmly on the security map. Intelligence interest is apparently focused on cities such as Glasgow, with its large Asian population, and other centres such as Dundee University, identified by the Brunei Centre for Intelligence and Security Studies as one where fundamentalist groups are notably active in recruiting. How and where future terrorist threats will emerge within the UK, or from without, remains a matter of speculation, but there is nothing which rules out the possibility of a seaborne threat. In late spring 2002, a newspaper reporter was able to gain access to Rosyth Naval Base (as reported in *Scotland on Sunday*, 16 June 2002), using only a false ID and an out-of-date parking permit! A further fear arose in that UK targets could be subjected to attacks using 'dirty' bombs and that components for such a device would possibly be smuggled in by sea. Britain, as an island, and Scotland, either as an independent state or remaining part of the whole, will always be vulnerable to attack from the sea. The current position is not an ending, merely a pause.

The story continues.

Glossary

Balinger: A large double-ended oared boat, used in the medieval era as a fighting vessel

Barque: A vessel with three or more masts, the foremast square-rigged and the others rigged fore and aft

Beam: A vessel's width on the beam at right angles to the fore and aft line

Bearing: The compass direction for a place or object

Birlinn: A general name for the West Highland Galley

Boom: This can mean an obstruction rigged over a harbour entrance to obstruct entry by hostile ships or the spar forming the lower edge of a sail

Bowsprit: The timber spar which projects forward from the bows of a sailing vessel

Brig: Two-masted square-rigged vessel

Brigantine: Two-master with the foremast square-rigged, the main rigged fore and aft (front to rear or prow to stern)

Carrack: The European round-ship, developed by the Portuguese and also northern European mariners

Carvel-built: A vessel constructed with fitted, flush planking

Clinker-built: Where the ship's planking is constructed in an overlapping manner

Cog: The medieval round-ship, flat-bottomed; essentially a merchantman, she would be converted for war with the building of 'castles' for and aft

Con: To steer a vessel

Creach: Gaelic term describing a raid or foray

Currach: A skin and wicker boat, intended as seagoing

Destroyer: A fast and highly manoeuvrable warship capable of long voyages

Dreadnought: A large heavily armoured battleship of the early twentieth century, carrying a very heavy armament of large calibre guns

Freeboard: The height from the lowest point of the gunwale admidships to the waterline

Frigate: A smaller fast, warship of the age of sail and later, smaller than a ship of the line; see 'rates' below

Galleass: A type of sailing galley which also carried a broadside, guns mounted above or below the oars

Galley: General descriptive term for a large oared vessel

Galleon: A large, multi-decked sailing ship used for both commerce and war; see chapter 7

Gunwale: Additional wooden planking affixed to the sides of the ship and positioned above the top row of planks

Longship: A clinker-built oared galley, developed in Scandinavia and fitted with a single, square sail,

Lugger: A ship or vessel with a rectangular sail hoisted on a yard (this is a beam slung from the mast to hang the sail)

Nyvaig: A Gaelic term used to describe a smaller oared galley

Privateer: One who sails under a commission or a letter of marque from the national government that authorises him to prey upon enemy vessels in time of war; this is private enterprise as naval action, the line between legitimate privateering and outright piracy can be somewhat thin

Rates: These may be defined as follows:

    1st-rate: 180 feet long, 900 crew, 100+ guns, 2,500 tons

      2nd-rate: 170 feet, 750 crew, 90+ guns, 2,000 tons

      3rd-rate: 160 feet, 600 crew, 64+ guns, 1,700 tons

      4th-rate: 150 feet, 350 crew, 50 guns, 1,100 tons

      5th-rate: 130 feet, 250 crew, 32+ guns, 800 tons

      6th-rate: 120 feet, 160+ crew, 20+ guns, 600 tons

Rutter: A pilot book used for navigation in the Middle Ages

Schooner. Two-master with fore and main masts, rigged fore and aft

Ship of the Line. A battleship of the Age of Sail; one that formed line of battle prior to and during a fleet engagement, categorised according to the rates (above)

Trireme. Classical galley of Greece and Rome; see chapter 2

U-Boat (Untersee Boot): German submarine of both world wars

Notes

ONE   *Introduction: A Thundering of Waves*

1. For a fuller consideration of the career of Sawney Bean, see R. Holmes, *The Legend of Sawney Bean.*
2. Compton Mackenzie's novel *Whisky Galore* was published in 1947 and an Ealing comedy of the same name released in 1949, both now classics of the genre.
3. Wilfrid Wilson Gibson's famous ballad 'Flannan Isle' was published in 1912; for an objective examination of the evidence, see C. Nicholson *Rock Lighthouses of Britain; the End of an Era.*
4. For a fuller background discussion, see D.J. Sadler, *Clan Donald's Greatest Defeat: the Battle of Harlaw 1411.*
5. As mentioned, traces of the sixteenth-century fort are visible, and the restored eighteenth-century 'Smuggler's' house, Gunsgreen amply repays a visit.
6. The Imperial War Museum in Edinburgh Castle (formerly the United Services Museum) retains some excellent uniform and equipment.
7. Kisimul Castle on Barra, stronghold of Macneil, was restored by a US descendant, Robert Lister Macneil, beginning in 1937 and largely complete by the date of his death in 1970. The fortress was leased to Historic Scotland in 2001.
8. See S. Kirsty, 'Battlelines drawn at British Submarine base: Local workers defy protestors over Trident's role in theatre of war' (*Guardian* 23 October 2001).

TWO   *Kingdom by the Sea*

1. For a fuller discussion on this fascinating subject, see L. Casson, *Ships and Seamanship in the Ancient World* and 'Age of the Trireme', a special issue of *Ancient Warfare* 2(3) (June/July 2008).
2. Visit http://www.nydam.nu/eng/nydambog.

3. In addition to Tacitus himself and the secondary sources, there is a very good overview of Roman Scotland to be found at http://www.romanscotland.org.uk.
4. For a fuller description of this early phase of Dalriadic history, refer to Sadler, *Clan Donald's Greatest Defeat*. The whole area including nearby Kilmartin contains a treasure trove of early historical traces, set in an enchanting landscape.
5. See P. Wagner, *Pictish Warrior AD 297–841*.
6. See C. Cessford, 'Pictish Art and the Sea'.
7. See also J. Bannerman, 'The Lordship of the Isles'.

THREE *Scotia: Coming of the Longships*
1. See M. Lynch, *Scotland: A New History* for a fuller picture of early Scottish society.
2. Details of the battle and the era are to be found in the classic primary sources, the *Anglo-Saxon Chronicle*, William of Malmesbury, Snorri Sturluson's *Egil's Saga* and, as a major secondary source, the *Oxford History of England*, Vol. 2.
3. See P. Sawyer, *The Oxford Illustrated History of the Vikings*.
4. See I. Heath and A. McBride, *The Vikings*.
5. G. Griffith, *The Viking Art of War*.
6. A commanded party is a force assigned to a particular mission. The term implies a group of chosen men rather than a particular size or composition.
7. Onund's exploits are set down in the anonymous early fourteenth century Icelandic work, *The Saga of Grettir the Strong*, trans. G.H. Hight (London, 1914).
8. See *The Orkneyinga Saga: The History of the Earls of Orkney*, trans. H. Palson (London, 1978).
9. For a fuller description, refer to the invaluable guide for such craft: D. Rixson, *The West Highland Galley*.
10. See G.M. Gathorne-Hardy, *King Sverre of Norway*.

FOUR *Lord of the Isles: The Hebridean Galley*
1. For greater detail, see R.A. MacDonald, *The Kingdom of the Isles: Scotland's Western Seaboard 1100 to c.1336*.
2. Refer to D. Rixson, *The West Highland Galley*.
3. See 'The Death and Burial of Somerled of Argyll', *West Highland Notes and Queries* (1991).
4. See E. Linklater, 'The Battle of Largs' *Orkney Miscellany* 5 (1973).
5. See C. McNamee, *The Wars of the Bruces: Scotland, England and Ireland* and P. Traquair, *Freedom's Sword: Scotland's Wars of Independence*.
6. See Sadler, *Clan Donald's Greatest Defeat*.

7. See J.P. MacLean, *A History of the Clan MacLean from its First Settlement at Duart Castle in the Isle of Mull to the Present etc* (Cambridge, 1889).

FIVE   *For Freedom: Ships and the Wars of Independence*

1. For a fuller discussion see Traquair, *Freedom's Sword,* and McNamee, *The Wars of the Bruces,* also D.J. Sadler, *Border Fury: England and Scotland at War 1296–1568.*
2. See Sadler, *Border Fury,* chapter 4.
3. Inverlochy Castle still stands just north of the main settlement of Fort William, rather indifferently signposted and located in a somewhat run-down industrial area. Nonetheless, the shell remains as a very fine example of its type and repays the effort of seeking it out.
4. Comyn was assassinated on consecrated ground, which led to Bruce's excommunication. The dispute between the former allies is said to have arisen from a suspicion that Comyn had betrayed Bruce's intentions to the king.
5. Bruce was to swiftly become a master in the dire art of economic warfare. His campaigns and raids into northern England after Bannockburn were aimed at inflicting maximum economic loss.
6. See Sadler, *Border Fury,* chapter 4.
7. See E.H.H. Archibald, *The Wooden Fighting Ship in the Royal Navy AD 897 – 1860.*
8. James II had a fascination for artillery and by cruel irony died when one of his own pieces exploded while firing a salute to the queen during the siege of English-held Roxburgh.
9. Quite how the Red Douglas earned his epithet of 'Bell-the-Cat' is unsure, but, following the fall of Black Douglas, the Douglas earls of Angus came to the fore, and it was he who led the pogrom of James's low-born favourites at Lauder.
10. Edward IV had sent this formidable train north to cow those Lancastrian garrisons then holding the key border fortresses of Alnwick, Bamburgh and Dunstanburgh.
11. Pitscottie placed the location of James's death at Milltown near Bannockburn; though it may be he died on the field.
12. See D.J. Sadler, *Scottish Battles* (Edinburgh, 1996), chapter 6.
13. Ibid.

SIX   *The Old Scots Navy*

1. For a fuller account of James's path to Flodden, see N. Barr, *Flodden,* or D.J. Sadler, *Flodden 1513.*
2. See Archibald, *The Wooden Fighting Ship in the Royal Navy.*
3. See Raleigh's report, *A Report of the truth concerning the last sea-fight of the Revenge* originally published in 1591 (New York, 1902).

4. The Age of Forays was synonymous with internecine violence as the influence of the Lordship disappeared and royal rule through surrogates proved a poor substitute.

5. Mingary Castle also survives in a most dramatic coastal location by Ardnamurchan, though, at the time of this writer's last visit in 2010, in a rather parlous state.

6. For James's policy towards the Highlands, see N. Macdougall, *James IV*, chapter 7.

7. For James's obsession with Scotland's navy, see Macdougall, *James IV*, chapter 9.

8. See C. Falls, *Elizabeth's Irish Wars*.

9. See A. Chambers, *Ireland's Pirate Queen: the True Story of Grace O'Malley*.

SEVEN   *Letters of Reprisal: The Privateers*

1. The French equivalent was a *Lettre de Course* from which the term 'corsair' derives; the custom was finally abolished by the terms of the Treaty of Paris 1856, which brought the Crimean War to an end.

2. The Scottish High Court of Admiralty was abolished by the Court of Sessions Act of 1830.

3. The Dutch Wars came about firstly as a consequence of the revival of more cordial Anglo-Spanish relations in the early seventeenth century and secondly as rivalry between England, whose naval power dipped during the Civil Wars, and the Dutch whose commercial, maritime interests grew exponentially, developed over the course of that century.

4. See, Archibald, *The Wooden Fighting Ship in the Royal Navy*.

5. The French War of 1627–1629 was part of the wider struggle of the Thirty Years War (1618–1648) and centred upon a series of minor naval engagements and the siege of the great Huguenot redoubt of La Rochelle, immortalised by Dumas in *The Three Musketeers*.

6. A 'flyboat' (from the Dutch *vlieboot*) was a form of shallow draught carrack, two- or three-masted with a high board and capable of mounting a dozen guns.

7. The Treaty of Breda, entered into by England, the United Provinces and France, was little more than a ceasefire as many of the major differences between the parties were not reconciled.

8. The Pentland Rising ended in a skirmish at Rullion Green where the king's forces were led by the formidable if somewhat eccentric Tam Dalyell who had made a fortune in the Russian service and was reputed by his enemies to have sold his soul to the devil.

9. The Killing Time marked the persecution of the more extreme Presbyterian sects by government forces under John Graham of Claverhouse, later Viscount Dundee, another who was said to be

shotproof as a consequence of his diabolical bargain. His enemies like Dalyell's might have confused this with their own poor marksmanship!

10. See J. Prebble, *The Darien Disaster.*

11. S. Meneke, 'Gow, John', in the *Oxford Dictionary of National Biography,* Vol. 23, pp. 92–3.

12. The term 'buccaneer' derives from the Arawak word 'buccan' referring to a wooden frame for curing meat, used by French hunters or *boucaniers*; the term has become synonymous with pirate but referred originally to larger, well-armed forces who preyed upon mainland targets.

13. See R.C. Ritchie, *Captain Kidd and the War Against the Pirates.*

EIGHT   *Ships of the White Cockade*

1. There were more Jacobite disturbances; Claverhouse had led the clans to a posthumous victory at Killiecrankie in 1689, another of history's 'what-ifs'.

2. The Tory clans were those identified with the Stuart cause, an affiliation that only really dated back to the mid seventeenth century, during the Civil Wars and after. The Whig clans were typified by the Campbells who had pursued their own agenda of aggrandisement resisted by Clan Donald.

3. See Archibald, *The Wooden Fighting Ship in the Royal Navy.*

4. Much has been written upon the military events; see S. Reid, *1745: A Military History of the Last Jacobite Rising.*

5. For a detailed, readable and fascinating account of maritime events for this period, see J.S. Gibson, *Ships of the '45.*

6. Cumberland proved no match for the master of war Maurice de Saxe, and the Allied army from England, Holland, Hanover and Austria suffered upwards of 12,000 casualties.

7. 'Raking' occurs when one warship successfully manoeuvres so as to deliver its broadside against the stern of its opponent, the shot thus crashing down the length of the enemy gun deck creating a ghastly shambles and dismounting guns.

8. There is an excellent model of the *Du Teillay* in the National Trust for Scotland Visitor Centre at Glenfinnan adjacent the monument.

9. MacGregor was in fact in the pay of the Hanoverians.

10. Another spy, Dudley Bradstreet, was instrumental in persuading the Jacobite officers at Derby that their path towards London was blocked by strong forces, far stronger than were then in position, though the decision to retreat was still the correct one.

11. 'Hangman' Hawley has the reputation of a brutal martinet; he was certainly far from young in 1745 as his commission dates from half a century before, though he may have been misjudged, affecting a

rather grim and earthy gallows humour.

12. Captain Fergusson's ruthless harrying is graphically described in John Prebble's classic account of Culloden and its aftermath.

13. The legend of Bonnie Prince Charlie as the romantic lead in a Disneyfied version of the 1745, engendered by the nineteenth-century romantic revival, spearheaded by Scott and which has sustained Scottish tourism since, bears only a passing likeness to the altogether grimmer historical reality.

NINE   *Band of Brothers*

1. The New Town of Edinburgh was built between 1765 and 1850, a neoclassical masterpiece designated, together with the Old Town, as a UNESCO World Heritage Site in 1995.

2. See, Archibald, *The Wooden Fighting Ship in the Royal Navy.*

3. The battle was fought on 20 November 1759 off St Nazaire in the turbulent Bay of Biscay; six French ships-of-the-line were lost and one taken for the cost of two British capital ships severely damaged.

4. The Carron Gun Works on the banks of the River Carron by Falkirk was officially begun in 1759 and remained a major European iron foundry for 223 years till it finally went into liquidation in 1982.

5. See, Mackay, J., *I Have Not Yet Begun to Fight: A Life of John Paul Jones.*

6. Spoken by Admiral Jervis in 1801; Napoleon had likened the Anglo-French conflict to a battle between 'the Elephant and the Whale'.

7. The ill-starred Walcheren Expedition was a failed attempt to open a second front in Europe to relieve pressure upon Austria. Britain in fact committed more troops than later served in the successful Peninsular Campaigns. Of the 4,000-odd casualties only just over 100 were caused by enemy fire, the rest by hunger and disease.

8. The Battle of Corunna, fought on 16 January 1809, saw the battered British forces saved from annihilation but at the cost of their commander's life.

9. The French defeat left Napoleon's expeditionary force bottled up in Egypt and contributed to their further defeat during the Siege of Acre.

10. The episode features in the first of the Aubrey novels by Patrick O'Brien: *Master and Commander.*

11. The great Japanese victory of Tsushima was won between 27 and 28 May 1905 – the 'Trafalgar of the East'; the Japanese ships had mainly been built in Britain.

TEN   *First Battle of the Atlantic*

1. See Archibald, *The Wooden Fighting Ship in the Royal Navy.*

2. John Arbuthnot 'Jackie' Fisher, 1st Baron Fisher of Kilverstone (1841–1920), famous for his influential reforms and widely regarded

as second only to Nelson.

3. The naval arms race engendered by the Kaiser's hubris proved fatal to Germany's best interests, diverting resources from the army which might otherwise have ensured a swift victory in 1914.

4. The battle fought on 20 October 1827 was an action between an Anglo, French and Russian fleet against that of the Ottomans and Egyptians, resulting in the destruction of the latter with the loss of over 4,000 sailors. The fight was an episode in the Greek War of Independence.

5. The sinking was carried out by Kapitanleutnant Schwieger commanding *U-20*.

6. Q-ships were so called as their home port was Queenstown in Ireland, though they were also known as Q boats, decoy vessels, special service ships and mystery ships. The Germans referred to them as *U-Boot-Fallen* (traps).

7. This notion was part of the package Haig offered to ensure cabinet support for the Third Battle of Ypres, an ill-judged attempt at breakthrough in Flanders which sank into the dismal mud and petered out in November when the scarcely visible remains of the village of Paschendaele were finally taken by the Canadians.

8. In addition to the blockships, indicator nets were also employed to trap enemy submarines.

9. See the *Edinburgh Evening News*, 19 July 2006.

ELEVEN   *Wolf Packs*

1. Operation 'Claymore', the commando raid on the Lofoten Islands, took place on 3–4 March 1941 and while the attackers did destroy installations and resources it was primarily a much needed morale booster. Some 314 Norwegian volunteers were brought back along with 225 German and 60 Quisling prisoners.

2. The Telemark raid, a series of SOE/Norwegian sabotage attacks on the Vemork Power Station by the Rjuken Waterfall in Telemark, have collectively been described as the most successful raid(s) of the war.

3. The *Royal Oak* was sunk by Gunther Prien commanding *U-47* on 13 October 1939; 833 lives were lost.

4. *Hood* was a First World War battlecruiser which had seen two decades of service. Pride of the Royal Navy, she was outmatched by *Bismarck*. Of the 1,418 crew, only three survived the sinking.

5. The Battle of Cape Matapan fought over 27–28 March 1941 was a decisive Allied victory with heavy losses inflicted upon the Italians and hugely disproportionate casualties; three RN killed and over 2,300 Italians.

6. The Battle of Taranto, 11–12 November, was an all aircraft attack

which inflicted severe damage upon the Italian warships in the port for the loss of two men dead and two captured. One battleship was sunk and two others severely damaged.

7. Hitler had, in fact, to a considerable degree neglected the U-boat arm during the pre-war build-up. Had the fleet been even more potent, the consequences for the Allies would have been catastrophic.

8. *Materielschlacht* = a battle of attrition.

9. The Enigma machine was an electro-mechanical rotor machine designed for the encryption and decryption of messages. For the full, remarkable story of the cracking of Enigma, see P. Calvorcessi, *Top Secret: Ultra.*

10. ASDIC: see W.D. Hackmann, *Seek and Strike, Sonar, Anti-Submarine Warfare and the Royal Navy.*

11. The Invergordon Mutiny of 15–16 September 1931 when some 1,000 sailors took industrial action was one of the very few such instances in British military and naval history.

12. The U-boat pens at St Nazaire were the target of Operation 'Chariot', launched on 28 March 1942 during which no fewer than five VCs were won – consequently dubbed, 'the Greatest Raid of All'.

TWELVE   *Cold Warriors: The Nuclear Age*

1. Some useful further information may be found at http://www.rnopsscotland.com.

2. The Cold War, 1945–1991, has been defined (Random House, 2009) as a continuing state of political conflict, military tension, and economic competition between the Soviet Union together with its satellites and the democratic countries of Western Europe.

3. ROTOR was a post-war UK response to the perceived threat from Russian bombers and was largely based around war era radar stations, see http://www.thetimemachine.co.uk.

4. Visit http://www.secretbunker.co.uk.

5. See M. Spaven, *Fortress Scotland: a Guide to the Military Presence.*

6. See B.P. Jamison (ed.), *Scotland and the Cold War.*

7. *Eilean Ghruinneard* is a small island more or less midway between Gairloch and Ullapool, only 2km by 1km in size. It was judged suitable by Portland Down as a site for experiments in biological warfare from 1942 when a virulent strain of anthrax bacilli (Vollum 14578) was introduced, even with the knowledge that contamination could ensue indefinitely. As a result of some stirring by eco-terrorists in 1981, serious decontamination got underway in 1986.

Bibliography

Archibald, E.H.H., *The Wooden Fighting Ship in the Royal Navy AD 897–1860* (London, 1968).

Armstrong, R. and Osborne, B.D. (eds), *Echoes of the Sea: An Anthology* (Edinburgh, 1998).

Baird, R., *Shipwrecks of the West Coast of Scotland* (Glasgow, 1995).

Balfour-Melville, E.W.M., *James I King of Scots 1406–1437* (Aberdeen, 1936).

Bannerman, J., 'The Lordship of the Isles' in *Scottish Society in the Fifteenth Century*, ed. J.M. Brown (London, 1977), pp. 209–40.

Barr, N., *Flodden* (London, 2000).

Barrow, G.W.S., *Robert Bruce* (Edinburgh, 1965).

——, *The Kingdom of Scots* (Edinburgh, 1973).

Behrens, C.B.A., *Merchant Shipping and the Demands of War* (London, 1955).

Bingham, C., *The Stewart Kingdom of Scotland* (London, 1974).

——, *Beyond the Highland Line* (London, 1991).

Black, C.S., *Scottish Battles* (Glasgow, 1936).

Boardman, S., *The Early Stewart Kings* (Edinburgh, 1996).

Boswell, J., *Journal of a Tour to the Hebrides* (New Haven CT, 1993).

Brander, M., *The Making of the Highlands* (London, 1980).

Brown, M., *James I* (Edinburgh, 1994).

Calvorcessi, P., *Top Secret: Ultra* (Kidderminster, 2001).

Campbell Paterson, R., *The Lord of the Isles* (Edinburgh, 2008).

Casson, L., *The Ancient Mariners*, 2nd edition (Princeton NJ, 1991).

——, *Ships and Seamanship in the Ancient World* (Baltimore, 1995).

Cessford, C., 'Pictish Art and the Sea', *The Heroic Age: Journal of Early Medieval Northwestern Europe* Issue 8 (June 2005), available online at http://www.mun.ca/mst/heroicage/issues/8/cessford.html.

Chambers, A., *Ireland's Pirate Queen: The True Story of Grace O'Malley* (New York, 2003).

Chadwick, H.M., *Early Scotland* (Edinburgh, 1949).

Chalmers, M. and Walker, W., 'The United Kingdom, Nuclear Weapons, and the Scottish Question', *The Nonproliferation Review* 9(1) (Spring 2002), pp. 1–15.

Coates, J.F., 'The Trireme Sails Again', *Scientific American* 261(4) (April 1989), pp. 68–75.

Cordingly, D., *Under the Black Flag* (New York, 1995).

Cunliffe, B., *The Ancient Celts* (London, 1999).

Davidson, J.D.G., *Scots and the Sea* (Edinburgh, 2005).

Devine, T.M., *The Scottish Nation 1700–2000* (London, 1999).

Duncan, A.A.M., *Scotland, the Making of a Kingdom* (New York, 1975).

Falls, C., *Elizabeth's Irish Wars* (London, 1950).

Foley, V. and Soedel, W. 'Ancient Oared Warships', *Scientific American* 244(4) (April 1981), pp. 116–29.

Fry, M., *The Scottish Empire* (East Linton, 2001).

Gathorne-Hardy, G.M., *King Sverre of Norway* (London, 1956).

Gibson, J.S., *Ships of the '45* (London, 1967).

Grant, I.F., *The Lordship of the Isles* (Edinburgh, 1935)

Grant, J., *The Old Scots Navy from 1689–1710* (London, 1904).

Gregory, D., *History of the Western Highlands and Islands of Scotland* (Glasgow, 1881).

Griffith, G., *The Viking Art of War* (London, 1995).

Hackmann, W.D., *Seek and Strike, Sonar, Anti-Submarine Warfare and the Royal Navy* (London, 1984).

Haswell Smith, H., *The Scottish Islands; A Comprehensive Guide to Every Scottish Island* (Edinburgh, 1996).

Heath, I. and McBride, A. *The Vikings*, Osprey 'Military' Series, (Oxford, 1985).

Hill, J.M., *Celtic Warfare 1595–1763* (Edinburgh, 1996).

Holmes. R., *The Legend of Sawney Bean* (London, 1975).

Jamison, B.P. (ed.), *Scotland and the Cold War* (Dunfermline, 2003).

Johnson, S., *A Journey to the Western Isles of Scotland* (London, 1984).

Jones, G., *A History of the Vikings* (Oxford, 1968).

Lane, E. and Campbell, E., *Dunadd: An Early Dalriadic Capital* (Oxford, 2000).

Lynch, M., *Scotland: A New History* (London, 1991).

MacDonald, R.A., *The Kingdom of the Isles: Scotland's Western Seaboard 1100 to c.1336* (Edinburgh, 1997).

Macdougall, N., *James IV* (London, 1989).

Mackay, J., *I Have Not Yet Begun to Fight: A Life of John Paul Jones* (Edinburgh, 2000).

Mackie, J.D., *A History of Scotland* (London, 1964).

Mackie, R.L., *King James IV of Scotland* (Edinburgh, 1958).

McNamee, C., *The Wars of the Bruces: Scotland, England and Ireland* (Edinburgh, 1997).

Marsden, J., *The Fury of the Northmen* (New York, 1993).

Miller, J., *Salt in the Blood* (Edinburgh, 1999).

Moyse-Bartlett, H., *A History of the Merchant Navy* (London, 1937).

Munro, R.W. and J., 'MacDonald, Donald Dubh *d.* 1545', *Oxford Dictionary of National Biography* (Oxford, 2004).

Newark, T., *Celtic Warriors* (Poole, 1988).

Nicholson, C., *Rock Lighthouses of Britain: The End of an Era* (Caithness, 1995).

Nicholson, J., *Historical and Traditional Tales Connected with the South of Scotland* (Kirkcudbright, 1843).

Norman, A.V.B. and Pottinger, D., *English Weapons and Warfare 449–1660* (Poole, 1966).

Palsson, H. (trans.), *Orkneyinga Saga: The History of the Earls of Orkney* (London, 1978).

Prebble, J., *Culloden* (London: Secker & Warburg, 1961).

——, *The Darien Disaster* (London, 2002).

Raleigh, Sir Walter, *A Report of the truth concerning the last sea-fight of the Revenge*, originally 1591, ed. S. Rhoads (New York, 1902).

Reid, S., *1745: A Military History of the Last Jacobite Rising* (Gloucester, 1996).

Ritchie, R.C., *Captain Kidd and the War against the Pirates* (Cambridge, MA, 1986).

Rixson, D., *The West Highland Galley* (Edinburgh, 2003).

Rodger, N.A.M., *The Safeguard of the Sea* (London, 1997).

Roskill, S.W., *The War at Sea*, 4 vols (London, 1954–1961).

Sadler, D.J., *Scottish Battles* (Edinburgh, 1996).

——, *Border Fury: England and Scotland at War 1296–1568* (London, 2004).

——, *Clan Donald's Greatest Defeat: the Battle of Harlaw 1411* (Gloucester, 2005).

——, *Flodden 1513*, Osprey 'Campaign' Series (Oxford, 2006).

Sawyer, P., *Oxford Illustrated History of the Vikings* (London, 1997).

Scotcrown Limited, *Scotland's Secret Bunker 1951–1993: A Guide and History* (St Andrews, 2007).

Smout, T.C., *History of the Scottish People* (London, 1969).

Spaven, M., *Fortress Scotland: A Guide to the Military Presence* (London, 1983).

Tabraham, C., *Scottish Castles and Fortifications* (Edinburgh, 1986).

Traquair, P., *Freedom's Sword: Scotland's Wars of Independence* (London, 1998).

Vinn, Sir Philip, *Action This Day* (London, 1960).

Wagner, P., *Pictish Warrior AD 297–841*, Osprey 'Warrior' series, (Oxford, 2002).

Index

Arnason, Kalf 42–3
Aros 60
Arran, Isle of 3, 7, 103–4, 116
Arthur 190
artillery at sea 86, 90–92
  powder ('serpentine') for 91–2
ASDIC (possibly for British Anti-
  SubmarineDetection Investigation
  Committee) 195
Askerhus 107
Asleifsson, Sweyn 40–41
SS *Athenia* 188
Athens 157
d'Athy, John 87
Atlantic, first battle of the 171–85
Atlantic, second battle of the 193–4,
  198–203
Aubrey, Jack 167, 168
Auchmoutie, Rear Admiral 122
HMS *Audacious* 175
Austria 164
  Empire of 171
Aviemore 188
Ayrshire 4–5, 6

B-24 Liberator 201
Bahus 107–8
Bain, Ranald 69
Balliol, Edward 77, 88
Balliol, John ('Toom Tabard') 64, 65,
  66, 76, 81
Balloch, Donald 68
Baltic Fleet 163
Baltimore 154
Bamborough 92
Bangor 27
Bann 23
Bannane Head 5
Bannockburn, battle of 65, 66, 77, 83
Baralong 178
Barbara 128
Barbour, John 83–4
Barnstaple 83
Barra 7, 15, 25, 59, 67, 148
Barton, Andrew 92, 95, 96–7
Barton, John 92, 95, 96
Barton, Robert 95–6, 106, 108
Barton family 106, 109, 119
Bashaw (and Bashaw's squadron) 134,
  135
Bass Rock 12
Battle in the Sound 54–7, 58
Beachy Head 150
Beaker peoples 19
Bean(e), Alexander 'Sawney' and family
  5–6
Beatty, Admiral 173, 174, 181

Beaumont, Henry de 88
Belgium 187, 205
Belle Isle 148, 165
Bellone 153
Ben Loyal 153
Benbecula 7
Bennet, James 128
Bergholm 188, 190
Berwick 12, 76, 77, 78, 83, 88, 89, 93,
  129
  sacking of (1296) 64
Berwick Castle 12
Betsy 134
'Big Blockade' 210
Binning, James 121
Bishops Wars 124
Bismarck 196
Bisset, Hugh 79, 82, 84
Bjorn 'Cripplehand,' bard of Norway
  33–4
Black Douglases 89
Blackadder, Captain Patrick 120
Blackness 93
Blar na Pairc, conflict at 72
Blenheim 165
Blessing 121, 125
Bletchley Park 199
Blitzkrieg 187
Bloody Bay, fight at 58, 68–73
'Blue Streak' 209
Boisdale, Laird of 149
Bonaparte, Napoleon 164, 165, 167,
  169
Bordeaux 119
Borthwick, Richard 130
Botecourt, John de 84, 86
bows 16, 20, 23, 39, 85, 100
  crossbows 94
  longbows 85
  see also archery
Brander, Pass of 82
Brattholm 190
Brazil 168
Breda, Treaty of 129
Bressay, Sound of 127
Brest 141, 144, 148, 198
Brest squadron 143
Brian Boru 31–2
British Empire 175, 178
Britons of Strathclyde 23
Brochel Castle 15
Brodick Castle 108
Bronze Age 19, 23
Brown, Captain 152
Brown, John 128
Browne, James 134
Brownhill, Captain William 104, 109